AN ANTHOLOGY OF INDIAN MUSIC

AN ANTHOLOGY OF INDIAN MUSIC

Edited by
DR. GOWRI KUPPUSWAMY

DR. M. HARIHARAN.

SUNDEEP PRAKASHAN
DELHI

First Published: 1989

ISBN 81-85067-22-8
Published by:
SUNDEEP PRAKASHAN
B-3/53, Ashok Vihar, Phase-II,
Delhi - 110 052
Phone: 7112866

Printed at
Efficient Offset Printers, Delhi.

AUTHORS'S PREFACE

The main objective of presenting this volume to the lovers, scholars and students of music is to bring under one cover several facets of our Indian musical heritage. The articles included in this publication cover a wide range of subjects of diverse and intrinsic value. These articles had earlier been published in several Journals and Souvenir Publications from 1977 onwards. Many of them were also presented in Conferences and Seminars in different parts of India.

There are nine sections in this volume - Composers and their contributions, Musical forms, Music Education, Dance, Comparative music, Historical analysis, Epigraphy, Devotional aspects and Physics of music. Under these divisions a total of 30 articles are included. Some of them deal with a few rare subjects such as - on Margadarsi Seshayyangar, Tiruvottriyur Tyagayyar, King Shahaji, Daru, Tillana etc.

For readily agreeing to publish this volume we are most grateful to Mr. A. Singhal of M/s. Sundeep Prakasan, Delhi, who has been engaged in fruitful efforts in bringing out several worthy publications on Indian Music. We are also highly thankful to Mr. P. Natarajan of Mysore for neatly executing the typing and preparation of the Manuscript with utmost accuracy and care.

AUGUST 1988

GOWRI KUPPUSWAMY

M. HARIHARAN

ACKNOWLEDGEMENTS

We acknowledge the Publishers/Editors of the following Journals wherein some of the articles included in this Volume have been published earlier :

* Acoustical Society of India Souvenir	An Ideal Concert Hall - 1987;
* College Book House, Trivandrum	Rādhā-Kṛishṇa Cult in Gīta-Gōvinda, 1980;
,,	Haridāsās of Karnataka, 1980;
* Geetha Book House, Mysore	Kshētra Kṛitis of Dīkshitar, 1978;
* Guruguha Sangeet Sammelan, Calcutta	Navagraha Kṛitis of Dīkshitar, 1986;
* Inter-State Music Dance Festival, Trivandrum	Origin and Development of Tōḍi Rāga, 1980;
* Indian Musicological Society, Baroda	Rare Rāgas Dealt by Musical Trinity, 1982 June 13(1)
,,	Kuchipuḍi Dance-Drama, 1980 September 10 (3 & 4);
,,	A New Theory of Kuḍumiyāmalai Inscription, 1985 June 16(1);
,,	Musicology in Tamilnadu
* Indian & World Arts & Crafts, New Delhi	Two Systems of Music Education, 1985 (4 & 5)
* Journal of Indian History, University of Kerala	Royal Patronage to Indian Music, 1982 Silver Jubilee
* Journal of Music Academy, Madras	Compositions of Mārgadarśi Sēsha Iyengār, 1986;
* Sawai Gandharva Kala Mandir, Hubli	Dīkshitar and Hindustani Music, Souvenir, 1985;
* Shanmukha, Bombay	Musical Compositions of King Shāhaji IX (3) 1983 July;
,,	Padavarṇas of Swāti Tirunāl, IX (2) April 1983;
,,	Darus in Carnatic Music, XII (4) 1986 October;
,,	Tamil Padas - XI (2). 1985 April;
,,	A Comparative Study of Indian and Western Musical Scales, VI (2) April 1980;

* Sangeet Natak, New Delhi	Pallavi in Carnatic Music [illegible] 74 - 1984 Oct.-
,,	Bhajana [illegible] in Carnatic Music - 1982 64-65 April-June;
* Swati Tirunal Jayanti Committee, Trivandrum	Rare Rāgas handled by Swāti Tirunāl - 1988 - Souvenir.

: oOo :

CONTENTS

I. COMPOSERS AND THEIR CONTRIBUTION

: oOo :

JAYADĒVA AND RĀDHĀ-KRISHṆA CULT

The tradition of verse compositions in Sanskrit remained supreme in India till the 12th century, but even though their output did not diminish thereafter, the Mohemmadan invasion coupled with the increasing prominence of the Indo-Aryan and Dravidian language (vernaculars) reduced to a significant extent the popularity of poetical works in Sanskrit subsequently. That is why Jayadeva--who lived during the later part of the 12th century and early part of the 13th century—has been called the 'last of the Ancients and the first of the Moderns'. Jayadēva was essentially an inspired poet who revelled in the theme of mundane and profane love. It is well to remember that Gītagōvinda was written at a time when Krishṇa and Rama burst into prominence as the celestial heroes for a new-Hindu revival calculated to resist Muslim dominance. Gitagovinda was looked upon as the religious work and Jayadēva came to be revered as a Vaishnavite devotee who had received the special grace of Lord Krishṇa himself.

The important point is that in the Gitagovinda, Radha is depicted as Lord Krishna's mistress and not consort. Jayadeva portrays Rādha merely as an ordinary woman whose company Krishṇa enjoys for a short while. Her passions are entirely human and nowhere is there the slightest hint that she is divine. The main theme of the Gītagōvinda is the estrangement of Rādha and Krishṇa caused by the latter's solicitude for other Gopis, Rādha's anguish, Krishṇa's indifference towards her and lastly the rapture which attends their final reunion.[1] Jayadēva's main object appears to have been to create a beautiful work of lyrical, pictorial and verbal splendour. Because of his emotional temperament, Jayadeva evidently chose an erotic theme and found the fascinating story of Rādha and Krishṇa most absorbing.

The source of the Rādha cult in Gītagōvinda still remains a puzzle and no satisfactory theory has been put forward in this context. A very significant fact is that Radha is not mentioned in the <u>Bhāgavata Purāṇa</u>, <u>Mahābhārata</u>, <u>Harivaṁsa</u> <u>Purāṇa</u>, <u>Vishṇudharmōttara</u> <u>Purāṇa</u> and <u>Brihatdharma</u> <u>Purāṇa</u> in spite of the fact that all of them deal with the Rasakrida of Krishna with the Gopis.[2] The name Rādha, is derived from the Sanskrit verb root 'Radh' meaning pleasing or conciliatory. Rādha therefore denotes one who pleases. Even though Radha is not mentioned by name in the <u>Bhāgavatā</u>, there is a story therein where mention is made of a particular Gopi who is Krishṇa's special favourite and keeps his company exclusively so much so that the rest of the Gopis surmise that she must have worshipped Krishṇa with particular devotion in her previous birth. However, Jagannatha Dasa in his Oriya translation of Śrīdharasvām's commentary of the Bhāgavata refers to this Gopi as Vṛindavati, which shows the identity of the favourite Gopi of Bhāgavata with Radha was not known.

Sri J.C. Roy, the formulator of the Astrological theory connecting the Rādha-Krishṇa myth, identifies Rādha with Vaiśāka (Libra) nakshatra on the authenticity of a verse in the Atharva vēda.[3] According to this theory, Krishṇa is Sūrya (sun) surrounded in the firmament by Gopis who symbolise the stars.

Radha plays a prominent role in the Brahmavaivarta Purāṇa[4] wherein Krishṇa is described as a young boy and Rādha as a much older woman in much the same way as represented by Jayadeva in his Gītagōvinda. According to this Puranic work, the Gods went to Lord Nārāyaṇa and begged him to destroy the demon Kamsa. Lord Nārāyaṇa gave them two hairs from his body one of which was born as Krishṇa and the other as Balarāma. They went to Lakshmi and entreated her to be born as Rādha so as to enable Krishṇa to have a companion.[5]

The Vaishnavites usually regard Gītagōvinda as a literary sequal to the Bhāgavata and during the interval between the composition of the two epics, there have been quite a large number of references to the love of Rādha and Krishṇa. The name Rādha has been associated with that of Krishṇa from ancient times and the earliest poet to make such a reference was Hala, the author of Gatha Saptasati,[6] who flourished in the 2nd century A.D. Another early reference to Rādha is found in three inscriptions of Vākpati-Muñja, a Paramāra king of Malwa.[7] An author, with a similar name Vakpati, in his Gauḍavaho written during the middle of the 8th century mentions Radha in a solitary verse which describes the marks made on Krishṇa's chest by Rādha.[8] The Kashmiri poet Anandavardhana (9th century A.D.) mentions Rādha in his Dhyānaślōka and refers to her as the creeper grove on the Kalinadi river.[9] In the Vēṇisaṁhāra of Bhaṭṭa Nārāyaṇa, we find a reference to Rādha as the beloved of the enemey of Kamsa. Hēmachandra, the author of Kumārapālacharita, mentions Rādha in two verses.[10]

It is interesting to note that both immediately before Jayadēva's time and immediately thereafter, there are

instances where the love play of Rādha and Krishṇa is portrayed in
an exalted divine plane, in contrast to Jayadeva's treatment of the
theme. Thus the sect founded by Niṁbārka ,(12th century) in the
Telugu country worshipped Rādha as Krishṇa's eternal consort who
lives for ever with him in the Gōlōka, far above the other worlds.
Nimbarka's followers believed that like her Lord Radha too became
incarnate in Brindavan as his wedded spouse. To Niṁbārka, Krishṇa
was more than a mere incarnation of Vishṇu. He was the eternal
Brahman from whom spring Rādha and numerous other Gopas and Gopis
who sport with him in the Gōlōka. Similarly in the Rādha-Krishṇa
hymns of Chaṇḍidāsa (14th century) in the Bengali language of the
romance of Rādha and Krishṇa attains a divine lyrical quality. Thus
one finds that the conception of the Rādha Krishṇa cult by Niṁbārka
as well as Chaṇḍidāsa vastly differs from the eroticism depicted by
Jayadēva in the Gītagōvinda.

The Sāduktikarṇāmṛita[11] of Śrīdharadāsa (early 13th century)
contains in addition to 13 verses of Jayadēva including 5 from the
Gītagōvinda, another verse attributed to Abhinanda which describes
the dalliance of Krishṇa and Rādha in a solitary grove on the banks
of the river Yamuna. After Chaṇḍidāsa, the next important poet who
dwelt on the Rādha-Krishṇa cult was Vidyāpati who flourished in
the middle of the 15th century in Bengal. Vidyāpati became famous
for his Chāryapadas which contain an excellent description not only
of Radha's adolescent youth but also her ecstatic encounters with
Krishṇa. In other parts of India also, the Rādha-Krishṇa cult became
highly developed. Mīrabai, the Queen of Rajasthan, wrote and sang
her immortal Mīra Bhajans on Rādha and Krishṇa. She was followed by
Sūrdas who distinguished himself by linking the thirtysix different
modes—the Rāgas and Rāgiṇis of North Indian Music—with love poetry
of Rādha and Krishṇa. Bilvamaṅgaḷa, the poet from Kerala, wrote the
Bālagōpalastuti based on the Rādhakrishṇa cult which made him famous
as the 'Jayadēva of the South'.

Within a hundred years of the appearance of the Gītagōvinda
Jayadēva's fame had spread to every nook and corner of the country.
At least a hundred and fifteen post-Jayadēva poets have paid him
tribute by extensively imitating his style. A verse from the
Gītagōvinda finds place as a benedictory invocation in an
inscription in Gujarat during the reign of Sāraṅgadēva (1292 A.D.).[12]
More than fifty commentaries on the Gītagōvinda have been listed by

Dr. Mukherji.[13] One of the earliest of these commentaries is by Rāṇa Kuṁbha of Mēwar (1433-63 A.D.) entitled Rasikapriya which is quite an exhaustive work. According to an Oriya inscription in the famous Jagannath Temple at Pūri[14] (believed to be dated 1499 A.D.) only the songs and poems from the Gītagōvinda are to be sung exclusively by the Dēvadāsis and other singers of that Temple by the orders of Gajapati Pratāparudradēva (the original inscription is reproduced).[15]

Jayadeva is generally believed to belong to the Kenduli village in the Birbhuṃ district of West Bengal. His memory has been kept afresh for nearly eight hundred years through the Annual fair in that village on the banks of the Ajay river. However K.N. Mahapatra[16] has adduced extensive evidence to show that Jayadēva as well as a number of his contemporaries flourished in Orissa. According to his version the Kenduli Bilva of Jayadēva is identical with a village known as Kenduli in Pūri District. However, irrespective of Jayadēva's place of origin, Gītagōvinda is a work which has profusely and extensively influenced North Indian literature in general and Bengali literature in particudlar.

Gītagōvinda represents Krishṇa as the seasonal God of Spring characterised by extreme sweetness which is conductive to his love play with Rādha. It is in this manner that the erotic theme (Śriṅgāra rasa) is brought out by Jayadēva. Throughout Gītagōvinda, Rādha plays the role of the classical heroine (Nāyaki)[17] in several forms with Krishṇa. It is therefore no wonder that the heroine of Jayadēva has become the model for the later Bengali and Hindi authors and the legend that it was Jayadēva who invented Radha still persists.

NOTES

1. W.G. Archer, The Loves of Krishṇa, 1957, London, p. 76.

2. For a fuller account of Rasakrida as found in various Puranas, refer Tadapatrikar's article vide— Annals of Bhandarkar Oriental Research Institute, Vol. X, p. 269.

3. Ch. XIX, 7.3 (c-d) Ed. by W.D. Whitney and R. Roth, 1856, Berliṇ, p. 356.

4. Brahmavaivarta Purāṇa, Krishṇa-Janma Khaṇḍa, Anandasrama Series, No. 102, Ed. by V.G. Apte, 1935, Poona, Vol. II, pp. 433-911.

5. Srikrishna kirtana, p. 202.

6. I. v. 89; II. vv. 12 & 14.

7. Indian Antiquary, Vol. VI, p. 5) and Epigraphia Indica, Vol. XXII, p. 108, 111 (The dates of the three inscriptions being 974, 982 and 986 A.D.).

8. Gauḍavaho : A historical poem in Prakrit, Ed. by S.P. Pandit, Bombay Sanskrit Series, No. 34, 1887, p. 7.

9. Dhvanyalōka, Ed. by P. Durgaprasad and K.P. Parab, Kavyamala Series, No. 125, Nirnayasagara Press, 1891.

10. Kumārapālacharita of Hemachandra (1936) Appendix p. 621, v. 2 and p. 622, v. 5.

11. Saduktikarṇāmirita of Sridharadasa, Ed. by Prof. S.C. Banerji, 1965. These verses are: 1.4.4; 1.50.3; 1.59.4; 1.60.5; 1.85.5; 2.37.4; 2.72.4; 2.77.5; 2.132 .4; 2.137.5; 2.170.5; 3.5.4; 3.9.4; 3.9.5; 3.10.4; 3.11.5; 3.15.5; 3.19.5; 3.20.5; 3.23.5; 3.29.5; 3.34.3; 3.34.4; 3.34.5; 3.38.3; 3.39.4; 3.40.5; 3.52.5; 5.16.4; 5.18.2.

12. Indian Antiquary, Vol. XLI, p. 20 with a slight variation.

13. Pandit Hare Krishna Mukhopadhyaya in his Kavi Jayadera O Sri Gīta-Gōvinda, Calcutta, 1965, 4th edition.

14. Cf. Manmohan Chakravarti in Journal of Asiatic Society of Bengal, Vol. LXII, 1893, pp. 96-97.

15. Left side of the temple (3'-3" x 1'-3" - Lines 10)

Vīra śrī gajapti gauḍēśvara navakōṭikarṇāṭa kalavaragesāra vīravara Śrīpratāparudradeva. 1

Mahārājankara samasta 8 Aṅka śrāhi kakaḍā su 10 Budhvāre Avadharita Ārdhvagā pramāṇe vaḍa. 2

Thākurānka gītagōvinda thākura bhōgavēle e nāta hōiva samjhadhupa sarilā ṭhāru. 3

Vaḍa śiṅgāra pariyante e nāṭa hōiva vaḍa ṭhākurānka samparadā kapilēśvara ṭhākurāṅka vandhā. 4.

Nāchaṇīmāna purushā samparadā tēlangi samparadā emāne savihēm vaḍa Ṭhākurāṅga gītagō-- 5

vinda jam(jham ?) Ānagīta na sikhive Ānagīta na gāyive Āna nāṭa hōyi paramēśvarāṅga chchāmure na. 6

Hava ye nāṭa vitarakẹ vayishṇamạ gāyana chārījana achchanti yēmāne Gītagōvinḍa gītahi sē gāyive. 7

Ēhānka ṭhāru Aśikshitamāne ēkaśvarare śuṇi gītagōvinda gītahimse. 8

Sikhive ānāgita na śikhive ēhā. 9

Je parīksha ānāgīta nāṭa karāyile jani se jagannāthanka drōha karayi. 10

16. cf. Article No. 1 in the book "Jayadeva and Gitagovinda - A Study". Edited by the present authors.

17. Virahōtkanṭhita, Abhisārika, Viprālabdha, Kanḍita svādhīnabhartarika, etc. Each of these is mentioned by Jayadēva.

PURANDARADĀSA AND CARNATIC MUSIC

The keynote of Indian life has been spirituality. And leaders of spiritual thought—the saints and holy men who lived in the country in every age bearing witness to the supremacy of spiritual values in life—have helped to shape the life outlook of our society. We had thus in South India the Saivite, Veerasaivite and Vasihnavite seers right from the eighth century onwards.

The Haridasas of Karnataka belong to the lineage of wandering mendicant ascetics for whom India has justly been as famous from times immemorial as for her religious myths and legends. The term Haridasa itself is a compound phrase made up of the two words Hari and Dāsa—denoting servants of God. When the Haridasas became an organized group, they came to be known as the Dāsakūṭa (brotherhood of God's servants).

Like the Vaikāris of Maharashtra or the Nāyanmārs and Āḷwārs of Tamil Nadu, the Haridāsas spread the cult of devotion to God or Bhakti by singing devotional songs in every nook and corner of the Kannada country. They were of the Vaishnavite sect, devoted to the worship of god Viṭṭhala or Pāṇḍuranga of Pandharpur and other manifestation of Lord Krishṇa or Vishṇu.

Faith and prayer were the essential constituents of the Bhakti of the Haridāsas. The Ankitha or title was conferred by the guru after duly assessing the merit of the aspiring to become a member of Haridāsa Pantha. Each Haridasa is distinguished by his own independent title or Mudra. The vast majority of these Mudras or Ankithas end with the suffix Viṭṭhala. It is significant that Pāṇḍuranga Viṭṭhala or Purandhara Viṭṭhala Pandharpur was the family deity--Kuladēvata--of the saints of Karnataka (and neighbouring Maharashtra as well). He is also the deity sacred and dear to the Kannada people.

The doctrine of Bhakti or devotion is based essentially on the idea of a supreme God towards whom the devotee looks with reverence and awe and seeks protection after total surrender. The Haridāsas have given pride of place to Bhakti-marga as the supreme path of attaining salvation, although they have not spurned altogether the other two Paths to Mōksha--Jnana-marga and Karma-marga.

From the Vedic times down to the period of the great Āchāryas and saints, we find a gradual development of the Bhakti cult ultimately culminating in the idea of Vasudēva-Krishṇa (or Rudra-Śiva) as the supreme God. During the Vedic period we find how the Vedic seers sang hymns of devotion addressed to various deities like Agni, Vāyu, Indra, etc. However, it is only in the Upanishadic period that we find a definite mention of the word Upāsana as also of Vasudēva (and Śiva) as the supreme gods on earth. The doctrine of Bhakti has been beautifully dealt with in the Bhagavad gita, according to which even by offering the leaf of a holy plant, a flower, a fruit or even a handful of water to Krishṇa, one would attain Nirvāṇa. While the various Āchāryas tried to propound their own religious theories in the light of Gīta itself, the undercurrent of the Bhakti cult is inescapable in all their precepts. Mainly drawing inspiration from the teachings of the Āchāryas, the saints endeavoured to make the Hindu religion popular by singing songs of devotion at the doors of the rich and the poor alike.

To Madhvāchārya (who appeared on the scene in the 13th century) in particular goes the credit for having brought the cult of Bhakti to perfection while propounding his theory of Dvaita or dualism. The essence of Madhva's philosophy is the adoration of Hari or Krishṇa through Bhakti. This doctrine of devotion necessarily implies the concept of the superiority of God and the consequent inferiority of individual souls (Jeevas), or more simply the difference between God and man. Madhvā postulated the idea of Mōksha is interconnected with devotion towards the overlord of the universe. Hari (Krishṇa) was the supreme or prime reality and all souls were dependant on his grace. According to Madhvā, every devotee should surrender himself absolutely to the Lord. This concept is upheld by the Haridasas who were all faithful disciples of Madhvācharya. The religious disciplines characteristic of the Madhva school were conducive to foster the spirit of the Haridasas and it was therefore but natural that they were all ardent followers of the Madhva faith.

The Haridasas introduced the Dvaita tenets extensively in their works and spared no pains to spread the Madhvā doctrine of devotion throughout Karnataka. Like their great preceptor, the Haridāsas were also devotees of Lord Hari and his ten Avatāras. They always looked towards Hari as their father, mother, brother and all in life; but still they remained at a respectable distance from Him and showed a peculiar kind of reverence towards him. They were also great believers in the value of Nāma Sankeertana or meditation by means of the name of the Lord as the surest means of attaining salvation.

The works of the Haridāsas are varied and numerous. The number of their songs available to us even now runs to many thousands. They contain innumerable references to the Purāṇas, the Mahabharata, and the stories of Vasihnavite devotees and philosopher-saints such as King Prithu, Bāli, Śibi, Prahlāda, Dhruva, Gajēndra, Ajāmiḷa etc. The majority of the songs are on Krishṇa and Rādha. Their subject matter covers the Bhāgavata-upākhyāna Upanishadsāra and the thoughts of the great seers.

The contribution of the Haridāsas to the enrichment of the Kannada language cannot be exaggerated. However they deserve even greater praise for using Kannaḍa as the medium for spreading the knowledge of Hindu philosophy, which, till their time, was the exclusive prerogative and domain of the Sanskrit-knowing segment of the population.

The Haridasas comprised two divisions--Dāsakūṭa and Vyāsakūṭa. The terms Dāsari and Vyāsari came into vogue first at the time of Purandaradāsa and his religious preceptor Vyāsarāya. Originally the disciples of Purandaradāsa were designated Dāsakūṭastha. Later on the terms Vyāsakūṭa and Dāsakūṭa came to assume different meanings altogether. Vyāsakūṭa denoted the branch of Haridasas who were well-versed in Sanskrit and as such had first-hand knowledge of our philosophy from the original texts. Being intimately conversant with the Vedas, Upanishads and other Darsanas they claimed to be strict votaries of the Vēdavyāsa tradition. The adherents of Dāsakūṭa systematized all elements of value enshrined in our scriptures as involved in the Vyasa tradition and sought to explain to the masses the implications and significance of this great tradition through the medium of Prakrit Kannada, the language of the region. They conveyed the message of Dvaita philosophy and imparted moral instruction and insight into profound metaphysical truths through the vernacular which was the really intelligible medium for vast sections of the masses who had no access to the Sanskrit texts.

The Haridāsas threw open the doors of the Hindu religion to all the different castes and communities and also made it a faith for the poor. In this way the Haridāsa movement has done a great service to the masses in Karnataka by laying emphasis on the doctrine of equality in society. The Haridāsas preached that neither sex nor social position nor the ordinary barriers of caste and creed could come in the way of realization of the supreme bliss.

The works of Haridāsas also contain a complete code of morality for all mankind. They made it abundantly clear in their works that orthodoxy or mere observance of religious rites without true devotion towards Hari is of no avail and that a life of morality is the <u>sine qua non</u> for the attainment of salvation.

The teachings of each Haridasa are inevitably influenced by his personal experiences which are by their very nature varied and numerous. This is because the joys and sorrows or failures and uncertainities in the life of a particular Dāsa would obviously be different from those of another. In fact the environment in which a particular Haridāsa was born and bred as well as the agonies and travails which he had to experience while treading the path of Samsara necessarily gave a new and different colouring to his teachings, thereby creating a distinct philosophy of his own. However, it should be said to the credit of the Haridāsas that they never fell prey to pessimism. The darker or more tragic aspects of mundane existence could never make them lose heart. Probably on account of their utmost devotion towards Lord Hari, they did not feel worried even by the extraordinary calamities in life. In spite of dealing with the dreary aspects of Saṁsāra, their works nevertheless contain a strong note of optimism.

The works of the Haridāsas are also characterized by a happy blend of poetry and music. One of the most valuable contributions of Karnataka to world culture is the system of music described as Carnatic music or Dakshiṇādi (south Indian) music as distinct from Hindustāni or Uttarādi(north Indian) music. It is said that the soul of a nation is enshrined in its temples, its literature and arts. All these were venerated in India and regarded as emanations of God, the fountainhead of all that is true, good and beautiful in life--Satyam, Śivam, Sundaram. This idea was symbolically and beautifully expressed when the sages described Saṅgeeta and Sāhitya as two limbs of goddess Saraswati.

Music in south India was never divorced from devotion. All the great composers were men of extraordinary transcendental experience, drunk on devotion. They were sages for whom Bhakti through music was the ideal path of salvation. It was the firm conviction of Madhvācharya and the followers of the Dvaita philosophy that God would manifest Himself when the soul craved for His company through music and dance. The philosophy of the Haridasas was based on the realization of Paramātma through poetry and music, for the Lord is Saṅgītapriya and both poetry and music are the Sādhana of Adhyātma Vikās: 'Mad Bhakta yatra gāyanti tatra tishṭāmi". Bhakti was enshrined in poetry and transmitted through music, for poetry and music are both dear to the Lord. To the Haridāsas they were twin-born and one could not exist without the other. Śrīpādarāya says in one of his Ūgabhōgas that Dhyāna in Krita Yuga, Yagña in Treta Yuga, worship in Dvāpara Yuga and Gāna in Kaliyuga are the favoured forms of devotion to Kēśava.

Music was the most powerful medium of communication of great and vibrant ideas among the masses of Karnataka. The Haridāsas resorted to music to enlighten the people on the sublime precepts of the Vedas and the Upanishads. They carried the great intricacies of philosophical thought to all classes of the common people far and wide in Karnataka through Geeta and Prabandha characterized by the dominance of Laya and Tāḷa (Laya-tāḷa-pradhana) and through Ūgabhōga characterized by the dominance of Svara and rāga (Svara-rāga-pradhana). They regarded the Kīrtana mode of approach to reality as one of the nine forms of Bhakti (Navavidha-bhakti) and effectively used this form for conveying the message of Dvaita philosophy and love of the divine Krishṇa to those for whom the scriptures were remote and incomprehensible.

In contrast to contemporary saints in other parts of India, the Haridasas composed songs in a variety of forms--Pada, Sūlādi, Ūgabhōga, Tatvasuvaḷi, Ślōka, Kanda, Vachana, Gadya, Sīsapadya, Vritta, Dvipadi, Tripadi, Chaupadi, Satpadi, Ashṭapadi, Ragaḷe, Yalapada, etc.

The names of nearly 200 Haridāsas are known including three female Haridāsas. In general the Haridasas can be divided into three groups : the first group represented by Vijayadāsa, Jagannāthadāsa, Venkaṭēśa, etc. who mainly produced literature which was more or less specifically meant for the Madhvās; the second group represented by Vyāsarāya, Gōpāladāsa, Subbaṇṇadāsa, etc. who created a literature which was meant for the Brahmanical world in general based on the main tenets of Hindu ethics; and the third group represented by Śrīpādarāya, Purandaradāsa, Kanakadāsa and Vādirāja who preached the ordinary code of morality for people of all castes and communities.

The earliest known Haridāsa was Narahari Tīrtha of whose works we have at present only very scanty information. Purandaradāsa's guru's guru Śrīpādarāya may be regarded as the real progenitor of the Haridāsas. However, it is an incontrovertible fact that the most well-known as well as the most outstanding of them all was Purandaradāsa.

The personality of Purandaradāsa is a product of great spirituality, art and culture. To dedicate himself to God he gave up untold wealth for which he was known as Navakōṭi Nārāyaṇa. In music his achievements are vast and magnificent. His compositions number 475000, each with numerous Charaṇas. He is the father of the Carnatic system of music, his compositions ranging from the simplest Svarāvaḷis and Gītas to elaborate and complex Sūlādis. His synthesis of Sāhityākshara and Svara-rasa-laya is the very acme of perfection. His language is poetic, adorned with rich imagery and pithy sayings. His parables and allegorical utterances have all the fascination and depth of the scriptures. As a religious teacher he is second to none. He pursued his gentle methods of instruction through the most attractive and congenial channels of music. His eminence was undisputed, all his contemporaries, not excluding his own guru Vyāsarāya, according him the highest praise and homage.

Dāsas who came after Purandaradāsa deified him as an incarnation of Narada. It is no disparagement even to Tyāgarāja to say that Purandaradāsa's compositions in the main furnished the inspiration for his outpourings. It is learned on good authority that Tyāgarāja's mother was familiar with a large number of Purandaradāsa Kīrtanas; her frequent singing of these left a lasting impression on the young Tyāgarāja and in later life helped in shaping his style. Muthuswāmy Dīkshitar, though a composer with a distinctive, original style of his own, was yet a faithful adherent to the tradition of Purandaradāsa in the frequent use he made of the Sūlādi Saptatāḷas and in the shaping of melodic forms of ragas embodied in the Dēvarnāmas. A comparison of the archaic Sanchāras in familiar rāgas of Dīkshitar's composition with corresponding phrases in Purandaradāsa's Kīrtanas will reveal a remarkable identity. An examination of certain Padas of Purandaradasa with those of Kshētragña will establish the closest identity between them. Vyāsarāya, the preceptor of Purandaradāsa, was so profoundly impressed with the greatness of his Shishya that he paid him his tribute in the form of a Kīrtana. In this lyric, Vyāsarāya speaks of who is and who is not a Dāsa and concludes that only Purandaradāsa can be called a Dāsa. Purandaradāsa's own foremost disciple Vijayadāsa gives a glowing account of his master in his composition 'Banda duritha vināsana'.

Purandaradāsa, whose original name was Śrīnivāsa Naik, was born exactly 500 years ago at Purandaragaḍ near Puṇe into a rich family of diamond merchants. To start with he was as miserly as his wife was generous. The episode of the old man who, after futile appeals to Śrīnivāsa Naik, approached and obtained from his wife her nose-ring in order to tide over financial difficulties in connection with his grandson's Upanayanam is too well known to warrant repetition. On coming to know of this Śrīnivāsa Naik was stupefied and his mind received a rude shock. He ruminated over his own baseness as against the devout and noble spirit of his wife and a remarkable change came upon him. In a flash of intuition he discovered for himself the marvellous web of his own spirituality which had remained dormant. Tormented by anguish, he frantically struggled to wrench himself from the intolerable veil of Saṁsāra and distributed all his wealth to the poor and the needy. It was clear to him that the old man was none other than the Father of Universe come to teach him the great truth of a life of love and sacrifice. Overcome by an unquenchable desire to see the old man who had given him a glimpse of the eternal, to be realized through piety, probity, renunciation and contentment, he left Purandaragad, shorn of all possession, along with his wife and sons.

His destination was naturally Haṁpi which was then the centre for all religious and cultural activities under the benign rule of Emperor Krishṇadēvarāya. When Purandara reached the Vijayanagar capital, he needed a competent guru to harness his wandering mind and channelize all his ecstacies in accordance with the prescribed principles of yōga and other esoteric sciences. There was none more fit to fill this role than Vyāsarāya, the imperial preceptor and pontiff. Purandara obtained his holy initiation from Vyāsarāya who gave him his Ankita and he started composing innumerable Kīrtanas under the Mudra of Purandara Viṭhala. Vyāsarāya also provided him appropriate insight with the Darśanas, Vedas, Upanishads and other Śastras. The association of Purandaradāsa with Vyāsarāya was a communion of like minds and symbolized a beacon light appearing at a critical juncture in south Indian history.

Purandaradāsa owed his conversion to a Haridāsa to his wife and he was ever grateful to her for bringing about the change in his outlook and way of life. In one of his earliest compositions beginning with the words 'Ādaddhalla holithe āyyithu' he pays a glowing tribute to his noble wife whose merit it was to cause light to dawn on his: 'Heṇḍathi saṁthathi sāviravāgalu daṇḍige betha hiḍisadalayya'.

Purandaradāsa's daily routine was one of going from door to door singing his compositions, collecting alms and maintaining his family through what was collected thereby. There are many stories current, including references in some of his compositions, to these daily rounds, his embarrassment at the visits of rich relations, his extreme struggle to wean himself and his family from the temptations of wealth and fortune and his conflicts with the orthodox and the rich who were disdainful of his casteless catholic outlook and of his Bhajan Gōshṭi which consisted of all classes of people. His Dāsakūṭa was the target of opprobrium and Purandaradasa had a very hard time with the ignorant and the obstinate who missed no opportunity to malign him and his mission.

Purandaradāsa went on an extensive pilgrimage to holy places in south India. He travelled over the whole land—over tirtha and kshētra—observing men and their ways of living. Wherever he went he composed songs on the presiding deities of these sacred places. He seems to have visited, among other places, Mysore, Nañjanguḍ, Śrīraṅgapaṭna, Mēlkoṭe, Abbur, Mulabāgal, Kāñchipuram and Tirupati besides Pandharpur. It is said that Beṭṭada Chāmarāja Woḍeyār welcomed Purandaradāsa with special honours at Mysore. His sojourn at Pandharpur—the earthly home of his patron Lord—must have been far more prolonged as compared to other places, as borne out by the very large number of his compositions on this deity. After a life of unparallelled service to the cause of religion, social justice, philosophy, literature and music, Purandaradāsa returned to Hampi to spend his last days in perfect peace. And on Pushya Bhahula Amāvāsya of the Raktākshi year corresponding to 1654 A.D., he left his world with the image of the Lord in his mind and His name on his lips.

There are many points of similarity between Purandaradāsa and the saint-singers of north India. While Tulsidās stayed at the Saguṇa level and Kabīr at the Nirguṇa level, Purandaradāsa started at the Saguṇa level, later equated the Saguṇa and Nirguṇa, and ultimately became a great yōgi and mystic. Through Yōga, Gñāna and Bhakti he attained the Sākshātkāra of Nirguṇa Paramātma.

Purandaradāsa preached the loftiness of Bhakti in eloquent words and phrases. We notice in his songs an appeal to the evil-minded to give up bad ways and become good men and to good men to strive still further and lead saintly lives. We find numerous practical hints scattered in his songs to the way we should live in this world and develop good social relations with our fellow men.

One of the aims of Purandaradāsa was to convey to the masses the finest thoughts and truths of Hindu culture and dharma. It will be no exaggeration to say that what is not contained in his composition is not worth knowing. His utterances were even in conformity with Śruti and Smriti. Of all the Vāggēyakāras Purandaradāsa has the greatest claim to be regarded as an Āchārya or teacher. His religion on ethics have universal appeal. His works are replete with aphorisms, epigrams and parables. They breathe the fiery spirit of the prophet as well as the fervour of the poet. There is an appropriateness in Purandaradāsa's works being classed 'Purandarōpanishad' by no less a person than his own preceptor Vyāsarāya and valued as scripture. The Upanishads set forth the profound truths of religion and philosophy as do Purandaradāsa's compositions. Though devotion to God is the main theme of his works Purandaradāsa made liberal use of the modes and techniques usually adopted in Vedantic exposition. He also gave a secondary role to rituals and religious observances and laid emphasis on the importance of knowledge as the means of salvation even as the Upanishads did. As in the Upanishads, Purandaradāsa also made liberal use of allogories and metaphors in his compositions.

Allusions and references to Puranic stories are found scattered all over Purandaradāsa's compositions, Purandaradāsa drawing upon them for the characteristic tenets of the Dwaita faith. The Bhagavatha Purāṇa is regarded to possess as much sanctity as the Srutis themselves. Purandaradasa has dug into this mine and embedded its teachings with profound artistry in his compositions. The babyhood of the divine Krishṇa is particularly dear to Purandaradāsa and he has composed numerous songs describing the fascinating episodes of Bālakrishṇa. They are rhapsodies of vivid realization of divine Krishṇa; the Mystic sees Him, sports with Him, enjoys His company and incessantly cries for perennial companionship. The description of the ten Avatars of Vishnu frequently recurs in his songs. One of his most delightful pieces, 'Gokula dhoḷagōrva rākēndumukhi thanu'. conjures a romantic situation and elaborates on the ten incarnations of Vishnu.

We are left in no doubt as to the number of pieces composed by Purandaradasa. Apart from the testimony of others, we have his own song which classifies his four lakh seventy-five thousand pieces according to subject matter. When it is remembered that most of them have several Charanas, the mere volume of his productions is apt to bewilder one's imagination. There is a popular belief that of all the most prolific poets and writers, Purandaradāsa came next only to Vedavyasa—'Vyāsaranantara dāsare'. It is not, however, the stupendous quantity of his work that make us wonder but the sustained level of merit in ideas, language and music.

Purandaradāsa's compositions fall mainly in the category of Kīrtanas of which he was a master along with his illustrious senior contemporary Annamāchārya. He was the creative progenitor of the musical form Krithi immortalized by the trinity of Carnatic music--Thyāgarāja, Muthuswāmy Dīkshitar and Syāmā Sāstri. Purandaradāsa's influence on Tyāgarāja is borne out by the vast similarity of ideas in the songs of the two composers. Thyāgarāja also makes a eugolistic reference to Purandaradāsa in one of his Gēya Nāṭakas—Prahlāda bhakthi Vijayam.

Purandaradāsa is also said to have composed 'Draupadi vastrāpaharaṇa' and 'Sudhāma charitra' in prose and verse in the Yakshagāna style of song sequence. None of these is now extant. There is another Yakshagana play Anasūya charitre containing his Mudra at the end of the songs which are still in vogue.

Purandaradāsa has ben justly termed the father of Carnatic music. He was not merely a composer but a Lakshaṇakāra of the highest calibre. The system of south Indian music as we know it is entirely his gift. The separation of the northern from the southern system is nearly a thousand years old. In the absence of regularized bases of Lakshaṇa, both the systems were concurrent, though nebulous, for several centuries. It was the work of Purandaradāsa that imparted a distinct individuality to Carnatic music, which, after the labours of Vēnkaṭamakhi, became even more pronounced.

The first great change effected by Purandaradasa was the introduction of the Māḷavagauḷa scale as the basic for music instruction. The ancient Suddha scale was Kharaharapriya. It was derived by the application of a Chatuśruti interval to Shaḍja, Pañchama and Madhyama. Purandaradāsa adopted the Māḷavagauḷa scale as its derivation from Shaḍja, Pañchama and Madhyama was based on a process identical with the derivation of the ancient classic scale, the only difference being that in the derivation a Dviśruti instead of a Chaturśruti interval was used. A Dviśruti interval is beyond question easier to negotiate than a Chatuśruti interval. And that is the reason which underlines the selection of the Māḷavagauḷa scale. It is significant that the Māḷavagauḷa scale paved the way for the enunciation of the 72-mēḷakartha scheme by Vēnkaṭamakhi later. In the process of modal shift of tonic, the Rishabha of Māḷavagaula yielded the 72nd Mela, Rasikapriya, while the Nishada of Pantuvarali, which is the parallel of Māḷavagauḷa in Prathi madhyama, yielded the first Mēḷa, Kanakāngi. When the Ādi and Antya Mēḷas with distinct Pūrvāngas and Uttarāngas were isolated, it became easy for Venkatamakhi to evolve the system of 72 Mēḷas.

Not content with prescribing the scale Purandaradāsa framed a graded series of lessons which even today prevails in the teaching of Carnatic music. The Svarāvalis, Alankāras and Gītas form the surest road to mastery over Carnatic music with all its intricacies of Svara- and Tāla-prastāras.

In the number of compositional types he created, Purandaradāsa has no equal. In every one of these the same perfect commingling of sense, word and music is noticeable. He was a renowned composer of both Lakshya and Lakshaṇa Gītas. Apart from Kīrtanas, he was also a prolific composer of Tāna Varṇas and

Tillānas. It is stated that Adiappa Iyer modelled his Tāna Varṇas on those of Purandaradāsa. A great number of his Kīrtanas are in Madhyamakāla. All varieties of tāḷa are used though Chapu and Jhampa Tāḷas are more favoured. It is significant however that as compared to his predecessors he employed the Ādi Tāḷa in greater measure. In this respect Saint Tyāgarāja's affinity to Purandaradāsa is closer. Purandaradāsa was equally facile in composing Chowkha-kāla Kīrtanas. Some of his compositions are replete with Nāyaka-nāyika Bhāva and but for the language they are apt to be mistaken for Kshētragña's. In Bhāva, rāga and tāḷa, they are the model for all Padā composers.

The type of composition which exhibits Purandaradāsa's extraordinary mastery over the technique of music is the Sūlādi. This is the exclusive preserve of the Haridasas and among them Purandaradasa was the most prolific composer in this musical form; he is reputed to have composed as many as 64000 Sūlādis. The term Suladi itself occurs in the Sahitya of one of Purandaradāsa's compositions starting with the words 'Vasudēvana nāmāvaliya'. The Sūlādis owe their origin to the Sālaga Sūḍa Prabandhas which in general gave greater prominence to the tala than the raga (Ālapthi) aspect. The medieval Gēya Prabandhas were classified in three broad groups—Sūḍa, Alikrama and Viprakīrna. Among these the first variety—Sūḍa Prabandhas—was further subdivided into Suddha and Chāyālaga, the latter term in course of time degenerating into Sālaga. The Sālaga Sūḍas were Niryuktha with respect to drakshaphala (latent auspicious power) sentiment as well as tāḷa. They were seven in number, known as Dhruva, Mantha, Pratimantha, Nihsārika, Rasa, Aḍḍatāli and Ēkatāli, and formed a distinct group of special compositions that were sung in a prescribed manner to Dēsi tāḷas. This conventional prescription and practice with regard to talas became so rigid in course of time that eventually they came to be named Sūlādi or Sūḍādi tāḷas, again seven in number, called Dhruva, Maḍhya, Rūpaka, Jhampa, Triputa, Aṭṭa and Ēka. It would seem to be more than sheer coincidence that the name of the first Sālaga Sūḍa Prabandha as well the first Sūlādi tāḷa is identical : Dhruva. The Sālaga Sūḍa Prabandhas were also known collectively as Sūlakrama. The term Sūlādi (or Suḍādi) itself emerged from Sūḍa, which became Sila, and is derived from the root Sul meaning to sound and to occur in a pre-ordained manner; this indicates that all these songs were rendered in a set sequence to the seven specific Sūlādi tāḷas. While to start with the Sālaga Sūḍas were regarded as seven separate and distinct entities, by the 15th century they came to be designated and sung as one single Prabandha called Sūlādi, its seven parts considered stanzas or equivalents of Charaṇas, each set to one of the Suladi talas. Apart from this change form a multitude of Desi talas to the seven specific Sūlādi tāḷas, another change which the saints of the Haridāsakūṭa of Karnataka were instrumental in bringing about was the fusion of the seven Sālaga Sūḍa Prabandhas into a composite whole. The Sūlādis in their present form and structure were created and propagated by the Haridāsas during the 15th and 16th centuries, so that both this term and musical form have come to be identified today with these saint composers; the Sūlādi remains a distinct form characteristic of Dāsa Sāhitya and the devotional music of Karnataka. Another alteration that the Suladis underwent in the course of their evolution from Salaga Suda Prabandhas—for which too the Haridasas were solely responsible—was with regard to theme. Whereas the Sālagas embraced any topic ranging from mundane love to the adulation of patrons and kings, the Sūlādis pertained largely to divine praise and glory in addition to social and moral uplift. This is in harmony with the belief that Sūlādi is derived from the terms Suluhu (easy) and Hadi (pathway), suggesting that devotion or Bhakti, Sūlādi's keynote, is also the easy path to salvation.

Besides the Haridasas, Annamāchārya and Shāhaji Mahārāja are also known to have composed Sūlādis. A very valuable treatise in the context of Sūlādis is Tulaja's <u>Saṅgītasārāmṛitha</u> while quite a few compositions also figure in Subbarāma Dīkshitar's <u>Saṅgīta Sampradāya Pradarśani</u>. Tulaja considers Purandaradāsa to be the foremost authority and exponent of both the theory and practice of this musical form. The Sūlādis comprise several stanzas, the number of which varies from five to nine or ten. The number of lines differs not only from Sūlādi to Sūlādi but even from stanza to stanza in the same Sūlādi. Sūlādis are essentially Tāḷamālikas and would appear to contain a traditionally predetermined tala pattern. This includes a minimum of five and a maximum of eight tāḷas (made up of the seven Sūlādi tāḷas and an eighth called Jhompaṭa tāḷa), Dhruva and madhya being invariably used in all Sūlādis. However, the prescribed order of tāḷas is not strictly followed, nor does the repetition of tāḷas vitiate the composition.

The Sūlādi is a learned, elaborate and difficult piece giving a most comprehensive view of all the important rāga-sañcharas. Many Sūlādis are also rāgatāḷamālikas in structure; in other words, a multiplicity of rāgas is used, each stanza being set to a different raga in addition to a different Sūlādi tāḷa. It is said that whereas Śrī Pādarāya and Purandaradāsa composed their Sūlādis as rāgatāḷamālikas, this practice was modified by Purandaradāsa's disciple Vijayadāsa, who set an entire Sūlādi to a single rāga. The specifications regarding rāgas are not however as stringent as those with respect to the tāḷas. This is indeed surprising considering that musicologists like Tulajā have cited Prayōgas from several Sūlādis of Purandaradsa as authoritative examples to illustrate the Lakshaṇas of rāgas then in vogue.

Yet another compositional form exclusive to Dāsa Sāhitya and the devotional music of Karnataka--of which too the Haridāsas, Purandaradāsa in particudlar, have been the exclusive architects--is the Ūgabhōga. But in contrast to Sūlādi, the term Ūgabhōga does not find mention in any of our musicological treatises. The term is considered to be a corruption of the compound Udgrahābhōga formed by the combination of two of the Avyayas of the medieval Prabandha, Udgraha and Ābhōga, with some of its midle letters getting obliterated with time. Another view is that Ūgabhōga is derived from Ug and Ābhōga. Everything that falls within the ambit of man's experience is Ābhōga and the narration of such experience through words is Ūgabhōga. When the Haridāsa was in a trance in communion with his Ishṭadēvata, his innermost thoughts and experiences spontaneously poured forth in literary and musical forms. This is the genesis of the Ūgabhōga.

It may therefore be described as the essence or epitome of exalted experience. From the point of view of Bhāva it is deemed to be the direct translation of the thoughts of the composer in the ecstasy of inspiration. The theme is short and simple but varied and is invariably religious, ritualistic, spiritual or divine. The composition is essentially prose though occasionally one encounters a prosodical structure. In this respect as well as in certain basic ideas the Ūgabhōgas resemble the Vachanas of Basavēśvara and Akkamahādēvi. However, it is a moot point whether Purandaradāsa and other Haridāsas actually derived inspiration from these Vīraśaiva saints to model their Ūgabhōgas. The Ūgabhōga differs from the Sūlādi in being essentially an Anibaddha Prabandha. It is an extremely simple type of composition undefined into parts and almost nebulous in structure. As a musical form it is even more elementary than the Gīta. The Ūgabhōga is not associated with any specific raga or with any particudlar mode of rendering. It is usually sung in a single rāga with or without tāḷa. When sung without tala the Ūgabhōga sounds like Bhāratavachana (Gamaka) or the Kannada counterpart of Ślōka. In current concert practice, it is customary to preface a Dēvarnama with a Ūgabhōga conveying the same idea and the same rāga is used for both. In short the Ūgabhōga is a piece of Dāsa Sāhitya on a usually religious theme which is rendered in a more or less extempore musical manner. Whatever its origin and history it is a beautiful musical form, unique to its native Karnataka.

It is usual to estimate a composer's contribution to the system of music he practised. But what words can adequately describe the achievements of one who was the author and founder of that very system, of which we are the proud inheritors? His place as a Vāggeyakāra and Lakshaṇakāra is unique. He is to Carnatic music what Vālmīki is to Sanskriti literature. Such a collossus appears but infrequently on the cultural scene of a nation.

MUSIC OF THE HARIDĀSAS OF KARNATAKA

The Haridāsas of Karnataka belong to the holy lineage of wandering mendicant ascetics for whom India has been justly as famous from times immemorial as for her religious myths and legends. Like the Vaikaris of Maharashtra or the Āḻwārs and Nāyanmārs of Tamil Nadu, the Haridāsas spread the cult of Bhakti (or devotion to God) by singing devotional songs in every nook and corner of the Kannada country. The doctrine of Bhakthi or devotion is based essentially on the idea of a supreme God towards whom the devotee looks with reverence and awe and seeks protection after abject surrender. In fact, when a logical turn is given to the emotional side of man, we designate the same as Bhakthi. The Haridasas have given the pride of place of Bhakthi Mārga as the supreme path of attaining salvation, although they have not spurned altogether the other two aspects of Hindu Ethics viz., Jñāna Mārga and Karma Mārga.

From the Vedic times, down to the period of the great Āchāryas and Saints, we find a gradual development of the Bhakthi cult ultimately culminating in the idea of Vasudeva-Krishṇa (or Rudra-Śiva) as the supreme God-head on earth. During the Vedic period, we find how the Vedic seers sang songs of devotion addressed to various deities like Agni, Vayu, etc. However, it was only in the Upanishidic period that we find a definite mention of the word 'Upāsana' as also of Vasudēva (and Rudra-Śiva) as the supreme Gods on earth. The doctrine of Bhakthi has been beautifully dealt with in the Bhagavatgīta, according to which even by offering the leaf of a holy plant, a flower, a fruit or even a handful of water to Sri Krishṇa one would attain Nirvāṇa. While the various Āchāryas tried to propound their own religious theories in the light of the Gita itself, the undercurrent of the Bhakthi cult is inescapable in all their precepts. Mainly drawing inspiration from the teachings of the Āchāryas, the Saints tried to make the Hindu religion popular by singing songs of devotion at the doors of the rich and the poor alike.

To Madhvāchārya, in particular, goes the credit for having brought the cult of Bhakthi to perfection while propagating his theory of Dvaita or Dualism. The essence of Madhvā's philosophy is the adoration of Hari or Krishṇa through devotion or Bhakthi. This doctrine of devotion (Bhakthi) necessarily implies the idea of the superiority of God and the consequent inferiority of the individual souls (Jīvas), or more simply the difference between God and man. Madhvāchārya postulated that the idea of Mōksha is interconnected with that of pure devotion towards the over-lord of the universe. According to him every devotee should surrender himself completely to Lord Hari or Krishṇa. This idea is upheld by the Haridasas who were faithful followers of Madhvāchārya. Like their great preceptor, the Haridāsas were all devotees of Lord Hari and his ten Avataras. They were also great believers in the value of Nāma Sankīrthana or the efficacy of meditation by means of the Nāma of the Lord as a means of attaining salvation. They always looked towards Hari as their father, mother, brother and as their everything in life; but still they remained at a respectable distance from Him and showed a peculiar kind of reverence towards Him. They have introduced the Dvaita element extensively in their works and spared no pains to spread the Madhva doctrine of devotion throughout Karnataka. They preached the creed of Bhakthi in the Kannada country and inculcated that by following the path of Hindu Dharma, one is sure of attaining the ultimate goal.

The works of the Haridāsas are varied and numerous. The number of their songs available to us even now runs to many thousands. They contain innumerable references from the Purāṇas and Mahabharatha to the stories of Vaishnavite devotees and philosopher-saints such as King Prithu, Bāli, Śibi, Prahlāda, Dhruva, Gajēndra, Ajāmila, etc. The majority of the songs of the Haridasas are on Krishṇa and Rādha and in their very names and meritorious deeds, many devotees find solace.

The contribution of the Haridāsas to the enrichment of the Kannada language and literature cannot be exaggerated. However, the Haridasas deserve even greater credit for using the Kannada language as the medium for spreading the knowledge of Hindu philosophy which, up till their time, was the exclusive prerogative of the Sanskrit-knowing segment of the population. They threw wide open the doors of the Hindu religion to all the different castes and communities and also made it a faith for the poor. In this way the Haridāsa movement has done a great service to the masses in Karnataka by laying emphasis on the doctrine of equality of status in society. The Haridāsas preached that neither sex nor social position nor the ordinary barriers of caste and creed could come in the way of the realization of the supreme Bliss.

The works of Haridasas also contain a complete code of morality for all mankind. They have made it abundantly clear in their works that mere outward show of orthodoxy or observance of religious rites without true devotion towards Hari is of no avail and that a life of morality is the sine-qua-non for the attainment of salvation.

The teachings of each Haridasa are inevitably influenced by his personal experiences which are by their very nature varied and numerous. This is because the joys and sorrows or failures and uncertainties in life of a particular Dasa would obviously be different as compared to that of another. In fact, the environment in which a particular Haridasa was born and bred as well as the agonies and travails which he had to experience while treading the path of samsara necessarily give a new and different colouring to his teachings thereby creating a distinct philosophy of his own. However, it should be said to the credit of the Haridasas that they have never fallen a prey to pessimism. The darker or more tragic aspects of the mundane existence could never make them lose heart. Probably on account of their utmost devotion towards Lord Hari, they do not feel worried even by the extraordinary calamities in life. In spite of dealing with the dreary aspects of samsara, their works nevertheless contain a strong note of optimism.

The works of the Haridasas are also characterized by a happy blend of music and poetry. In contrast to contemporary saints in other parts of India, they composed songs in a variety of metres viz., Pada, Suladi, Ugabhoga, Tatvasuvali, Sloka, Kanda, Vachana, Gadya, Sisapadya, Vritta, Dvipadi, Tripadi, Chaupadi, Satpadi, Ashtapadi, Ragale, Yalapada, etc.

The Haridasas were first and foremost the followers of God Vithala or Panduranga of Pandharpur. The names of nearly 200 Haridasas are known, including three female Haridasas. Each Dasa is distinguished by his own independent Title or Mudra or nom-de-plume. While some of these Titles end in the suffix Vithala, others do not.

The terms "Dasaru" and "Vyasaru" first came into vogue at the time of Purandaradasa and his religious preceptor Vyasaraya.

Originally the disciples of Purandaradāsa were designated as dāsakūṭasthas. Later on the words Vyāsakūṭa and Dāsakūṭa came to assume a different meaning altogether. "Vyāsakūṭa" meant the branch of devotees who were well-versed in Sanskrit and knew the philosophy in the original while "Dāsakūṭa" meant that branch of the devotees who conveyed the message of Dvaita philosophy and religion through the vernaculars.

In general, the Haridāsas can be divided into three groups: (i) the first group represented by Vijayadāsa, Jagannāthadāsa, Vēnkaṭēśa, etc., who mainly produced literature which was more or less specifically meant for the Madhvās; (ii) the second group represented by Vyāsarāya, Gōpāladāsa, Subbaṇṇadāsa, etc., who created a literature which was meant for the Brahminical world in general based on the main tenets of Hindu Ethics; and (iii) the third group represented by Śrīpādarāya, Purandaradāsa, Kanakadāsa and Vādirāja who preached the ordinary code of morality for people of all castes and communities.

Belonging to the early part of the 15th century, **ŚRĪPĀDARĀYA** is chronologically one of the earliest among the Haridasas. He was born in a poor family at Mulbāgal in Kolar district and his original name was Lakshmīnārāyaṇa. He became a disciple of Svarṇavarṇatīrtha, the pontiff of the Śrī-Raṅga Maṭh, whom he succeeded later. Śrīpādarāya was the first among the Haridāsas to introduce Kannada in his Math and thereby inculcate the doctrine of Dvaita in Kannada. In fact, his three Kanarese works, viz., Bhramara Gīta, Vēṇu Gīta and Gōpi Gīta were required to be sung every day at the time of prayers in his Maṭh at Śrī-Raṅga. The first work, Bhramara Gīta, in particular, contains some of the most beautiful pieces of lyrical poetry on the meritorious deeds of Krishṇa comparable to Kāḷidāsa's Mēghadūtha. His nom-de-plume was Raṅganātha Viṭhala. The songs of Śrīpādarāya are characterized not only by a strong fervour of devotion but also a happy blend of rhythm and meaning, thereby creating a very pleasing sensation both in the minds and ears of the listeners. However, as ill luck would have it, only a few songs of Śrīpādarāya are at present available to us.

The period of **VYĀSARĀYA** (late 15th century and early 16th century) was the age of renaissance throughout the world. Karnataka was no exception and it too enjoyed its golden age in the cool shelter of the reign of Krishṇadēvarāya of Vijayanagar. Vyāsarāya, later known as Chandrikāchārya, was born at Bannur in Mysore district and became the spiritual adviser to the Rāyas of Vijayanagar. Having himself received initiation at the hands of Śrīpādarāya, Vyāsarāya had a number of famous and illustrious disciples including Purandaradāsa, Kanakadāsa and Vādirāja. Krishṇa Chaithanya of Bengal is also reputed to be Vyasarāya's disciple. Vyāsarāya stands supreme among the Haridāsas as being the pioneer in doing away with the prejudices of caste and creed. In spite of adorning the exalted pontificial throne of Madhvā, he allowed the low-born Kanakadāsa into the fold of the Dāsakūṭa in the face of vehement opposition from the orthodox Brahmins of the day. Though Vyāsarāya was a great Sanskrit scholar with many outstanding works in Sanskrit to his credit, he has also composed a number of devotional songs in Kannada, thereby catering to the needs of the lay public in Karnataka. The Mudra of his songs is Sri Krishṇa.

PURANDARADĀSA—easily the most widely known of the Haridāsas—was born towards the end of the 15th century in a family of wealthy merchants at Purandaragaḍ in the Poona district of Maharashtra. He was originally known as Śrīnivāsa Naik. It is said that he was initially a miser, but due to a miraculous event which was displayed to him by Pāṇḍuraṅga who appeared before him in the guise of a Brahmin, Śrīnivāsa changed the course of his life, gave away his belongings in charity to the poor and became a Dasa singing the praise of God and preaching His glory to the people through his songs. Purandaradasa was the first and foremost disciple of Vyāsarāya who also confered on him his nom-de-plume viz. Purandara Viṭhala. The admiration of Vyāsarāya for his disciple is admirably portrayed in his well-known song 'Dāsarendhare Purandaradāsarayya'. It is said that Saint Thyāgarāja Swāmy of Thiruvayāru in Tamil Nadu was an ardent admirer of Purandaradāsa and received inspiration from him through a dream for composing Kīrthanas. Well-versed in the art of music, Purandaradasa is famous as the author of the Piḷḷāri Gīta (collection of musical exercises). He is reputed to have composed 4,75,000 songs in addition to other original works like Draupatī Vashtrābaraṇa, Sudhāma Charithra and Paratatvasāra. Purandaradāsa's songs are characterized by extreme lucidity and simplicity of style. They reveal a mind familiar with the world and its ways and inclined as much to see without as within. Wide knowledge, deep experience and a profound love of humanity are evident in them and their range is great. Purandaradāsa was one of the foremost devotional saints of Karnataka as also a poet of varied genius. He deserves special credit for laying down the foundations of the school of devotion on a broader basis in Karnataka.

KANAKADĀSA, a contemporary of Purandaradāsa was, also born towards the end of the 15th century. His birth place was Baḍa in Dharwar district. He was by birth a hunter or shepherd (Kuruba). It is said that God Channakēśava frequently used to appear in his dreams and persuade him to become a Dāsa but Kanaka persistently refused to do so. Later Kanaka seems to have sustained a terrible defeat in battle after which he directed his attention unflinchingly towards the path of devotion. He became a disciple of Vyāsarāya who offered him the holy water (Thīrtha) and thereby accepted him into the fold of the Dāsa-kūṭa. A story is current that when, due to his low caste, Kanakadāsa was denied entry into the temple of Krishṇa at Uḍipi, he went to the back side of the temple and stood there praying. God Krishṇa is then said to have turned round and stood facing Kanakadāsa. Even today one can see a small window known as Kanakana Khiṇḍi at the rear of the temple through which devotees can have Darśan of the deity. Kanakadāsa was one of the most sublime thinkers and mystics of his age. He was an eminent writer in Kannada. Besides many devotional songs, he has also a number of other works to his credit like Haribhakthisāra, Naḷacharitre, Narasiṁha Stōtra, Rāmadhyāna Mantra, Mōhanatharaṅgiṇi, etc. Kanakadāsa's songs are known for their simplicity of style and deep religious import. The Mudra of his songs is either Kāginele Ādikēśava or Baḍada Ādikēśava.

VĀDIRĀJA TĪRTHA, also known as Sōderajāru, was a contemporary of both Purandaradāsa and Kanakadāsa and like them, a disciple of Vyāsarāya. Vādirāja also was born towards the end of the 15th century and his birth place was Hūvinakere in South Kanara district. He was a worshipper of Haya-Grīva and his nom-de-plume was Hayavadana. He was both an eminent Sanskrit scholar and a poet of high order in Kannada. Besides many Sūlādis and devotional songs, twenty-two works are attributed to his authorship including six in Kannada, viz., Tātparya-Nirṇaya, Vaikuṇtha Varṇane, Guṇḍa Kriyā, Lakshmī-Sobhana, Svapna Gadya and Bhramara Gīta. He has also composed a number of devotional songs in the Tuḷu language for the benefit of people belonging to the Scheduled castes. Vādirāja was also a social reformer and was responsible for converting the entire goldsmith class of North and South Kanara districts to the fold of Vaishnavism.

The passing away of the above three illustrious disciples of Vyāsarāya, which coincided with the fall of the Vijayanagar empire, also witnessed a decline in the Haridāsa movement. In fact, throughout the 17th century, there was a comparative lull in the Bhakthi wave in Karnataka, but is soon revived at the end of the century with the birth of **VIJAYADĀSA.** Vijayadāsa was born at Chikalparvi in Raichur District and his original name was Dāsappa. Quite early in life, Dāsappa went to Benares in search of education. It appears that while meditating on the banks of the Ganges, Purandaradāsa appeared before him in a day dream and blessed him with the nom-de-plume 'Vijaya Viṭhala'. It is said that immediately after this incident Dāsappa began composing songs and also came to be known as Vijayadāsa, Vijayadāsa is reputed to be a prolific composer and his songs rank in number next only to Purandaradāsa's. It is believed that he composed 25,000 songs. They are not only imbibed with a strong fervour of devotion but also characterized by originality of thinking. Even the subjects dealt with by other Haridasas received a novel approach at the hands of Vijayadāsa.

GŌPĀLADĀSA, originally known as Bhāgaṇṇa, was born early in the 18th century at Masarukallu in Raichur district. He received initiation at the hands of Vijayadāsa who also conferred on him the title 'Gōpāla Viṭhala' and thereafter Bhāgaṇṇa came to be known as Gōpāladāsa. In the whole range of Haridāsa literature,Gopaladāsa's devotional songs are outstanding. They are characterized by a rare combination of extreme simplicity and sublimeness and cover a wide range of topics in the domain of mysticism.

Like Gōpāladāsa, **JAGANNĀTHADĀSA** was born in the early part of the 18th century and he too belonged to the Raichur district. His original name was Śrīnivāsa. Being an eminent scholar in Sanskrit, Śrīnivāsa looked down upon Kannada and hated the Haridāsas in general and Vijayadāsa in particular for conveying the teachings of Madhvā in Kannada. It is believed that because of this he suffered an attack of consumption which threatened to become fatal. Becoming overpowered with repentance, Śrīnivāsa expressed a wish to see Vijayadāsa and he was taken in a cradle to the latter's residence. Finding that Śrīnivāsa had completely surrendered himself before him,

Vijayadāsa asked his disciple Gōpāladāsa to part with 40 years from his own life span in favour of Śrīnivāsa. In deference to his preceptor's wish Gōpāladāsa did accordingly and saved Śrīnivāsa. Gopaladasa also blessed Śrīnivāsa with the nom-de-plume Jagannātha Viṭhala and henceforth the later came to be known as Jagannāthadāsa. As if to make amends for his initial aversion towards his mother tongue, Jagannāthadāsa turned out to be a composer and writer of great merit in the Kannada language. In addition to hundreds of devotional songs and Tattvasuvalis, he is also the author of the well-known Harikathāmṛitha Sāṛa which propounds in a nut-shell the tenets of Dvaita. They bear eloquent testimony to his learned scholarship and perfect grasp of the religious and philosophical lore in regard to Vaishṇavism.

The Haridāṣa movement made an effort to place a complete code of morality and religion before the people. Its main object was to condemn formalism and ritualism in religion and a too arduous pursuit of worldly prosperity. It preached, instead, devotion to God and recognition of spiritual values. It preached also that the better life was not meant only for a few people but was meant for all and should be striven after by all. Imbued with a spirit of equanimity, dispassionateness(virakthi), universal love and kindness towards mankind, the Haridāsas, like all the mystics of the world, have proved themselves to be torch bearers to those who wander in the dim darkness of dreary saṁsāra. Their experiences and sublime spiritual teachings have proved solace to millions of people. The names and works of the Haridāsas would be remembered by the rich and poor alike in every home in Karnataka as long as the Kannada language survives.

MĀRGADARŚI SĒSHAYYANGĀR AND HIS COMPOSITIONS

As pointed out by Subbarāma Dīkshitar in his Sangeeta Sampradāya Pradarśini Sēsha Iyengar was a Śrīvaishṇavite. That he must have been well versed in Tamil though all his compositions are invariably in Sanskrit, is evident from the fact that he has praised the beauty of Nālāyira Divya Prabandham in numerous Kritis besides referring to Ramanuja's commentary on Brahmasūtra. He also makes a mention of Vipranārāyaṇa in one of his kritis and this saint is none other than Toṇḍar Aḍippaḍi Āḷwar. Now the cult of Vipranārāyaṇa is confined to South India. All these unequivocally point to the fact that Sēsha Iyengar must have belonged to South India, most likely to Tamilnadu.

In the history of South Indian Music, three Mārgadarśis are known to us. Margadarsi Virabhadrayya, otherwise known as Melaṭṭūr Vīrabhadrayya, was the pioneer composer of Svarajatis by adopting the format of the Padas of Kshetragna with the addition of Jatis. Round about the same period Mārgadarśi Gōvindaswāmayya emerged at Karvēṭinagar with the compositional form Tānavarṇam representing a fusion of the three styles of Padam, Svarajati and Śabdam. Besides being unique in their aesthetic appeal, his varnams are uniform with respect to their Anāgata eḍuppu. While the Svarajati is essentially a dance musical form the Tānavarṇam is an art musical form which finds only a limited place in music concerts accounting merely as the invocatory piece, it is the Kriti which represents the major art musical form accounting for the lion's share of the duration of music concerts. It was given to Mārgadarśi Sēsha Iyengar to introduce the Kriti into the fabric of Carnatic Music. It is a point of interest that these three Mārgadarśis, who were respectively responsible for the emergence of Svarajati, Varṇam and Kriti, were contemporaries during the later half of the 17th century just like the Musical Trinity who followed them a century later and it is also significant that these musical forms are taught to students of music in just the same order in which they became current.

Mārgadarśi Sēsha Iyengar was instrumental in innovating the current framework of the Kritis consisting of the Pallavi, Anupallavi and Charanas. Pallavi is the prop of the kriti to be repeated at the end of each one of the other sections. The anupallavi completes the picture of the melodic theme which the Pallavi starts delineating. The Charaṇas represent a combination of the structural features of the Pallavi and Anupallavi and may be either single or multiple in number. Sēsha Iyengār's Kritis with a single charaṇam served as the model for Muthuswāmi Dīkshitar's Samashṭi charaṇa compositions while those with multiple Charanas were the forerunner of the Kritis of eminent composers like Tyāgarāja, Syāmā Sāstri and Swāti Tirunāḷ. However the vast majority of Sēsha Iyengar's kritis have three or more charanas which are invariably quite long replete with compound phrases.

Most of these kritis are in praise of his Ishṭadēva Śrī Raṅganātha. Even now they figure prominently among the items rendered during the Ekānta Sēva of the Śrīraṅgam temple and this holy tradition is being continued to this day, by the sons of the late Vidwān Rāmaswāmi Iyengar who still enjoy the hereditary rights of the temple. They are based on Madhura bhakti which deals with the dignified and lofty love symbolizing the yearning of the self for communion with the Supreme Lord. Thus Sēsha Iyengar has portrayed śriṅgāra rasa coupled with Bhakti in his compositions. He has employed diverse ragas for his kritis including some apūrva rāgas like Karṇaṭaka Sāraṅga, Ghaṇṭa, Gauḷipantu and Jujāvanti. Many of his compositions have no indication of tāḷa; however tāḷas like Ādi, Rūpaka, Jhampa and Chāpu are mentioned in other cases.

Sēsha Iyengār's pioneering role in the evolution of the Kritis as a dominant art musical form, in addition to his lofty diction and remarkable mastery over phrases which sound bold and fresh even today, mark him out as a trail-blazer of Mārgadarśi. He steadfastly stuck to the rule that the starting notes of the Pallavi and Anupallavi should bear either the Samasvara Saṁvādhithva or Stāyisvara relaționship (as excellently portrayed in his Ānandabhairavi kriti 'Pāhiśēsha').

In addition to poetic excellence, the Sahityas of Sēsha Iyengar's kritis are outstanding examples of verbal felicity emanating from assonance, alliteration and rhyme. They abound in prosodical and rhetorical beauties such as Prasa, Yati etc. The fact that in his treatise 'Muhanaprāsa antyaprāsa vyavastha', Swāti Tirunāḷ copiously quotes examples of different phrases from Sēsha Iyengar's kritis bears testimony to their pre-eminence in this respect. Some beauties in Sēsha Iyengar's kritis are as follows :

DVITĪYĀKSHARA PRĀSA :

Sēsha Iyengar was also the innovator of Dvitīyākshara prāsa also known as Ādi prāsa or Edukkai. It is significant that this type of rhyme is not to be found in earlier masterpieces such as even the Gītagōvinda of Jayadēva. Muthuswāmi Dīkshitar implicitly followed Sēsha Iyengār in this respect and has composed many kritis with Dvitīyākshara prāsa. Examples of this prosodical beauty in Iyengar's kritis are as follows :

1) Śrī Raghuvara - Ghaṇṭa rāga - 8th Charaṇa : Bhāsura bāṇa...
lāsamanujakāya...
kōsalapuravāsa...
nāsakausalēya...

2) Raṅgapate pāhi - Darbār rāga - Anupallavi : nandakara...
nandakadhara...
mandaradhara...
sundaravadana...

paṅkaja bhava...
paṅkaja sadana...
śaṅkara sakha...
śaṅkaṭa hara...
kiṅkara jana...

ANTYAPRĀSA :

Antyaprāsa refers to the rhyme inherent in the ending syllables of a line or prasa. The following are some of the examples found in Iyengar's kritis :

1) Nāthavāsmin - Tōḍi rāga : Vipranārāyaṇe
kainkarya racana parāyaṇe

Śrī kāmitanēna santi vidhānēna
karadhatēna Samstutēna

2) Sīte Vasumati - Asāvēri rāga : Vasumati saṁjāte ...
guṇajāte
kāruṇya pūrna śānte...
Śrīnidhana lōchanānte...

3) Śrīraṅgaśāyinam - Dhanyāsi rāga : sanutam...
logathēvāsitam...
samāgatam..
vimānastitam - shōbitam...

4) Vandē Gōvindarājam - Śaṅkarābharaṇa rāga : Gōvindarājam suravarasasam...
vararājam - puṇyaślōkam...
sakalalōkam - maṇipravēkam...
guṇavadyam śeshavadyam...
pratipādyam - śrayamādyam...
guṇajālam - varapālaṁ...

MUHANA

Muhana refers to the prosodical beauty wherein the same or similar syllable or phrase occuring at the commencement of the first avarta of a section of a musical composition is featured also in the second āvarta of the same section.

An example of Muhana in a Sēsha Iyengar's kriti is as follows:

Raṅgapate Pāhi - Darbār rāga : Maṅgaḷa kara saṅga....
Gaṅgā janakagaruḍa.... Pallavi

Vrindāvana lōla...
vanditamunijanapāla.... Charaṇa-1

Kuntisutamōda....
chintitakārya.... Charaṇa-2

ANTARUKTI

For the first time we find Antarukti, a type of prosodical usage, in Sēsha Iyengar's kritis. Antarukti denotes the use, for the purpose of facilitating Tāḷa, of one or more syllables, or words between phrases which are in Muhana. It may be used in any part of a composition; if it is used in one charaṇa it should be used in other charaṇas as well. Some instances of Antarukti in Sēsha Iyengar's kritis are given below :

Raṅgapate -	Vrindāvana lōla Ā nandakara suśīla	(Charaṇa - 1)
Darbār rāga	Kuntīsutamōda Ā krūravinutapada	(,, 2)
	Paṅkēruhanētra Ā pannasujanamitra	(,, 3)
Bhajēham -	Pālitadinakaragōtram sadā pari pālita	(Charaṇa - 1)
Gauḷipantu	Vīkshāraṇyaśayanam-Sadā vrilidahari	(,, 2)
	Gōpayitadēvēśam Śrī kōsalanagara	(,, 3)

Let us now consider the influence of Sēsha Iyengar on some composers who were his contemporaries as well as some of those who came after him. Among his contemporaries striking similarities are found between the sāhityas of Sēsha Iyengar's kritis and some sāhityas of King Shāhaji. For example :

Iyengar	Shāhaji
Gōpālaka pāhi - Dhanyāsi rāga	Dharmasamvardhani - ? rāga
Gōpālaka pāhi	Induvadane aravindanayane nava
brindāraka hitabrinda vidāra	kundaradane suchimandahasane ripu
vaindavana nivāsa	brindaharane surabrindaśaraṇe bhakta
nandagōpasadānanda gōvinda	kuruvindabharaṇe
natamuchikunta	
nandakayudha purandaranandana	
vandita pādāravinda mukunda	
Śrīraghuvara - Ghaṇṭa rāga	Karuṇāsāgara - Āhiri rāga
Śrīraghuvara	Karuṇāsāgara
Karuṇavaruṇālaya parivārita	karuṇāsāgara garaḷakandhara
haraviranikaya	dharajāmanōhara haranagadharaśara
saraṇāgatabhayaharaṇa sukha	śaraṇāgata trāṇapara parapavana
parivarakāñjanēya	karadhritasuravara varadaparātpara

Passing on the post-Sēsha Iyengar composers, a striking influence is found on the compositions of Tyāgarāja. For instance there is a strong similarity between Iyengar's kriti 'Raṅgapatē' in Darbār and Tyāgarāja's kriti 'Pāhi parama dayālo' in Kāpi rāga.

Iyengar	Tyāgarāja
Pankajāsana kaḷatra	Pankajāpta hariṇāṅka nayana śrī
śaṅkarasakha kiṅkarajana	śaṅka suguṇa makarāṅka janakamām
sankaṭaharadhanuja jayabha	
yaṅkara gōpījana maka	
rāṅka nissaṅka	

There is also a striking resemblance between Sēsha Iyengar's kriti 'Māmavaraghuvara' in Asāvēri rāga and Tyāgarāja's Sāranga kriti 'Māmava raghurāma'; each comprising a pallavi followed by seven charaṇas.

Iyengar	Tyagaraja
Māmava raghuvīra mānita	Mamavaraghurāma marakatamaṇiśyāma
munivara garvita sītārāma	pāmarajanabhīma pālitasutārāma
tanayavirāma	
nripati lalāma daśaratha	
rāma samarōddhāma	

Tyāgarāja's Maṅgaḷa kriti in Dhanyāsi 'Jānakī Nāyaka nīku jayamaṅgaḷam' is very similar to Iyengar's 'Jānakī manōharāya jayamaṅgaḷam' in the same raga.

Dikshitar	Iyengar
Śrī Sarasvati hitē	Sitē vasumatisañjāte
śivachidānande śivasahitē	ramaṇīyaguṇajāte
vāsavāthimahite	rakshita sārvabhūte
vāsanādi rahitē	paripāhi mām.

However, it is on Swāti Tirunāḷ that Sēsha Iyengar's influence is most patent. There is a remarkable resemblance in the theme, content as well as construction of their compositions. As already pointed out most kritis of Sēsha Iyengar contain three or more long charaṇas with compound phrases and this is also the format adopted by Swāti Tirunāl. While the former's kritis are mainly on Raṅganātha, the songs of the latter are invariably on Padmanābha who is just another variant of Vishṇu also in a reclining posture. A close similarity is found between the kriti 'Bhōgīndraśāyinam' in Kuntaḷavarāḷi rāga of Swāti Tirunāḷ and Iyengar's kriti 'Śrīraṅga śāyinam' in Dhanyāsi. (This has been brought to notice earlier by Sri T.S. Parthasarathy in his paper on Iyengar).

Sēsha Iyengar's Punnāgavarāḷi kriti 'Pāhiśrī rāmachandra' and his Kalyāṇi piece 'Yōjayapadanaḷinēna' with seven long charaṇas following Pallavi and Anupallavi contain a gist of the Rāmāyaṇa and closely resemble Swāti Tirunāḷ's Sāvēri kriti 'Bhāvayāmi'. Swāti Tirunāḷ has composed many songs in Sanskrit which bear such close similarity to the songs of Sēsha Iyengar as to cause confusion regarding their actual authorship. For instance in the kritis 'Jayasuguṇālaya' in Bilahari, 'Yōjayapadanaḷinēna' in Kalyāṇi and 'Kōsalēndra' in Madhyamāvati the mudra 'Padmanābha' is absent and only the mudra 'Kōsalēndra' occurs. But still they have been included among Swāti Tiruna!'s compositions in some published texts. As already pointed out, Swāti Tirunaḷ has quoted profusely from Sēsha Iyengar's compositions for the lakshya aspect in his treatise 'Muhanaprāsa antyaprāsa vyavastha'. This would show that he was conversant with a large number of Iyengar's kritis. According to Subbarāma Dīkshitar, out of numerous kritis presented by Sēsha Iyengar for approval by Lord Raṅganātha, only 60 were returned while the rest were either not approved or missing. It is known that Shaṭkāla Gōvinda Mārār, who visited Tanjore and adjoining areas, introduced to Swāti Tirunāḷ many kritis of Iyengar from the manuscripts he acquired during his trip. It is highly probable that Sēsha Iyengar's missing kritis formed part of the manuscripts which Gōvinda Mārār took back with him to Travancore and consequently Swāti Tirunāḷ had access to a number of Sēsha Iyengar's kritis which were not current in Tamilnadu.

The Telugu work 'Saṅgīta Sarvārtha Sāra Saṅgrahamu' published in 1859 by Vīṇa Rāmānujāchārya mentions 18 kritis of Sēsha Iyengar.

In 1979 the late Prof. T. Kodandaramiah presented a paper on a certain manuscript dated 1869 belonging to Madurai Anantagōpāla Bhāgavatar containing among others 26 kritis of Iyengar. The texts of these kritis known as Kōsala Kirtanas have been recently brought out in a book form the Saraswathy Mahal Library. Five of these kritis already find place in the 'Saṅgīta Sarvārtha Sāra Saṅgrahamu' while 21 are new kritis.

'Gāyakalōchanam' of Tachchūr brothers gives a set of 9 Sēsha Iyengar's kritis, three of which are new compositions not found elsewhere - 'Śrīraghukula' in Sāvēri, 'Kalayāmi Dāśarathe' in Suruṭi and 'Bhajēham Vīrarāghavam' in Gauḷipantu.

Chinnaśwamy Mudaliar mentions two songs of Sēsha Iyengar including a new piece in Ānandabhairavi. This kriti has been published in 1982 by Dr. T.S. Ramakrishnan in the Music Academy Journal.

Two new kritis are wrongly printed as those of Swāti Tirunāḷ by Gaṇapati Śāstri in his book 'Saṅgīta Kritis' published in 1906. They are 'Jayasugunalaya' in Bilahari and 'Yōjayapadanaḷinēna' in Kalyāṇi. Another song 'Kōsalēndra' in Madhyamāvati is found in this book and also in the Madurai Manuscript brought to light by late Prof. Kōdaṇḍaramiah. Thus we have 48 kritis of Sēsha Iyengar available to us according to the following list :

Beginning of the song	Rāga	Tāḷa
Ānjanēya	Mōhanam	--
Bhajēham	Gauḷipantu	Ādi
Dēvadēvanupama	Bhairavi	--
Gōpālapāhi	Dhanyāsi	Ādi
Jānaki manōhara	Dhanyāsi	--
Jayajaya Śrī	Bhairavi	--
Jayasuguṇālaya	Bilahari	Ādi
Kalayē tāvakinā	Sāvēri	--
Kalyāmi daśaratha	Suruṭṭi	Jhampa
Kamalanayana	Pūrvikalyāṇi	--
Kamalanayana	Bēgaḍa	Ādi
Kalayēham	Suruṭṭi	Ādi
Karuṇābdha	Suruṭṭi	Ādi
Kōsalēndra	Madhyamāvati	--
Māmavaraghuvīra	Asāvēri	--
Narasiṁha bhava	Brindāvanasāraṅga	Ata
Nāthavāsmin	Tōḍi	--
Nīlajīmuta	?	--
Pāhimām śrīraghu	Bēgaḍa	Chāpu
Pāhimām Śrīrāma	Punnāgavarāḷi	--
Pāhiśēsha	Ānandabhairavi	Rūpaka
Pāhi śrīraghuvara	Tōḍi	--
Pāhigōpavēsha	Kalyāṇi	--
Pālayamām dēva	Karnāṭakasāraṅga	Chāpu
Pāhiśrīramāramaṇa	Aṭhāṇa	Tripuṭa
Raghunāyaka	Karnāṭakasāraṅga	Chāpu
Rāmapālaya māṁ	Bhairavi	--
Raṅganāyaka	Kēdāragauḷa	Ādi
Raṅganāyaka bhujaṅga	Kēdāragauḷa	Ādi
Raṅgapatē	Darbār	Rūpaka

Rē mānasa chintaya	Kalyāṇi	--
Sēvēham	Kēdragauḷa	--
Sēvē śrīcharaṇa	Darbār	Ādi
Sītevasumati	Asāvēri	--
Sārasadaḷanayana	Suruṭṭi	Ādi
Śrīraghuvara	Ghaṇṭa	--
Śrīraghukulavara	Sāvēri	Ādi
Śrīrangaśāyinam	Dhanyāsi	--
Śrīrangaśāyi	Kēdāragauḷa	--
Śrīrāma jayarāma	?	--
Śrīrukmiṇīśa	Athāṇa	Ādi
Śriraghuvara	Sāvēri	Ādi
Vandēham	Jujāvanti	--
Vandē gōvindarājam	Śankarābharaṇa	--
Vandē vakuḷābharaṇa	Mukhāri	--
Vāñchitapala	Kāmbōdhi	Jampa
Vāsavādi gēya	Karṇāṭakasāranga	Chāpu
Yōjaya padanaḷinēna	Kalyāṇi	Ādi

It has also been reported that there are a couple of manuscripts among the collections of the Kerala University Library which together contain 27new kritis of Iyengar not known hitherto. Hence at present we have access in all to 75 compositions of Sēsha Iyengar.

It is also interesting to note that many composers who followed Sēsha Iyengar have commenced some of their kritis with words identical with the initial phrases of Iyengar's kritis. A few examples are given below :

<u>Iyengar's</u>	<u>Other's</u>		
Ānjanēya paripālaya	Ānjanēya raghurāma	Sāvēri	Swāti Tirunal
Gōpāla pāhi	Gōpālaka pāhi	Bhūpāḷam	,,
Kalayēham	Kalayē dēvadēvam	Malahari	,,
Kalayāmi daśaratha	Kalayāmi hridi	Kannaḍa	,,
	Kalayāmi raghu	Bēgaḍa	,,
	Kalayāmi śrīrāma	Dhanyāsi	,,
Vande gōvindarājam	Vandē mahēśvaram	Ārabhi	,,
Māmava raghuvīra	Māmavaraghuvīra	Māhuri	Dīkshitar
Sārasadaḷayanayana	Sārasadaḷanayana	Khamās	,,
	Sārasadaḷanayana	Bilahari	Tiruvoṭṭiyūr Tyāgayyar

Jayajaya śrīraṅgēśa	Jayajaya śrīraghu	Gowri	Tyāgarāja
Pāhimām śrīrāma	Pāhimām śrīrāma	Kāpi	,,
Pāhi śrī rāma ramaṇa	Pāhiramāramaṇa	Varāḷi	,,
Rē mānasa	Rē mānasa	Tōḍi	,,
Śrī raghukula	Śrīraghukula	Haṁsadhvani	,,
	Sirraghukula	Bēgada	Mysore Sadāsiva Rao

Thus in the realm of Carnatic music Sēsha Iyengar happens to be a Mārgadarśi or trend-setter in many respects and consciously or unconsciously we have been his followers.

(This paper was presented at the Annual Conference of the Music Academy, Madras in 1984.)

MUSICAL COMPOSITIONS OF KING SHĀHAJI OF TANJORE

There have been many royal composers, royal musicians and royal musicologists. Among them king Shāhaji of Tanjore, the eldest son of king Veṅkōji occupies an honoured place. He was a great man of letters and patron of learning and fine arts. It was he who founded the colony of fortysix learned men in Tiruviśainallūr known by the name of Shāhajirājapuram. He has been eulogised in scores of kāvyas and hundreds of songs, all of which are now preserved in the Saraswathy Mahal Library at Tanjore. His period was the golden age of literature, art and philosophy in the Cauvery delta and the titles dakshiṇabhōja and abhinavabhōja that he earned are true tributes to his patronage and active participation in the great cultural renaissance and allround creative activity that were witnessed during his time.

King Shāhaji was a great scholar and poet. His interest in music, dance and drama was also equally great. During his time many of his dramas were enacted in his palace or in the temples under the control of the palace. He was also a prolific composer in Telugu and Sanskrit. He has to his credit nearly twenty dramas in Telugu interspersed with songs, in addition to hundreds of stray pieces in Sanskrit, Telugu and Marathi.

Tyāgarāja (Tyāgēśa), the presiding deity of the temple of Tiruvārūr was also the family deity of the Maratha rulers of Tanjore. King Shāhaji has composed in praise of Tyagēśa several Telugu and Marathi padas, Jāvaḷis, Gītas, Swarajatis, Kritis, Kīrtanas, Dance Pieces, Rāgamālikas and also literary forms like Sīsapadya, Dvipadi, Utpalamāla, Champakamāla, Daṇḍaka, Ashṭaka, etc.

Shāhaji's contribution to music and dance is no less important or abundant than that of the Trinity of Music of the subsequent age. But it has not been adequately recognised. He occupies a significant place in the history of Carnatic music of the pre-Trinity period. He had his own circle of musicians and collected almost all the gītas, traditional ālāpas etc. of all the ragas current in his time. They are in about twenty manuscripts consisting of more than 5000 pages of palm leaf, all of which are now preserved in the Saraswathy Mahal. They contain the results of the intensive researches in music carried out by his court musicians and further more one manuscript in fact contains Shāhaji's own observations and conclusions on the subject. In addition to this collection of lakshyas, King Shāhaji had, with the help of his musicians determined the lakshaṇas of all the rāgas in vogue during his time.

His younger brother King Tulajāji had freely drawn from these rāga-lakshaṇas while compiling his work Saṅgīta Sārāmruta.

A study of Shāhaji's works is bound to help us in understanding the state of Carnatic music during the pre-Trinity period and in judging how far, if at all, any departure was made by the Trinity and their contemporaries from the tradition as handed down through the generations immediately preceeding them. The yakshaganas and other musical operas known in his time were the forerunners of the operas of Sri Tyāgarāja and Swāti Tirunāḷ.

It is interesting to note that the Syānandūrapuravarṇana Prabandham of Swāti Tirunāḷ, has a striking similarity to the operas of King Shāhaji, especially the Pallaki Sēva Prabandham. The former's compositions too embrace a number of languages. King Shāhaji happens to be the forerunner of Muttuswāmi Dīkshitar in composing kritis in praise of deities enshrined in different kshētras or temples. While Dīkshitar composed them invariably in Sanskrit, Shāhaji composed them in Telugu. While we look into the compositions of Saint Tyāgarāja, we are surprised to see sets of phrases and lines borrowed from the compositions of King Shāhaji.

King Shāhaji was deeply devoted to the deity Tyāgarāja and must have realised that the knowledge of music, however profound, would be of no value and would lead one astray, unless it is properly used as an instrument of devotion to the Lord (Saṅgīta jñānamu bhaktivinā sanmārgamu galadē). Luckily for Carnatic music, the successors of Shāhaji followed the same liberal cultural policy and patronised music. Thus king Shāhaji may be rightly viewed as one of the most important personalities responsible for the Golden age of Carnatic music that culminated in the age of the Trinity.

It is worthy of note that Shāhaji as a composer and as mentioned before a staunch devotee of Tyagēśa of Tiruvārūr, that his devotion or upāsana of that deity therefore naturally turned out to be a nādōpāsana or worship by music and that all the three great vāggēyakāras known as the Trinity were born in Tiruvārūr itself. Is it a mere coincidence or else can a devotee be justified in concluding that being very much pleased with the nādōpāsana of Shāhaji, Lord Tyāgarāja soon blessed the Maratha kingdom of Tanjore with the three great nādōpāsakās all born in Tiruvārūr, near the Tyāgarāja temple itself? Is it not true that one has to reap as and where one has sown?

But the uniqueness in the case of the royal composer is this. The King's mother tongue was Marathi. His father was originally a feudatory of the Sultan of Bījāpur where the court language was Arabic or Hindustani. The language of the people of the country Shāhaji ruled was, of course, Tamil. Still Shāhaji chose Telugu to compose the majority of his songs. In Tanjore the Marathas succeeded the Nāyaks and whose court language was also mainly Telugu. Hence it is true that by Shāhaji's time, the court language of Tanjore was a mixture of the above mentioned five languages as evident from Shāhaji's own work 'Pañcha-bhāshā vilāsam'. Yet Shāhaji seems to have felt more at home in Telugu than in any other language in composing his songs.

Regarding his musical compositions the following select examples are noteworthy.

1. GĪTAM in Saurāshṭra rāga known as Ādyaswarākshara gīta

   Sārasāksha śara-sāṁbaśiva sarva
   Rī ramaṇaśēkhara śriṅ-gāranaya śarīra
   Māra harana dēva-parāgata sudha
   Dhara vāṇi dē sāha-nīrajamitra tyāgēśa.

   Note the swara mnemonics interspersed with the Sāhitya.

2. another GĪTAM IN Tōdi Rāga - Ādi Tāla

   Viḷṁbakāla

   Bhō gā yō gā bhō gā rā gā
   Nā gā vē gā dē gā tyā gā

<u>Madhyamakala</u>

Sara sija bhava nuta chara nala vavi hrita
Sara sija hrita nuta sara dhiśa radhi bhrta

<u>Duritakala</u>

nirupama muninuta varadasa tatanata
suranaga sucharitạ karimukha grihayuta
harihaya nutirata purahara navasita
karaḍhara sarakrita suruchira kritigata

3. **<u>VILŌMA DARU</u>** in Rēvagupti rāga - Ādi tāḷa

Nagutā dittēdi taguṇā
maguvaku lōkuvagumā ||
kanaru tirutiru naka
neneru pōnu pōrunene ||
melata mīri rima talame
kalaya manu maya leka ||
chēḍiya rādu rāyaḍiche
podimigāni gāmidi po ||
vade sāhēśa deva
rā dēva ravadēra ||
tyāga gavaya vagaga tyā
vēgada brovu brodagavē ||

S s r r g g P P g g r r s s
S r g p d d s S d d p g r S

Note : The text as well as the swara would read the same when it is read in the reverse direction.

4. **<u>MAṆIPRAVĀḶA KRITI</u>** (in 6 languages)
(Kannaḍa, Tamil, Sanskrit, Marathi, Hindi and Telugu)

Pallavi : Ārubhāshadalli nipuṇata, nōḍēnamma
Ārumukhasvāmimīdu ||

Anupallavi : Ghōra bhūtagale kondu kondu anudina
kōpamāḍi hōgēndu mātāḍidanu ||

Charana 1 : Vețțuni kațțeri munnaḍisandi
viranili sandi uṅgaḷai koḷḷuvēn ||
ghațțiyāy ennai ananjapērai piḍikka
kāraṇamēdenru māṭāḍidanu

Charana 2 : Sakini dakini bhīkaraghōra
jaḍa daiyamma kāminima bhaktula bēhi
pōkunṭe koṭṭuḍu pondayani tyāga
muddukumāruṇḍu māṭāḍidanu ||

The other three charanas are in Sanskrit, Marathi and Hindi.

5. <u>SAPTA RĀGA TĀḶA SULĀDI DARU</u>

Nārāyaṇagauḷa : Śrī tyāgēśa sāhēndra vinuta
Dhruvā-tāḷa Śrīdhara <u>nārāyaṇa</u> <u>gauḷa</u> <u>dhruva</u> atham
nitya jayavardhana ēkavitō-
nija santōsha paha sataha ||

Kannaḍagauḷa : Kanakavasanta śiva tyāgēśa
Maṭhya tāḷa <u>kannaḍagauḷa</u> <u>maṭhye</u> ēka viśrēsha
mana ullāsa dēvedēvēśa
majavati dayākari sāhadēva īśa ||

Māḷavagauḷa : Vara <u>māḷavagauḷa</u> sādara
Rūpaka tāḷa vanajāksha sara <u>rūpaka</u> dhīra
hara tyāgēsa dayākara
ēka sāha dēva chandraśēkhara ||

Rītigauḷa : <u>Rītigauḷa</u> <u>jhampe</u> yenērīti ēkavite kānta
Jhampa tāḷa Sitaśailasutēśa sitākaravanta
data tyāgēśa avadhūta mūrtivanta
bhūtanāyaka sāha bhūtalēśa hrinniśānta ||

Pūrvigauḷa : Saraṇāgatārthihara śaśiśekhara
Tripuṭa tāḷa śyāmaḷāṅgi dēvi prāṇēśvara
karuṇākara sāhanuta tyagēśvara
vara<u>pūrvagauḷa</u> <u>tripuṭa</u> ēka śankara ||

Chāyāgauḷa : Māyātīta nidhāna tyāgēśa
Aṭa tāḷa mahārāja sāhēndranuta viśvēśa
<u>chāyāgauḷa</u> <u>aṭatāḷa</u> ēka dēvēśa
sayamnata dayākari bhūtēśa ||

Kēdāragauḷa	:	Bhēdabhēdarahita ahitaraṇa
Ēkatāḷa		bhīkara bhavasāgarataraṇa
		kēdāragauḷa ēkatāḷa ēka nidhāna
		sādara sāhadēva tyāgēśa aridamana ||

Note : The rāgas are all set to end in gauḷa; the rāga and tāḷa names occur in each charaṇa simultaneously. Dīkshitar has also composed a set of Group kritis in these rāgas ending with gauḷa.

6. **SWARĀKSHARA DARU**

(In Tōḍi, Kalyāṇi, Kāpi and Śaṅkārabharaṇa rāgas)

Sa ri ga ma pa dha ni vīka paiḍika
taruṇalevvaru dā ni sarigāri ||
Alinīlavēṇuḷa abjanibhāsyulu-
kaḷakanṭhulu dā ni sarigāri ||
jalajadāḷakshulu sarasa biṁbōshṭulu-
mēlatalevvaru dā ni sarigāri || 1 ||

karikuṁbha kuchamulu karpūragandhulu-
hari madhyālu dā ni sarigāri ||
dharani nitambalu dhāvaḷyahāsalu-
darakanṭhalu dā ni sarigāri || 2 ||

Note : The ending of every second line with the same phrase which is also swarakshara for the sāhitya and swara for the phrases at the end of the song.

7. **JĀVALI** in Rāgamālika

(Kalyāṇi, Suraṭi, Asāvēri, Rēvagupti, Pantuvarāḷi rāgas).

Kalyaṇi : Ambānilaya chidaṁbara vilasita
lambōdara hēraṁba sallāmu |
Aṁbara maṇiruchi ḍambaviḍambana
aṁbuja hita chidambara sallāmu ||

Suraṭi : Sati nirmala sati chakrāṅga
gati sadguṇavati sallāmu ||
nati trijagadgati rūpa
sruti sarasvati sallāmu ||

Asāvēri : Nandanandana induvadana
Kundaradana gōvinda sallāmu |
mandahasana mandajōdbharaṇa
nanditagōpāla brinda sallāmu ||

Rēvaguptai : Vāsavahita kamalāsana kritabhrigu
pāsana sadguṇa bhāsure sallāmu |
Bhōsaladaivate śrisāhanute mahi
shāsuramardini dāsapale sallāmu ||

Pantuvārāḷi : Jati

Note : This seems to be the only Jāvaḷi available in Rāgamalika with a solkaṭṭu at the end.

8. CHATURDAŚA RĀGAMĀLIKA - Adi tala

Satata gaurīvara sarasa dayā kari
vitata kalyāṇi tujhēviraha tapate tapanavari ||
Sāraṅga ḍamarudhara
sakala nāṭaka sūtradhara
bhairavīśa anila anala jhala
bhāsura varāḷi sallāpana sāhēḍita || satata ||
lalitapañchamasvara na sāhētila
lavamātra ghaṇṭārava na shētila
sa lalita āharichcha na sāhētila
satvara madhyamāvati antara hiṭa jhala ||
Sāmagānapriya tyāgēśa
sakala ādinatabhūtēśa
vāmanārchita śrīrāga vardhana
vāmākshīśa anūrāga māḷavāśrīkari ||

Note : Dīkshitar has also composed the Chaturdaśa rāgamālika on the same lines and adopted most of the rāgas figuring in this rāgamālika.

9. DVĀDAŚA RĀŚI KRITI

Bararāśiyukta balēvari
paripūrṇadayākara svāmi |
dhirabrahmādiśa dēvatrayambakanātha ||

Mēshōnnēsha vilaṁbana sāhē
Mī saṅgato rāśitichi vṛishabha ||
Bhūshālankrita sthānadvaya kuṁbha
bhūritiche nayanayugaḷa mīna ||
varabhrūyugaḷa tiche dhanushya
sarasa kapōlim kastūri makara ||
taruṇi tanumadhye siṁha
darśanīya ghonte karkāṭaka ||
sārasa sundara kanyāsa
jagatraya tulā nahi īśa ||
viraha vēdanatīśa vrishçhika
vara tyāga trayaṁbakēśa mithuna hoya tīśa ||

Note : The names of each rāsi is coined with the sāhitya.

10. **TĀḶA PRABANDHAM** (Naḍai Daru)

Thū yē bhū śrī dhī tē
jaya bala kari maṇi haya yasa guṇa dhanā
naya pada kala sukha vaya muda subha kari || 1 ||

Sāraṅga : hara vara maja ase dēva dēhi ||
vanita kavita ghanata dhanata
anuja thanuja manuja hitaja || 2 ||
manasa vachasa sarasa vapusha
vinaya sunaya janaya dinaya || 3 ||

Kalyāṇi : ānanda ārogya abhaya karave ||
sitadēha jitamōha natasāha nagagēha
hritanaga dhritanaga atiyoga adityaga || 4 ||

Asāvēri : savinaya ghanōdaya jaganmaya vrajanaya ||
nagajadhara natamandara
suguṇōdara śubhakēdāra || 5 ||

Note : The increase of sāhityakshara from 1 to 2, 3, 4, 5 is highly praiseworthy. It leads to the change of naḍai.

11. **MAṄGAḶAM** (Maṅgaḷa Daru)

Mā pāli dēvuniki maṅgaḷam
mamu ganna talliki maṅgaḷam ||

Gaṅgādharuniki garuṇābdhiki
divyamaṅgaḷa dēvunikimaṅgaḷam ||
Saṅgītarasikaku jalajākshiki
sarvamaṅgaḷaku dēvuniki maṅgaḷam ||
Rahigala tyāgēśunaku radamauliki
Sāha mahipāla dēvuniki maṅgaḷam ||
guhya karimukhulanu kūrimito ganna
mahitaguṇādhyaku maṅgaḷam ||

12. **ĒKA ŚABDA DARU** (Ēka śabda prāsam)

Ambā rakshi satata maja amritakaṭākshi
Śambarāri jīvanadayini sadayē rājarājēśvari ||
Abjamukhabhāsure Abjakuṭila bhrūyugaḷe
Abjachanchalanētri Abjakanṭaśōbhite
Abjakōśaghanasthani Abjavallīrōmalatike
Abjāruṇatanukānte Abjasumadhuravāṇi ||
Abjāsanapūjite Abjalōchanasōdari
Abjagatigāmini Abjaharadhāriṇi
Abjatarudare Abjashaḍsadhatri
Abjabhūshabhūshite Abjavāsasahite ||
Abja javaharivāhine Abjamaṇitaraḷe
Abjatapanapratāpe Abjapanapramatte
Abjakuśale nrityalōlē Abja iva Ārōgyapradē
Abjahara tyāgēśa dayite Abjamitrānvaya sāhanute ||

Note : The song has been composed with the word 'Abja'.

13. **ANDHĀDI DARU** (Muktapadagrasta daru)

Karuṇāsāgara garaḷakandhara
dharajāmanōhara haranagadharasara
Śaraṇāgata trāṇapara paramapāvana śaṅkara
karadhritasulavara varada parātpara īśvara ||

Ghanabhaktavana vanajabhānutacharaṇa
raṇajitapura puṇyajana janapālana vichakshaṇa
kshaṇagarvitasamanadamana manasijahara bhaktaghana
ghanadamitra giriśarasana sanakādinuta nīranjana ||

Vāgīśanuta bhūshitanaga nagacharmāmbara ghanayōga
yōgjnadhyēya girijārdhabhāga bhāgadhēya natasatayāga
yāgadhvamsanavirāga rāganandavaibhōga
bhōgabhūshaṇa sāhadēvatyāgēśāsrtitānurāga ||

d d d p p m g m-g m p m p d d p
d p m g r r s n s - n s g m p p d p ||
d p s s s s r s - r s n s n d p n d p
d p s n d d p m p d - p d d p p m g r r s n s ||

Note : The beginning of a line commences with the ending of the preceeding line. This is the case with Swara also.

14. NAVAGRAHA KRITI (on 9 planets)

Mukhāri rāga - Ādi tāḷa

Navagraha māye kanyēvari nātha anugrahakāri
Ravikōṭisamatēja ranganāyaka swāmi ||
Bhāsvascharīrakāntichi paripūrṇachandravadana
sāsvadbhauma ghanajaghana saumyaguṇayukta ho ||
gurusthāna yugalate sarasakavya nipuṇate
vara mandayanate vāmākshi rāhu nenate
tyāgēśāpta śrīranga dēva sadayāntarāga
bhōgakāri kētu rōmavalisi mugdhākshi varakanyēśi ||

15. NAVARATNAPRABANDHAM (Svara, Śabda, Tāḷa artha daru)

Tōḍi, Dhruvatāḷa

sa ri Ga Ri sa ri Ga ri sa
sa ri Ga ri ga Ma pada Ni
sa ri sa ri ni da Pa pa ma ga ri sa ni ||

Karpūrānga ambikāsanga dēva
darpaka garvabhanga
tyāga valmīkalinga ||

ta ka ki ṭa je je kri tam tam thām
dhi ka na ta dha na ta tē |
te ta jhe na tōm dhi na to dha na tōm
Sa Ri Ma Pa pa Dha - Pa ma ri ma Ri Sa sa |

Sa ri ma pa Dha pa da - pa ni Sa Ni Sa ni
Sa ri sa ri sa ni sa ni - pa ma pa da Da pa
ma ro ||

Note : The composer has expressed the meaningful words for the Swaras, Sāhitya and Jatis. It is something unique which could not be found in any other compositions.

16. **SWARAJATI** - Dēvagāndhāri rāga, Āṭa tāla

kadhi karitila jana paratatvachinta ||
bālē ajñāna kaumārē krīdana
bala sanga taruṇapana paratatvachinta || 1 ||
Angagalita phalita vriddhapana
anika rōga bhajana te paratatvachinta || 2 ||
Atitvarita tyāmchi ayushyachi gati-
aharnisi ritusamvatsara jñali paratatvachinta || 3 ||
baganema visaratata īśhanatraya bhramatata-
tyāga tribhuvanānatha he paratatvachinta || 4 ||

Swara :

Ri ri Ri ma ga Ri - ma ga Ga Ri-
pamagari-magariSa-ririSa-maGariSa || 1 ||
Ri ma Pa ma pada da pa - pama gari Ri-
pamagari-magariSa-ririSa-maGariSa || 2 ||
Dada pamapa Dada pmgari-Rima pamapa-
Pama Ma ga ri Ri - pamagari-magariSa-ririSa-maGariSa || 3 ||
Sari ri sa- Rima maga Ripama pa da pa-
nisa Sa ni ri ri sa ni sa ni ri ri sa ri -sanisaSa || 4 ||

Swarajati :

ta ki da ta dim dim - gi nam gathom - dim dhim nam ga tom
sa sa sa Sa Sa ni . ni Da da da da da ma ga ri
ta kki da ta ka dim dhim- di ki da ta ka- ta kka jha nu
sa sasapa pa pa magaga ri sa dhalankutom ma ga tam risa
||

Nagaraja jati :

kida taka jheta jhe tari - ṭa kida ta ka dim dhim
dha na ta ta dhana dhana tom - dhalankutom || 1 ||

jhem ta ri ta dim - dim ku ta kki da ta ka - dhanatatom-
dhikitatom |

ja ga ja ga ta ka ta ka dhim - dhim - da kki da ta ka ta ka
dhi tta - dhalankutom ||

(This paper was presented at the Annual Conference of the Karnataka Gana Kala Parishad, Bangalore, 1985.)

KING SHĀHAJI'S CONTRIBUTION TO MUSIC

There have been many royal composers, royal musicians and royal musicologists. Among them king Shāhaji of Thañjāvur, the eldest son of king Venkōji occupies an honoured place. He was a great man of letters and patron of learning and fine arts. He has been eulogised in scores of kāvyas and hundreds of songs, all of which are now preserved in the Saraswathy Mahal Library at Thañjāvur. His period was the golden age of literature, art and philosophy in the Cauvery delta and the titles dakshiṇa bhōja and abhinava bhōja that he earned are true tributes to his patronage and active participation in the great cultural renaissance and allround creative activity that were witnessed during this time.

Tyāgarāja (Tyāgēśa), the presiding deity of the temple of Tiruvārur, had, according to the Puranas, been worshipped by god Indra and the emperor Muchukunda. He was also the family deity of the Maratha rulers of Thañjāvur. King Shāhaji is said to have composed in praise of Tyāgēśa about five hundred Telugu padās and kīrtanas and approximately a hundred Marathi padas, swarajatis and Tillānas in addition to many padas in Hindi. More than two hundred padas are found in the manuscripts preserved in the same Library. The collection includes fifty bhakti padās, five bhāva padās, nine vairāgya padās, hundred and three śringāra padās, fourteen hāsya padās, twenty four nīti padās and three mangaḷa padās. These padās are literary gems full of meaning.

Shāhaji's contribution to music and dance is no less important or abundant than that of the Trinity of the subsequent age. But it has not been adequately recognised. He occupies a significant place in the history of Carnatic music of the pre-Trinity period. He had his own circle of musicians and collected almost all the gītas, traditional ālāpas, etc. of almost all the rāgas current in his time. In addition to this collection of lakshyas, king Shāhaji had, with the help of his musicians, determined the lakshaṇas of all the rāgas in vogue during his time and there are ten manuscripts containing these lakshaṇas. He had himself written a treatise in Hindi giving the lakshaṇas of both the Hindustani and Carnatic rāgas. One uniform feature of these lakshanas in that the lakshya quotations are made from ālāpas, gītas, ṭāyas, sūlādis and prabandhas. It would appear that at one time these five lakshyas of each rāga were being regularly learnt and memorised by each musician.

A study of Shāhaji's works is bound to help us in understanding the state of Carnatic music during the Pre-Trinity period and in judging how far, if at all, any departure was made by the Trinity and their contemporaries from the tradition as handed down through the generations immediately preceeding them. The yakshagana which was also known in his time was the forerunner of the operas of Sri Tyāgarāja and Svāti Tirunāl Mahārāja.

It is interesting to note that the Syānandūrapuravarṇana Prabandham of Svāti Tiruṇāḷ, the royal composer of Travancore, has a striking similarity to the Pallaki Sēva Prabandham. Besides giving a detailed description of the Lord from head to foot and of the deities associated with Him, the drama of the Kerala ruler also describes in detail the dance of beautiful damsels in the front yard of the temple based on the songs set to śruti and laya along with the accompaniments of flute and mridangam. It also deals with the procession of the deity led by the Mahārāja to a hunting ritual. Like Shāhaji's compositions Svāti Tirunāḷ's compositions too embrace a number of languages. But unlike Svāti Tirunāl, Shāhaji has composed many kshētra kritis or kīrtanas in praise of the deities enshrined in different holy places. Some of the kshētra kritis of Shāhaji are listed below :

'Kaḷakanṭi' in Vasantabhairavi rāga is in praise of Lord Śingāperumāḷ, now in Veṇṇāṭṛraṅgarai on the outskirts of the town of Thañjāvur. It is said that a demon called Thañjāsura, who was responsible for Thañjāvur getting its name, gave so much trouble to the people of this town and that Lord Narayana took the form of Narasimha and killed him to save them. From that time the place came to be known as Thañjāvur.

'Ēmōyani' in Ghanṭārava rāga is in praise of Lord Brihadīśvara of Thañjāvur.

'Ikanē' in Mōhana rāga is in praise of Lord Koṇkaṇēśvara of the West street of Thañjāvur.

'Chāla dhanyulithinē' in Pūrvi rāga is in praise of Tyagēśa of Ṭiruvārūr.

'Nāmīda parākusēya' in Gowrī rāga is in praise of the goddess Kamalāmbā of Tiruvārūr.

'Champaka vanavāsi' and 'Vinta jūdare' both in Asāvēri rāga on god Rājagōpālasvāmi of Mannārguḍi.

'Nī pādābja' in Asāvēri rāga on goddess Brihatkuchāmbāl of Tiruvaḍamarudūr.

'Amba Varamulimma' in Gowḷipantu rāga is in praise of goddess Abhyāmbikā of Māyavaram.

'Ādarimpavē mā talli' in Asāvēri rāga on goddess Abhirāmavalli of Tirukkaḍaiyūr.

'Tyāga vaidyēśvara' in Pantuvarāḷi rāga is in praise of Lord Vaidyanātha of Vaithīśvaran koyil.

'Tyāgēśa Vaidyēśuni' in Pūrvi rāga is in praise of goddess Daivanāyaki of the same place.

'Mukkanṭi nīva' on god Muthukumārasvāmi of the same place.

'Iyakarādaiya' in Pantuvarāḷi rāga on god Chaṭṭanāthasvāmi of Śīrgāḷi.

'Daya sayavamba' in Nādanāmakriya rāga is in praise of goddess Kāḷi of Śīrgāḷi.

'Taruṇalavu manasu' in Kāpi rāga on god Vriddhagirīśvara of Vriddhāchalam.

'Inṭiki rārā' in Pūrvi rāga is in praise of Lord Ekāmbaranātha of Kāñchīpuram.

'Īlāgu tāḷunē' in Sāranga raga is in praise of Lord at Dharmapuri.

'Tirukkōṭīśvara nannu' in Bilahari rāga is in praise of Lord Tirukkōṭīśvara of Dīpāmbāḷpuram.

'Nī dayagaligite' in Kāmbhōji rāga is in praise of Lord

Mallikārjunasvāmi of Śrīśailam in Andhra Pradesh. This song is noteworthy for its rasabhāva and meaning.

It can be seen that Shāhaji employed popular rāgas as well as some apūrva rāgas in the above songs. It would appear that he had a partiality for some rāgas like Asāvēri and Pūrvi.

In addition to the above compositions, Shāhaji has to his credit the following :

Sanskrit songs in praise of gods Brihadīśvara, Shaṇmukha, Praṇatārthihara, goddesses Brihannāyaki, Ānandavalli, etc.

Twentyfive Telugu yakshagānas including Kirātavilāsamu, Krishṇa līlā vilāsamu etc.

The Sapta sūlādi Prabandha, the Sapta rāga-tāḷamālika, the Pañchatāḷa Prabandha in five Mārgi tāḷas, the Rāgamālikā daru, Śabdaṁ and the Pañcha bhāshā vilāsa nāṭaka using five languages viz., Tamiḷ, Telugu, Marathi, Hindustani and Sanskrit.

Dramas like 'Vignēśvarakalyāṇamu',[1] 'Śāchi Purandaramu', 'Vallī Kalyāṇamu'[1], 'Śāntakalyāṇa', 'Draupadi kalyāṇa',[1] 'Jala krīḍa', 'Satipati dāna vilāsamu', 'Sītā kalyāṇa', 'Rāma paṭṭābhishēka', 'Ratikalyāṇa', 'Rukmiṇi Sathyabhāma saṁvāda', 'Sati dāna sūra' etc. all in Telugu.

Prabandhas like 'Bhaktavatsala vilāsa', 'Gaṅgā Pārvati saṁvāda', 'Pañcharatna prabandha',[1] 'Tyāgavinōda-chditra-prabandha', 'Vishṇu Pallaki sēva prabandha' and 'Pallaki sēva prabandha'[2] — all in Telugu.

All the padās of Shāhaji bear the mudra or stamp 'Tyāga'; his other compositions bear his own name 'Sāha' as mudra.

Shāhaji's court was adorned by many scholars and poets. Some of them have compositions to their credit in praise of their patron. They are listed below :

Dhuṇḍi Rāja Vyāsa : He wrote some Sanskrit compositions known as Shāhavilāsa gīta and also some Ashṭapadis.

Chandraśēkhara Swāmiji : He composed a Tamil Kuravañji and a Tamiḷ Yakshagānam.

Vāsudēva kavi : He composed five padas known as 'Dautya pañchakam'. He is the author of Pārvatīpariṇayamu - a drama relating to the wedding of Śiva and Pārvati. It is dedicated to king Shāhaji.

Śēshāchalapati kavi : He bore the title Andhra Pāṇini and was considered the foremost poet in the court of Shāhaji. In his 'Kōsala bōsalīyam' he states that he was greatly honoured by Shāhaji who presented him a palanquin and showered gold on the poet (Kanakābhishēkam). He has also written two more works : (1) 'Shāharājavilāsamu' - a drama relating to the marriage of Līlāvati who falls in love with Shāhaji and (2) the 'Saraswatīkalyāṇamu'. Though the authorship of the latter is surrendered to Shāhaji, the colophon in the work shows that it is the work of Sēshāchalapati kavi.

Ashṭāvadhāni kavi : He was the author of 'Chandraśēkhara vilāsa nāṭakamu' and was patronised by Shāhaji. He has included Marathi passages in the drama.

Girirāja kavi : He was another well known court poet at the time of Shāhaji. His family name was Darbha. He was also the court poet of Śarabhōji, the brother of Shāhaji. His works are 'Shāhaji vijayamu', 'Shāharājakalyāṇamu','Shāharāja vilāsamu', 'Shāhēndra charitamu', 'Rāmamōhana Kuravañji' and 'Sarvāngasundari vilāsamu'. He has also composed a number of padas. It may be noted that this Girirāja kavi is the maternal grandfather of the well known musician Śrī Tyāgarājasvāmy.

Vēdasūri : He wrote a treatise Sangīta makaranda dedicated to Champu, the son of Shāhaji. Only the chapters on tāḷa and nritya of this work are available in the Thañjāvur Saraswathy Mahal Library. In the nāṭya cahpters the Carnatic style of dance is dealt with vividly.

The other court poets of Shāhaji included Rāmakavi, Kāśinātha kavi, Sōma kavi, Rāmabhadra Dīkshitar etc. Śrīdhara Vēnkaṭēśa alias Ayyāvāḷ of Tiruviśanalūr was not a court poet in the strict sense. But he composed the work Shāhēndra vilāsamu in praise of king Shāhaji.

Notes

1. These works are printed by the Andhra University.

2. This work was printed as early as 1896 by the well known musician Sri Subbarāma Dīkshitar and later in 1955 by the late Prof. P. Sambamoorthy.

RARE RAGAS DEALT WITH BY THE MUSICAL TRINITY

The glorious era of the Vijayanagar empire witnessed the bifurcation of our music into Carnatic or South Indian music and Hindustani or North Indian music. Carnatic music, which was a mere sapling to begin with, was assiduously sustained and nurtured by the Nayak and Marātha rulers of Tanjore as well as numerous versatile composers who followed them into the mighty and beautiful tree that it is today with highly scented multi-coloured flowers of diverse types of musical compositions and scores of melodic ragas.

During Vēṅkaṭamakhi's period, Carnatic music was confined to the four Daṇḍis - Gīta, Rāga, Ṭhāya and Prabandha - dealt with in his famous treatise Chaturdaṇḍi Prakāśika, of which Gīta and Rāga attained a higher status and prominance. However, as a landmark in our musical evolution, the importance of his magnum opus is due more to the 72 mēḷa scheme propounded therein, which is the foundation on which our present day music has been built and developed. Even though our rāga concept dates back to Mataṅga's time (5th century) and a rational system of raga classification was perfected by Vēṅkaṭamakhi, our ragas owe their identity and individuality exclusively to the several songs by gifted and inspired composers.

One can trace time-honoured rāgas like Kāṁbōdhi, Bhairavi, Madhyamāvati, Bēgaḍa, Sāvēri, Bhūpāḷam, etc., to comparatively early times. These are quite familiar and popular and easily comprehensible by the vast majority of the people. They not only lend themselves to spacious and elaborate exposition but also inspire the artistes with lots of innovative ideas in improvisation. This is not, however, the case with rare or apūrva rāgas, some of which have become even more or less obsolete at the present time. These have yet to be explored and understood sufficiently to develop such dimensions as to radiate their bhava or soul in the same measure. They have a comparatively restricted range. Attempts at detailed exposition of some of these rāgas are tantamount to a rather mechanical exercise in svara permutation which fails to bring into focus their broad melodic outline and character. It sometimes looks like tight rope walking within extremely narrow limits. To the musicologist, the few compositions in these apūrva or rare rāgas form the sole reliable basis for determining their characteristic ārōhaṇa - avarōhaṇa and svara sañchāras and formulating their authentic lakshaṇas.

Most of these apūrva or rare rāgas seem to have come into vogue after Vēṅkaṭamakhi's time - particularly during the golden age of Carnatic music spread over the second half of the 18th century and the first half of the 19th century (1750-1850). This was the period of the three greatest composers of South India - Tyāgarāja (1767-1847), Muthuswāmy Dīkshitar (1775-1835) and Śyāma Sāstri (1762-1827), collectively known as the Trinity of Carnatic music - who have greatly enriched our musical stock. They were all born at Tiruvārūr near Tanjore and the present lofty status of Carnatic music is in a large measure due to their unique and unrivalled compositions.

As composers, the Trinity possessed significantly different styles. While Thyāgarāja's songs are well known for their bhāva, Dīkshitar gave more importance to the rāga aspect whereas Syama Śāstri's songs are outstanding in rhythmic excellence. But all these three great composers had one thing in common. They not only revived many rāgas which were more or less dormant at their time but themselves invented many rare or apūrva rāgas and left for posterity a versatile treasure of compositions in these rāgas. It is worthy of mention that some of these rare ragas slowly gained currency after their time.

The purpose of the present paper is to focus attention on the rare janya rāgas exclusively employed by the Trinity for some of their compositions or, in other words several of these rare rāgas not handled by any other composers either before or after their time. There are some rāgas like Kalāvati, Ramāmanōhari, etc.,which have a mēḷakarta status according to the Asampūrṇa Mēla Paddhati followed by Muthuswāmy Dīkshitar but treated as janya rāgas by Tyāgarāja. Such mēḷakarta rāgas have necessarily been out of our purview.

Below is given a list of such rare rāgas (janya) exclusively handled by the Trinity along with the commencing words of the sāhitya of one song by each composer, the scale of the rāga as employed in his compositions in this rāga and the number (in brackets) of the corresponding mēḷakarta.

Name of the rare raga	Tyāgarāja	Dīkshitar	Śyāma Sāstri
Āndhāḷi	Abhimānamu S r m p n s S n p m r g m r s (28)	Brihannāyaki S r g m p n s S n p m g r s (28)	--
Ārdradēśi	--	Śrī Gaṇēśātparam S r g m p d n s S d p m g r s (15)	--
Bhairavam	Mariyāda gādayya S r g m p d n s S d p m g r s (17)	Kālabahiravam S r g m p d n s S d p m g r s (17)	--
Bhinnapañchamaṁ	--	Matsyāvatāra S r g r m p d p n s S n d p m g r s (3)	--
Bhinnashaḍjam	Sarivārilōna S r g r p m p n s S d p m g r s (9)	--	--
Bindumālini	Entamuddō S g r m p d n p n s S p n d p g r s (16)	--	--
Chandrajyōti	Bāgāyanayya S r g m p d s S d p m g r s (41)	--	--
Chāyānāṭa	Idisamayamurā S r g m p m p s S n d n p m r s (34)	--	--
Chāyātaraṅgiṇi	Kripajūchuṭaku S r m g m p n s	Sarasvatī chāyātaraṅgiṇi S r g m p n, s (p d n s) S n d p m g r s (28)	--

Chintāmaṇi	--	--	<u>Dēvibrōva</u> S r p m p d n s S p d p m g r s (56)
Chittarañjani	<u>Nāḍatanumaniśaṁ</u> S r g r g m p d N d p m r g r s(19)	--	--
Dēvagāndhāram	--	<u>Pañchāsathpīṭha</u> S r s g m p d p n s S n d p m g r s (22)	--
Dēvakriya	<u>Nāṭimāṭa marachitivo</u> S r m p n s S n d n p m g r s (20)	--	--
Dēvarañjani	--	<u>Namaste paradēvate</u> S g r m p d n s S d p m gr s (22)	--
Dīpakam	<u>Kaḷala nērchina</u> S g m p d p s S n d n p m g r s (51)	--	--
Gaṁbhīravāṇi	<u>Sadāmatiṁ</u> S g p m p d n s S d p m g r g r s (30)	--	--
Gānavāridhi	<u>Dayajūchuṭakidi</u> S m r g m p d n s S d n p m r s (34)	--	--

Jayantasēna	Vinatāsutavāhana S g m p d s S n p m g s (22)	--	--
Jīvandhika	--	Brihadīśa kaṭāksha S r m p d n s S n d p m r s (17)	--
Jujāhuḷi	Parākujēsina S m g m p d n s S d n d p m g s (13)	--	--
Kaikavaśi	Vāchāmagōchara S r m p d n s S n p m g r s (60)	--	--
Kaḷakanṭhi	Śrījanaka tanaye S r m p d n s S n d p m r s (13)	--	--
Kalagaḍa	Samayamu ēmarakē S r g p d n s S n d p g r s (13)	--	Pārvati ninnu S r g p d n s S n d p g r s (13)
Kalānidhi	Chinna nāṭena S r g m s p m d n s S n d p m g r s (22)	--	--
Kalāvati	Ennaḍu jūtuno S r m p d s S d p m g s r s (22)	--	--
Kannaḍabaṅgāḷa	--	Rēṇukā dēvi S r m p d s S d m p m g r s (15)	--
Kēsari	Nannukannatalli S r g m p m d p d s S d n d p m g r s (25)	--	--

Kiraṇāvaḷi	Eṭiyōchanālu S r g m p d n s S p m g r s (21)	--	--
Kōkilavarāḷi	Samukhānanilva S r g r m p d n d s S d n d p m r g r s (11)	--	--
Kōlāhalaṁ	Madilōnayōchana S p m g m p d n s S n d p m g r s (29)	--	--
Kumudakriya	--	Ardhanārīśvaram S r g m d s S n d m g r s (51)	--
Māhuri	--	Māmava Raghurāma S r g m p n s S d p m g r s (29)	--
Māḷava- pañchamam	--	Vāsudēvam upāsmahē S r g m p n s S n d p m g r s (15)	--
Māḷavaśrī	Evarunnāru S g m p n d n p d n s S n d p m g s (22)	Kanakasabhāpatim S g m p n s S n d p m p n d m g s (22)	--
Mañjari	Paṭṭiviḍuvarādu S g r g m p d n s S n d p m g r s (22)	--	--
Manōrañjani	Aṭukārādani S r m p d n s S n d p m g r s (5)	Bālāmbikē S r m p d n s S n d p m p m r g r s (5)	--

Mārgadēśi	--	<u>Maṅgaḷadēvate</u> S r g m p d n s S d m p g r s (15)	--
Māruva	--	<u>Māruvakādimālini</u> S g m d n s S n d p m g r g r s (15)	--
Māruvadhanyāsi	<u>Mridubhāshaṇa</u> S g m p d n d p n s S n d p m d m g r s (22)	--	--
Mēchabhauḷi	--	<u>Gōvindarājēṇa</u> S r g p d s S n d p d m g r s (34)	--
Mōhananāṭa	--	<u>Mōhananāṭa rāga</u> S g m p d p m p n s S n p d p m g s (9)	--
Nabhōmaṇi	<u>Nāyeḍavaṁśa</u> S r g r m p s S n d p m g r s (40)	--	--
Nādachintāmaṇi	<u>Evarani</u> S m g m p n d n s S n d p m g r g s (22)	--	--
Nādataraṅgiṇi	<u>Kripālavāla</u> S r g m p n s S n d p m g r s (22)	--	--
Nāgadhvani	--	<u>Brihadīśvaraṁ</u> S r g s m g m p d n s S n d p m g r s (29)	--

Nāgavarāḷi	--	Gānalōle S r g m p m d n s S n d p m g r s (8)	--
Pūrṇalalita	Kaluguṇapada S r g m p s S n d p m g r s (19)	--	--
Pūrṇapañchamaṁ	--	Sādhujanachithe S r g m p d s S d p m g r s (15)	--
Pūrvagauḷa	--	Nīlōtpalāmbikayāṁ S r m p d n s S n d p m g r s (29)	--
Pūrvavarāḷi	--	Paramēśvarēṇa S r m p d s S n d p m g r s (3)	--
Rāgapañcharaṁ	Sārvabhauma S r m p d n d s S n d m r s (28)	--	--
Rāmkali	--	Rāma rāma S r g p d s S n d p m g r s (45)	--
Ramāmanōhari	Sītāmanōhara S r g m p d n d s S n d p m g r s (52)	--	--
Rasāḷi	Aparādhamula S r g m p d n s S n p m g r s (22)	--	--
Rudrapriya	--	Rudrakōpa S r g m p d n s S n p m g r s (22)	--

Sāmanta	--	Praṇatārtiharāya S m g m p d n s S n d n p m g r s (30)	--
Siddhasēna	Evarainalēra S g r g m p d s S n d m p m r g r s (22)	--	--
Siṁhavāhini	Nenaruṁchara S g m p d n s S n d p m g r ṣ (27)	--	--
Śrīmaṇi	Ēmantunē S r g p d s S n d p g r s (2)	--	--
Śrutirañjani	Ētāri saṁcharintu S r g m p d n N d p m g s r s (61)	--	--
Sthvarāja	--	Sthvarāja S r m p d s S n d p m g s (46)	--
Suphōshiṇi	Rammiñchuvārevarurā S r s m p n d s S d n p m r m s (28)	--	--
Suddadēśi	Raghunandana S r m p d n s S n d p m g r s (28)	Kāmākshī S r m p d n d s S n d p m g r s (22)	--
Suddhamāḷavi	--	Naraharim āśrayāmi S r g m p n s S d n p m g r s (29)	--
Suddhamukhāri	--	Muraharēṇa mukundēna S r m p d s S n d p m g r s (1)	--

Svarabhūshaṇi	Varadarāja S g m p d n s S n d p m g s(22)	--	--
Supradīpam	Varaśikhivāhana S r m p d n s S n d p m g m r s (17)	--	--
Svarāvaḷi	Prārabdhamiṭlu S m g m p n d n s S n p d m g r s (28)	--	--
Śarāvati	--	Śarāvati taṭavasin S m g m p d n d s S n d p m g r s (25)	--
Ṭakka	Rākā saśivadana S r s g m p m g m d n s d s S n d m p m g m r g s (15)	Sundaramūrtim S g m p m g m d n s S n d m p m r g s (15)	---
Taraṅgiṇi	--	Māyē tvaṁ yāhi S r g p d n d p d s S d p g r s r g m r s (26)	--
Tīvravāhini	Sarijēsivēḍuka S r g m p d p n s S n d p m g r g m r s (46)	--	--
Umābharaṇaṁ	Nijamarmamulanu S r g m p d n s S n p m r g m r s (28)	--	--
Vasantavarāḷi	Pāhirāmadūta S r m p d n N d p g r s n (20)	--	--

Vardhani	Manasāmanasāmarthya S g m p d n s S n p d p m g s (11)	--	--
Vēgavāhini	Challaganātho S r g m d n d s S n d p m g r s (16)	--	--
Vivardhani	Vinavē Ō Manasā S r m p s S n d p m g r s (29)	--	--

It can be seen from the above Table that while Tyāgarāja has composed in 50 rare ragas not handled by any other composer who either preceded or followed him. Dīkshitar and Śyāma Śāstri respectively have compositions in 34 and 2 such ragas to their credit. Again whereas the number of these rare rāgas in which both Thyāgarāja and Dīkshitar have songs to their credit is 6, there is only one such raga in which both Thyāgarāja and Śyāma Śāstri have composed. On the other hand there is none in which both Dīkshitar and Śyāma Sāstri - or, for that matter, all the members of the Trinity - have composed. It is worthy to mention that wherever the same rare rāga has been handled by more than one member of the Trinity, they do not at all differ in their parentage (i.e. corresponding mēḷakarta) but only in a majority of case, in their scalic structure or ārōhaṇa and avarōhaṇa.

We thus owe a deep debt of gratitude to the Trinity for enriching our musical heritage through ushering into our repertoire a number of rare rāgas not handled by other composers. A conspicuous feature which merits attention in this context is that some of these rāgas with the same name find a slightly different identity at the hands of different members of the Trinity. So in attempting exposition of these rāgas, a different melodic picture would have to be delineated depending on whether the artiste has Tyagārāja's, Dīkshitar's or Śyāma Sāstri's composition in perspective. And the appropriate identity and rāga bhāva cannot be portrayed faithfully except by bringing into play the artistes manodharma and powers of improvisation in the fullest possible measure.

KSHETRA PANCHARATNA KṚITIS OF TYĀGARĀJA

Indian music is based essentially on spiritualism. Our saint composers spread the cult of devotion through the medium of music. In south India, Purandaradāsa stands foremost and we regard him as Saṅgīta Pitāmaha. The compositions of the Musical Trinity are replete with the knowledge contained in our Vedas, Purāṇas, Āgamas, Epics, etc. Tyagarājaswāmi is by far the greatest and most celebrated name in the history of Carnatic music. Our composers were all Bhaktaṣ and employed the medium of music as the easiest path to attain salvation. Tyagarāja has chosen Telugu, the sweet musical language, for the majority of his compositions. Their variety is vast. Some of them can be learnt even by children. Many of them are worthy concert pieces. To ensure the success of any concert the artist would prefer a large proportion of Tyāgarāja's kritis. Tyāgarāja has also to his credit many Utsava Sampradāya Kīrtanas and Divyanāma Kīrtanas suitable for Bhajana in congregation. Besides he has also composed three musical operas - Nowkā Charitram, Prahlāda Bhakti Vijayam and Sītārāma Vijayam. In this respect one can find the similarity between Tyāgarāja and Swāti Tirunāḷ Mahārāja.

In south India musicians and music lovers celebrate Tyāgarāja Arachana with great fervour and enthusiasm. Whether it be at Tiruvaiyāru, where he attained Samādhi, or any other place, the main feature of the Tyāgarāja Ārādhana is the group singing of his Ghana rāga pañcharatna kṛitis.

Pañcharatna kritis belong to the genere of Samudāya kritis or group kritis. Among the Trinity Śyāma Sāstri has to his credit only a single set of group kritis - the Navaratnamālika comprising of compositions on Goddess Mīnākshi. Muthuswāmi Dīkshitar has composed the largest number of Samudāya Kritis in Carnatic music. Many of them like Navāvarāṇa kṛitis, Vibhakti kṛitis, etc., are groups of 8, 9, or 11 each. He has also composed groups of 5 kritis - the Pañchabhūtha and Pañchaliṅga kritis. However Pancharatna refers almost exclusively to the groups of 5 kritis, composed by Tyagaraja. Apart from the Ghanarāga Pañcharatnam, he has six sets of Kshētra Pañcharatna kṛitis to his credit on the presiding deities of five kshetras (1) Tiruvaiyāru (2) Tiruvoṭṭiyūr (3) Gōvūr (4) Lālguḍi and (5) Śrīraṅgam.

Tyāgarāja's sishya Veenai Kuppayyar has emulated his guru in composing two sets of Kshētra Pañcharatnas : Kāḷahasti and Vēṅkaṭēśa Pañcharatnam.

Pañcharatnas comprise groups of five kritis each. Let us now dwell on the greatness of number 5.

1) Pañchakṛityas denote the 5 functions of the Universe viz. Sṛishṭi, Sthithi, Laya, Tīrōbhāva and Anugraha. Lord Vināyaka holds these pañchakṛityas in his five hands and hence is known as 'aiṅkaran'.

2) Our sensory organs are five in number called Pañchēndriyas.

3) Among the Navagrahas the number ascribed to Budha is five. Budha means learned and He is the giver of wisdom.

4) Bhūtas are five in number i.e., Pañchabhūthas. They are Prithvi, Appu, Tēyu, Vāyu and Ākāśa.

5) The five Bījāksharas of Mantraśāstra are Ōṁ, Aiṁ, Hrīṁ, Klīm and Sauṁ.

6) The possessor of Pañchabāṇas Goddess Aṁbikā is called Pañchabāṇēśvari.

7) Manmatha's bāṇas are five in number : Aravinda, Aśōka, Chuta, Navamallika and Nīlōthpala.

8) In Smārtha saṁpradāya daily worship is done to 5 dēvathas. This pañchāyatana pooja is to Śiva, Vishṇu, Sūrya, Gaṇapati and Dēvi.

9) Pañchakavyas consist of milk, curd, ghee, gōmūtra and gōmaya.

10) The reputed pañcapatras are chuta, bilva, āmalaka, kuśa and apamārga.

11) The pañcha bhakshyas are Bhakshya, Bhōjya, Lēhya, Chōhya and Pāṇīya.

12) In Karnataka the pañchaliṅga darśana at Talakkāḍu is held sacred.

13) The five important rhythmic phrase groups in music - Nāgabandha, Swatika, Ālagna, Śuddha and Samaskalika - are said to have emerged from the five faces of Lord Śiva - Sadyōjātha, Vāmadēva, Aghōra, Tatpuruṣha and Īśāna respectively.

14) The notes of music scales are also believed to have emanated from Lord Śiva's five faces. Tyāgarāja makes this clear in the charaṇa of his Chittarañjani kṛiti 'Nādatanumaniśaṁ'.

15) The five instruments - mṛidaṅga, conch, trumpet, drums and blow pipe - together are known as Pañchavādyam.

16) The pañchamahā śabda refers to the music played during royal processions to the accompaniment of the 5 instruments - trumpet, tambour, conch-shell, kettle drum and gong.

17) The pañchamukha vādyam for which Tiruvārūr is famous is a five faced drum.

In Carnatic music, Shāhaji Mahārāja was the originator of Kshētra kritis. The most prolific composer of Kshētra kritis is beyond doubt Muthuswāmi Dīkshitar. He travelled widely and his kṛitis are full of details of the Sthala purāṇa, Sthala virksha, Tīrtha, Temple festivals etc. On the other hand, Tyāgarāja visited only a few Kshētras. Upanishad Brahma Yōgin, who was the foremost exponent of Rāma Bhakti and the advaitic doctrine of the time, was a class mate and close friend of Tyāgarāja's father, Rāmabrahmaṁ. He sent word to Tyāgarāja that the latter should visit Conjeevaram and see him. So in 1837, when Tyāgarāja had already attained the ripe old age of 70, he embarked upon a tour to the northern districts of Tamilnadu. His distinguished disciple Veenai Kuppayyar, who had by then became the saṁsthāna vidwan to Zamindar Sundarēśa Mudaliar of Gōvūr, undertook to look after Tyāgarāja's comforts during this tour. Besides Conjeevaram Tyāgarājaswāmi also visited Tirupati, Shōliṅgapuram, Madras, Nāgapaṭṭiṇam and Śīrkzhi but he composed only two or three kṛitis on the deities at each of these places and not Pañcharatnas. He visited Tiruvoṭṭriyūr, Kuppayyar's bith-place as well as Gōvūr in deference to the wishes of Kuppayyar and Sundarēśa Mudaliar. During the course of the tour Tyāgarājaswāmi also visited

Lālguḍi and Śrīrangam. His visit to Lālguḍi was at the instance of his disciple Lālguḍi Rāma Iyer. He has composed kshētra pañcharatnas at all these places in addition to the deities enshrined in Tiruvaiyāru where he lived and attained Samādhi.

TIRUVAIYĀRU PAÑCHARATNAM

The name Tiruvaiyāru comes from 'Aiyāru' which in Tamil means 5 rivers. Tiruvaiyāru is in the midst of 5 rivers - Cauveri, Araśalār, Veṇṇāru, Vaḍayār and Kuḍamuruṭṭi. So the Lord of the place has taken the name Pañchanadīśa. His other name is Praṇatārthihara. Tyāgarāja's Pañcharatna kritis on this deity are

Śāriveḍalina in Asāvēri rāga and Ādi tāḷa
Ilalō Praṇathārthi hara in Aṭhāṇa rāga and Ādi tāḷa
Ēhi Trijagadīśa in Sāranga rāga and Chāpu tāḷa
Muchaṭa Brahmādulaku in Madhyamāvati rāga and Ādi tāḷa
Evarunnāru in Māḷavaśrī rāga and Ādi tāḷa

In the Asāvēri kriti Tyagārāja describes the grace of river Cauvery coming to see the beauty of Pañchanadīśa. In the Māḷavaśrī kṛiti Tyāgarāja prays to Pañchanadīśa to teach him the secret of controlling his mind to enable him to contemplate on the Lord whole heartedly. Māḷavaśrī is an apoorva rāga but also an ancient rāga which finds mention in our ancient texts. Even a composition of Śrīpādarāya - Sāsira Jihvegaḷuḷḷa - has been assigned this rāga. Śrīpādarāya lived before even Purandaradāsa. Some of Annamāchārya kṛitis also are in this rāga. But this ancient rāga has not gone almost out of use. No post-Trinity composer has composed in this rāga. Muthuswāmi Dīkshitar has composed two kṛitis in this rāga - Kanakasabhāpatiṁ and Mangaḷāmbikāyai namastē but these are very obscure. Tyāgarāja's kṛiti Evarunnāru is also very rarely heard and as in the case of many other apoorva rāgas, it is the only Lakshya now available for the Lakshaṇa of this raga.

Tyāgarāja's two sets of Pañcharatna kritis on Goddess Dharmasaṁvardhani are

1) Bāle Bālendu-Rītigauḷa-Ādi
2) Amma Dharmasaṁvardhani-Aṭhāṇa-Ādi
3) Vidhichakrādulaku-Yamunākalyāṇi-Rūpaka

1) Innāḷḷa valē-Dēśīyatōḍi-Chāpu
2) Māravairi-Nāsikābhooshaṇi-Rūpaka
3) Nannukanna talli-Kēsari-Dēśādi

4) Śivē pāhimāṁ-Kalyāṇi-Ādi
5) Karuṇajūḍavaṁma-Tōḍi-Ādi

4) Parāśakti-Sāvēri-Ādi
5) Nīvu brōvavaḷē-Sāvēri-Ādi

In the kriti Vidhichakrādulaku Tyāgarāja mentions about the golu of the Goddess and the greatness of the worship on Fridays. In the kriti Śivē pāhimāṁ the parrot in Dēvi's hands is described as always chanting Rāmanāma. It is noteworthy that Tyāgarāja, the devout Bhakta of Śrīrāma himself worshipped the Goddess. Tyāgarāja has composed as many as 28 kṛitis in Tōḍi but the kriti Karuṇajūḍavamma is a very rare kṛiti in this rāga.

GŌVŪR PAÑCHARATNAS

In this Kshētra Tyāgarāja has composed the pañcharatnas in praise of Lord Sundarēśa. They are :

Śaṁbhō Mahādēva in Pantuvarāḷi rāga and Rūpaka tāḷa
Kōrisēviṁparāre in Kharaharapriya rāga and Ādi tāḷa
Sundarēśvaruni in Śaṅkarābharaṇa rāga and Ādi tāḷa
Īvasudhā nīvaṇṭi in Śahāna rāga and Ādi tāḷa
Naṁmi vachchina nannu in Kalyāṇi rāga and Rūpaka tāḷa

When Sēkkizhar embarked on composing Periyapurāṇam it was Lord Sundarēśa who is said to have commenced the first line. Another name of the Lord here is Tirumēnisvarar. The word 'Gō' means cow. It also means Mahālakshmi. Parāśakti did penance at Māṅgāḍu sitting on Pañchāgni. All the dēvatas assembled there and Lord Śiva himself took up the responsibility of feeding the Dēvathas. For this purpose Śiva brought Kāmadhēnu down to the earth and made Her stay near Māṅgāḍu. That is the genesis of the name Gōvūr - the place where the divine Cow stayed. Lord Śiva is without any roopa and is worshipped only as a Liṅga in the mūlasthāna. The name of the Goddess of Gōvūr is Saundarya Nāyaki. According to inscriptional sources this temdple was built by Rājarāja Chōḷa. This is the only kshētra where Māṇickavāchagar festival is celebrated. During the nine days of this festival excerpts from the Tiruvembāvai of the saint are sung. Through the Gōvūr Pañcharatna kritis Tyāgarāja reveals his Śivabhakti.

TIRUVOṬṬRIYŪR PAÑCHARATNAM

This kshētra has been praised by Nāyanmārs. The name of the Lord is Tyagēśa and the Goddess is Tripurasundari. This place is reputed for the Haṁsanaṭana of the Lord who is here in the from of Svayaṁbhu liṅga. Ādi Śaṅkarāchārya has installed Śrīchakra pīṭhạ in this shrine. These pañcharaṭnas are all in praise of Dēvi Tripurasundari. They are

Dārinī Telusukoṇṭi in Śuddhasāvēri rāga and Ādi tāḷa
Sundarī nī in Kalyāṇi rāga and Ādi tāḷa
Kannathalli in Sāvēri rāga and Ādi tāḷa
Sundari nannindarilō in Bēgaḍa rāga and Rūpaka tāḷa
Sundari ninnu in Ārabhi rāga and Miśrachāpu tāḷa

The Kalyāṇi kṛiti has a chiṭṭaswara which has been in vogue for more than 40 years. For the Suddhasāvēri kṛiti Wālajapet Venkaṭaramana Bhāgavathar has added a beautiful chiṭṭaswara. Pallavi Gōpalayyar's kriti Nīdu Charaṇa paṅkaja closely resembles the Kalyāṇi kṛiti. All these kṛitis contain sthala mudras.

The Sāvēri kriti contains several proverbs like "will one search for butter when one has ghee?" ("Vennayuṇḍa nēṭikevaraina vēsana pāṭudura") "whyshould one simply imagine the mirage to be water?" ("Marīchikalanu jūchi nīrani bhramisi kandurā") etc.

In the Bēgaḍa kṛiti there are beautiful Anthya prāsas like vāṇi, śukapāṇi, varaśēshavēṇi, kalyāṇi, saṁbhaya śivunirāṇi, bālē, pālitasurajāle, svakrita akhila līlē etc., and Dvitīyākshara prāsas like Vārīśa, hari, mari, kori.

It is noteworthy that the Ārabhi kriti Sundari nannu contains innumerable references to Ādi Śaṅkarācharya's Saundaryalahari. The 2nd sloka of Saundaryalahari is as follows :

"Tanīyāṁśaṁ pāṁśuṁ tava caraṇa paṅkēruha bhavam viriñcih sañjīnvan viracayatilōkān avikalam" meaning :

'Brahma got the power of creation through worshipping Goddess Sundari is found in the following words of Tyāgarāja :

Sundari ninu varṇimpa brahmādi
Suralakaina taramā'

"tvakīyām saundaryam tuhinagirikanyē tulāyitum kavīndrāh"
(12th sloka)

The gist of 12th sloka is found in the words of Tyāgarāja as :
'kundaradana sanandakanādi vandita nēnenda'

The goddess herself is the Shōdasākshari svarūpa. The 16th letter in the mantra denotes the Chandrakalā. Here it is alluded that after seeing the Goddess's face, Manmatha made himself scarce.

The gist of the 6th sloka is found in the words of Tyāgarāja as 'Chelaku Nī lāvaṇyamu ganiyalanāḍe valarāju ..nakapōye" :

'Tanuḥ paushpam maurvi madhukaramayī pancavicikāḥ... apāngātte laptvā jagaditam anangō vijayatē" (6th soka in Saundaryalahari)

In one of the slokas of Śankarāchārya says "the brilliance of your smile made Lord Śiva himself white". Tyāgarāja gives the same idea in the words

"nī chiru navvu kāṇṭi sōki sivuḍanupamau śubhruḍāye"

The meaning of the 66th sloka is found in the words of Tyāgarāja as

"nī svaramunu vini vāṇi magani jihvanu gabhūni kāye"

meaning : Hearing the sweetness of Pārvati's voice Godess Sarasvati placed herself in Brahma's tongue. The gist of the 16th sloka 'Kavīndrāṇām chataḥ' is found in the kriti in the following words :

'Nīdayacēta satkavulella kāvyamulanu sēyanāye"

The gist of the last (102nd) sloka is found in the last part of the charaṇa in the following words :

"nīpadamuna tyāgarāju bhāvukamanukōnāye tripurasundari".

'Pratīpāḥ jvālābhiḥ divāsakara nīrajanavidhīḥ'
(102nd sloka in Saundaryalahari)

LĀLGUḌI PAÑCHARATNAM

As already mentioned Tyāgarāja visited Lālguḍi and stayed with his disciple Lālguḍi Rāma Iyer the great grand father of Padmasri Lālguḍi Jayaraman. The name of the Lord here is Saptaṛishīśvara and Goddess is Pṛavṛiddya Śrīmati. In this pañcharatna he has composed the first two kritis on the Lord and the next three on the Goddess making in all a set of 5 kritis. They are

Īśa Pāhimām in Kalyāṇi rāga and Rūpaka tāḷa
Dēvaśrī in Madhyamāvati rāga and tripuṭa tāḷa
Mahitha pravruddhe in Kāmbōdhi rāga and Chāpu tāḷa
Gathinīvani in Tōḍi rāga and Ādi tāḷa
Lalithē Śrīpravriddhē in Bhairavi rāga and Ādi tāḷa

The Madhyamāvati and Kāmbhōji kritis are in Sanskrit and the other three are in Telugu. The Dēvatā mudra is found in all the kṛitis. The compositions are full of Yati, Prāsa, Yamaka, etc. For example the Kāmbōdhi kṛiti is full of Yamaka.

'Vāhinīśa sannute na-
vāhibhīsha vallabhe pa-
vāhi nīlakanṭi simha-
vāhini janani'.

ŚRĪRAṄGA PAÑCHARATNAM

It can be seen that the Pañcharatna hitherto dealt with are all on Saivite deities. The Śrīraṅgam Pañcharatnas alone are on the Vaishnavite deity, Lord Raṅganātha. Śrīraṅgam is the most celebrated among the 'Svaṁ vyakta' kshētras. In Tamil Pēriya kōil refers only to Śrīraṅgam and the Lord is worshipped as Periya Perumāḷ. The five kritis are

Jūthā murārē in Ārabhi rāga and Rūpaka tāḷa
Vinarādana in Dēvagāndhāri rāga and Dēsādi tāḷa
Rājuveḍala in Tōḍi rāga and Rūpaka tāḷa
Karuṇajūḍavayya in Saranta rāga and Ādi tāḷa
Ō Raṅgaśāyee in Kāmbōdhi rāga and Ādi (Vilamba kāla) tāḷa

Tyāgarāja employs paryāya nāmas of the Lord such as Kastūri raṅga, Vaibhōga raṅga, Kāvēri raṅga, Raṅgaśāyi and Raṅgapati. The Lord is depicted as Śriṅgāra nāyaka. He has described the Lord's golden robes, and Ornaments, especially the dangling of pearl necklace. Though Lord Raṅganātha is called 'Ādipurusha' he is described here as a youthful deity. In his 'Bhagavad Dhyāna Sōpānam', Vedanta Dēśika calls the Lord as Raṅgayūnaḥ. This is also reflected by Tyāgarāja in the phrase 'paruvampuprāyamaṭa' (In jūthāmurāre - Ārabhi rāga kṛiti).

In the kriti Tyāgarāja says when one offers naivēdya to the Lord in the company of Śrīdēvi and Bhūdēvi, one's wishes will be fulfilled.

In the Kāmbhōji kṛiti he refers to Śrīraṅgam as Bhūlōka Vaikuṇṭha and complains that "if you are ever sporting with Lakshmi, when will you find time to think about me?". The Lord is described as going in procession on a Haya vāhana. It is worthy of note that the Lord is described throughout as a person young in age.

It is only after Tyāgarāja's visit to Viṇai Kuppayyar's house at Tiruvoṭṭriyūr that a son was born to the latter. This child was named Tyāgarāja who became a famous composer later as Tiruvoṭṭriyūr Tyāgayyar. Paying obeisance to Tyāgarājaswāmi his grand guru, as his own personal guru, Tiruvoṭṭriyūr Tyāgayyar has composed the Guru Kīrtana 'Tyāgarājaswāmi' set to Kharaharapriya rāga.

(This paper was presented at the Annual Seminar of Ganabharati Sangeeta Sabha, Mysore, 1986.)

MUTHUSWĀMY DĪKSHITAR'S NAVAGRAHA KṚITIS

Among the compositions of the Trinity, Muthuswāmy Dīkshitar's kṛitis possess both a popular and an erudite phase besides an esoteric approach - exclusive and individualistic, universal and all embracing. They reveal the connection between the divine in man and god and are intended to serve as vehicles in the sacred mission of the spiritual emancipation and rehabilitation of the masses through the medium of ennobling and soul-stirring music. This aspect is best brought out in his Samudāya kṛitis or group kṛitis on diverse themes.

Of all the Carnatic music composers, Muthuswāmy Dīkshitar has to his credit by far the largest number of group kṛitis which are exquisite examples of lofty musical architecture - as many as 12 sets, each consisting of 5, 8, 9, 11 or 16 songs. He scores over the other vāgēyakāras also in respect of the theme and scheme of his group kṛitis and emerges as unique and outstanding in this domain. The majority of these groups pertain to various topics/Gods presented according to attractively intellectual plans. The constituent kṛitis in each group are strikingly linked to one another through their subject matter and/or musical design. They provide a mine of information on different facets of Indian philosophy and religion in which Dīkshitar was adept. All his extensive esoteric knowledge on various religious lores as well as Yoga, Tantra, Mantra and Jyōtisha śāstras constantly keep surfacing in the Samudāya kṛitis.

Two among these groups comprise 5 compositions each - firstly the well known Pañchabhūta kṛitis on Lord Śiva's five elemental forms - Pṛithvi (earth), Appu (water), Tējas (fire), Vāyu (wind) and Ākāśa (sky) - enshrined respectively in the temples at Conjeevaram, Jambukēśwaram, Tiruvaṇṇāmalai, Kāḷahasti and Chidambaram and secondly the comparatively less familiar Pañchaliṅga kṛitis on the five Śivaliṅgas housed in the Tiruvārūr Tyāgarāja temple - Acalēśvara Hāṭakēśvara, Valmīkēśvara Ānandēśvara and Siddhēśvara.

A third set of 16 songs is made up of the Shōḍasa Gaṇapati kṛitis on different forms of Lord Vināyaka. Dīkshitar has composed eight of the remaining nine groups on the extra-musical principle of

Vibhakti or Sanskrit grammatical case which are eight in number including Sambōdhana (nominative, accusative etc. to vocative). Each of these eight sets is in praise of a particular deity viz., Lord Subramaṇya manifested as Guruguha, which incidentally is also Dīkshitar's mudra (Guru Vibhakti kīrtanas); Lord Śiva manifested as Tyāgarāja of Tiruvārūr (Tyāgēśa Vibhakti kīrtanas); Lord Vishṇu manifested as Rāma (Rāma navāvarṇam) and Krishṇa (Krishṇa Navāvarṇam); and lastly Dēvi in four manifestations - as Goddess Mīnākshi of Madurai (Madhurāmbā Vibhakti kīrtanas), as Abhayāmbā of Māyavaram (Abhāyāmbā Navāvarṇam), Nīlōtpalāmbā of Tiruvārūr(Nīlōtpalāmbā Vibhakti kīrtanas) and as Kamalāmba of Tiruvārūr (Kamalāmba Navāvarṇam). However, the Kamalāmbā Navāvarṇam actually forms a group of 11 compositions including, in addition to eight kṛitis in the eight Vibhakti corresponding to the eight Āvarṇas of the Śrī Chakra, a ninth in all the eight Vibhaktis coresponding to the ninth Āvaraṇa besides invoicatory (Dhyāna) and auspicious ending (Maṅgalam) compositions.

These Samudāya kṛitis reveal diverse facets of Dīkshitar's genius and learning. If the Tyāgēśa Vibhakti kṛitis unravel his experiences as a Yōgi, the Pañchabhūta kṛitis enlighten us about his profound knowledge regarding the Vēdāgamas and the Upanishads. The Kamalāmba and Abhayāmbā Navāvarṇams bear eloquent testimony to Dīkshitar's extraordinary perception of our Tantra and Mantra śāstras as a devout Śrī Vidyā Upāsaka ardently worshipping Śrī Chakra. In South India, in the tradition expounded by Bhāskarāchārya, Śrīvidya had long been practiced as a Sādhanamārga for salvation by the Advaitins. Dīkshitar has based his Kamalāmba and Abhayāmbā Navāvarṇams on Bhāskarāchārya's percepts. His last set of Samudāya kṛitis - the Navagraha kṛitis which form the subject matter of the kpresent paper possess astrological connotations and display Dīkshitar's deep insight into the ancient system of Hindu Jyōtisha śāstra.

It is but in the fitness of things that the Navagraha kṛitis possess an astrological bias because according to Jyōtisha Śāstra, the positions of the planets in a person's horoscope indicate their varying influence on the life course and one's fortunes and afflictions by diseases can be accurately predicted from the transit of the planets. If one considers the entire solar system as the body of God, planets signify definite centres or organs therein, each utilising and manifesting a different type of vitality or consciousness in which the Sun is the heart. And also if man is conceived to be the Universe in miniature, the Sun (Sūrya) would represent the Ātma or Soul; the Moon (Chandra), Manas or mind; Mars (Kuja or Aṅgāraka) Ahaṁkāra or ego; Mercury (Budha), Chith or intelligence; Jupiter (Guru), Buddhi or intuition; Venus (Śukra), worldly pleasures; and Saturn (Śani), Vivēka or balance of mind and discrimination. In this manner the planet deities are intimately linked with the evolutionary career of mankind and the passage of the Sun and the planets through the 12 signs of the zodiac mark of a person's progress in time and space.

Among Dīkshitar's Samudāya Kṛitis, his Navagraha kṛitis are the only group made of 9 components unlike other groups which contain 5, 8, 11 or 16 compositions each. Another point of difference is that every song in each Vibhakti group is in praise of the same deity in contrast to the Navagraha groups which are on the nine different planets. But the most important distinguishing feature of the Navagraha kṛitis is that they have not been composed according to any extra-musical plan but on the purely musical principle based on the Sūlādhi-sapta-tāḷas. This will be evident from the list of Navagraha kṛitis given below :

1.	Sun	SŪRYAMŪRTHE	Saurāshṭram	Dhruva
2.	Moon	CHANDRAṀ BHAJA	Asāvēri	Marṭhya
3.	Mars	AṄGĀRAKAṀ	Suraṭi	Rūpaka
4.	Mercury	BUDHAMĀŚRAYĀMI	Nāṭakurañji	Jhaṁpa
5.	Jupiter	BṚIHASPATE	Aṭhāṇa	Tripuṭa
6.	Venus	ŚRĪ ŚUKRA	Pharaz	Aṭa
7.	Saturn	DIVĀKARA	Yadukula-kāṁbōdhi	Ēka
8.	Rahu	SMARAMYAHAM	Ramāmanōhari	Rūpaka
9.	Ketu	MAHASURAM	Chāmaraṁ	Rūpaka

It can readily be seen that these Navagraha kṛitis constitute a set not on the mere basis that they pertain to the nine planets. Dīkshitar's genius has knit them together in a musical sense through adopting the order of the Sūlādi-sapta-tāḷas as enunciated in the well-known tāḷa aphorism (Dhruva, Maṭhya, Rūpaka, Jhaṁpa, Tripuṭa, Aṭa and Ēka) for the seven major planets from Sūrya to Śani in their accepted order. The adoption of this tāḷa principle for this set of group kṛitis bears testimony to Dīkshitar's outstanding attainments in music and unparalleled gifts as a composer. A noteworthy feature and interesting coincidence is that the sum total of the akṣharas of all the tāḷas used in these kṛitis is 81, which is again a multiple (square) of 9, the number of all the grahas - the potent number ! The composition of the Navagraha kritis on the basis of talas is particularly **appropriate** because tāḷa is a time measure and in astrology, periods of time have vital significance in the context of the influence of the different planets on man's fortunes and well being. According to astrology, each Graha determines a person's destiny during its daśa which in each case extends over a definite period of time (number of years). Tāḷa also being a time measure, it can indicate good or bad periods during which the planets hold sway over man's fortunes.

The rāgas of the Navagraha kṛitis too are not without significance. Dīkshitar has employed for his kṛitis on the seven major planets Saurāshṭra, Asāveri, Suraṭi Nāṭakurañji, Aṭhāṇa, Pharaz and Yadukulakāmbōdhi respectively. These are all Śuddha-madhyama rāgas as well as Sampūrṇa rāgas in the Asampūrṇa Mēḷa-Paddhati followed by Dīkshitar. Furthermore they are all Bhāsāṅga rāgas. The free unfettered movement of the Grahas is musically mirrored, as it were, by these Bhāshāṅga ragas which do not suffer from shackles of Janaka ragas but freely imbibe Anyasvaras.

From Muthuswāmy Dīkshitar's life history, one learns that he composed these Navagraha kṛitis for the purpose of alleviating the pain suffered by his favourite disciple Śudhamaddaḷam Thambiappan who was suffering from acute colic. It is said that the latter was cured of his malady by offering prayers through the medium of these kṛitis to those planet deities who were unfavourably positioned in his horoscope. The outstanding feature of this set of Samudhāya kṛitis is their healing value and powerful ability to propitiate the Navagrahas for an all-round betterment of life of everyone who has no easy access to Mantras. They enable everybody without distinction of caste or creed to win the favour and blessings of the planets. Mantra Śastra is an esoteric lore but its benefits can be derived even by the common devotees irrespective of status and learning if it comprises ordinary hymns and songs. Dikshitar's Navagraha kṛitis are easily accesible versions of Mantra and Tantra Śastras as they pertain to different planets. For the lay public they constitute effective prayers to various Grahas to earn their grace.

Another noteworthy feature of these Navagraha kṛitis is the literary beauty and appropriateness of their Sanskrit sāhitya. They are not based on phrases borrowed from the Navagraha stōtras or kavachas contained in our epics and Purāṇas. They are truly original compositions of Dīkshitar.

In astrology the different planets have been assigned powers to promote particular aspects of human life. For instance, the Sun is deemed to promote father, health, personal charisma etc.; the Moon : mother, mind; Mars : brothers, lands; Mercury : poety, intelligence; Jupiter : sons, wisdom, liking for righteous path; Venus : happiness from good family life; and Saturn : longevity. Dikshitar lucidly brings out these Kārakatvas (powers) of various planets in his Navagraha kṛitis. He calls Sūryamurtē Ārōgyādi phalada and Tēja spūrte (promoter of health and personal charisma). Significantly he commences his kṛiti on the Moon, the promoter of mind, with the words 'Chandraṁ bhaja mānasa' (pray to Moon, oh mind). Kuja is 'Bhṛāthṛukāraka' and 'Dharaṇīprada' (bestower of brothers and lands). Budha is 'Madhura kavitā prada' (conferer of poesy). Guru is 'Putra kāraka' (promoter of progeny/son) and Sukra is 'Kaḷatra kāraka' (bestower of spouse). Regarding Śanīśvara, Dīkshitar says that He is 'Ati krūra phalada' (cruel and threatening) to those who are immersed in the pursuit of worldly pleasures but the same planet pleasures but the same planet becomes 'Atiśaya śubha phalada' (extremely beneficial) to those who follow the righteous path and pray with sincere devotion. This is an interesting aspect of the Navagrahas dealt with by Dīkshitar.

Astrology also considers the Navagrahas to be friendly, neutral or inimical with the other Grahas. It is the combination of such friendly or inimical planets in a particular horoscope which augments or lessens the power of the individual planets to confer good or evil on that person. In some of his Navagraha kṛitis Dīkshitar includes this theme of mutual friendship or enimity among the Grahas beautifully woven into the sahitya fabric. In Aṅgārakam, Kuja is stated to be friendly with the Sun, Moon and Jupiter (Bhānu chandra guru mitram). In Budhamāśrayāmi, Mercury is referred to as the enemy of Mars (Kuja vairiṇaṁ). In Śrī Śukra Bhagavantaṁ, Venus is described as the enemy of the Sun and Jupiter (Ravi nirjara guru vairiṇaṁ). The 'Smarāmyahaṁ" Dikshitar mentions that Rāhu is friendly with Saturn and Venus (Śani Śukra mitram). In 'Mahāsuram',

Kētu is stated to be friendly with all planets (Navagrahayutaṁ sakaṁ).

The relationship between astrology and music dates back to very early times. The division of the octave into 12 units was employed by all the ancient nations and this is known as primordial division of the octave. The Zodiac has also 12 divisions which correspond to the same number of divisions of the octave and astrology has come in handy to explain the intervals of the octave and the effect produced by the svaras. The major seven planets represent the 7 svaras and the 12 divisions of the Zodiac are distributed among the 7 planets corresponding to the distribution of the 12 divisions of the octave among 7 svaras. Among the 7 planets, the sun and the Moon have each one of the divisions of the Zodiac corresponding to Sa and Pa in the musical octave. The remaining 5 planets have each two divisions as is the case also with the remaining 5 svaras in the musical scale. In astrology these divisions are known as Rāśis or houses (Mēsha, Rishaba etc., to Meena) belonging to the different planets. In this way one can readily perceive the connection between music and astrology. This coincidence between the divisions of the Zodiac and the division of the Octave serves as a facile means to explain the musical scales on a mathematical basis. The major planets being the Sun and the Moon, the basic note Sa is assigned to the prime Planet - Sun and Pa the second important note of the octave, to the Moon. The remaining 5 svaras are assigned in the following order - Ri to Budha, Ga to Śani, Ma to Śukra, Dha to Kuja and Ni to Guru. Next to Sa and Pa the most important svara is Ma and it is significant, that this svara is ascribed to Śukra among whose many portfolios, music itself is one.

The ownership of the different Zodiac houses by the various planets is invariably pinpointed by Dīkshitar in the appropriate Navagraha kriti. He thus mentions that the Sun is the Lord of Simha Rāśi (Simha rāśyādhipate); Mars is exalted in Makara and is the owner of Mēsha and Vrischika (Makarōtuṅgaṁ, Mēsha vrischika Rāśyāḥ dhipatim); Mercury owns Mithuna and Kanya (Kamanīyatara mithuna Kanyādhipaṁ); Jupiter is the lord of Dhanus and Mina (Mañju dhanur mīnādhipate); Saturn is the lord of Makara and Kumbha (Makara kumbha rāśi natham). Venus is the lord of Vrishabha and Thula (Vrusha Thulādīśa). The Chāyā grahas do not own any houses. Only in the kṛiti on the Moon, the mention of the house owned by the planet is missing. It is however understood in the Calcutta edition of the Navagraha kritis of the late Sri Anantakrishna Iyer, the sahitya of Chandram bhaja mānasa specifies Kaṭaka as the Rāśi owned by the Moon.

Let us now proceed to examine the salient features of the Navagraha kritis on the nine planets one by one.

1. **SŪRYA :**

The kriti on the first planet, Sun, starts with the words, "Sūryamurte Namastute'. It is set in Saurāshṭra rāga and Dhruva tāḷa. Though Saurāshṭra is currently being sung as a janya of Sūryakāntam, Dīkshitar must have conceived it only as a janya of Māyāmāḷavagauḷa while composing the kṛiti - a fact vouched for by the late Subbarāma Dikshitar in his magnum opus Saṅgīta Sampradāya Pradarśini. The composition of the kriti on this primary planet in a rāga which is a janya of Māyāmāḷavagauḷa is highly significant because Mayamalavagaula is the first raga taught to learners of music. Dīkshitar is also reputed to have composed in this rāga his very first kṛiti 'Śrī Nāthādi', heading his group of Guru Vibhakti kīrtanas. The uttarāṅga delineates vīra rasa and the Pūrvāṅga bhakti rasa. The phrase 'Namostute'has been cast in descending order from Madhyasthāyi to the Mandrasthāyi reflecting the singer's obeisance to the Sun. Not only as the first among the Sūlādi Sapta tāḷas but also as one with the maximum number of aksarakālas, Dhruva tāḷa eminently suits the composition on the great Sun who through his powerful radiation controls life here on earth.

The Sāhitya is replete with numerous beautifully apt phrases. Besides being reference to Mitra and Bhānu as in the vedas, the Sun is also described as the first and foremost Navagraha--'Sōmādi graha shikāmane'. The epithet Āryavinuta presumably refers to the widespread practice of sun worship among the early Aryans. The cult of Sun-worship is known as Souramata and its mantra, made up of 8 aksharas, is called the Sourāshṭrārṇa mantra. Dīkshitar describes the Sun as the embodiment of this mantra in the phrase 'Sourāshṭrārṇa mantrātmane' and thereby the Sourāshṭra rāga Mudra is introduced into the sahitya fabric. Apart from the Kētu kṛiti in Chāmaram, Sūryamūrte is the only other Navagraha kṛiti wherein the rāga mudra is introduced. Through the phrase 'Divyatara saptasvarāthine', Dīkshitar describes the Sun as riding a chariot drawn by 7 horses and this may also be interpreted to refer to the 7 rainbow colours constituting sunlight. By the phrase 'Bharatīśa hari harātmane', Dīkshitar praises the sun as the representation of the Trinity - Brahma, Vishṇu and Mahēśvara. He is also capable of conferring pleasures of the mundane world as well as salvation - Bhuktimukti vitaraṇātmane'.

2. CHANDRA :

The kṛiti on the second planet, Moon, is set to Asāvēri rāga Maṭhya tāḷa which is the second among the Sūlādi Sapta tāḷas. The commencing words ''Chandraṁ bhaja mānasa' calling upon the mind to pray to Moon emphasizes the latter's strong influence on the human mind. In fact the term 'mati' stands for both the Moon and the mind. The Moon is said to have been born out of Virāṭ Purusha's mind and Dīkshitar refers to this aspect in the words 'Viraṇmanō Jananaṁ'. Āsavēri is a very soft rakti rāga portraying karuṇa rasa and is eminently suited for the hymn on the Moon whom Dīkshitar describes to be pleasant and tranquil like the saint's heart (Sādhu hridaya sadruśam). Terms like Sudhākaram and Indirā sahōdaraṁ allude to the planet's birth in the ocean of milk.

3. AṄGĀRAKA (Kuja)

The kriti on the third planet, Aṅgāraka or Kuja is set to Suraṭi rāga and Rūpaka tāḷa, the third tāḷa among the Sūlādi sapta tāḷas. Despite the phrase 'Maṅgaḷavāram Aṅgārakaṁ āśrayāṁyahami Maṅgaḷavāraṁ is really not considered auspicious. Again suraṭi rāga is one sung for Maṅgaḷam; still nobody teaches this rāga directly to the students and in this way this rāga is also amaṅgaḷa. The selection of this rāga which is at once mangaḷa and amaṅgaḷa for a song on this graha which is also maṅgaḷa and amaṅgaḷa at the same time is a masterstroke of Dīkshitar's genius. In contrast to other Sūlādi-sapta-tāḷas, Rūpaka tāḷa begins with Dhrutam followed by Laghu. The use of this time beat with inauspicious vilakshaṇa for composition on this amaṅgaḷa graha also reveals Dīkshitar's skill and imagination as acomposer.

Aṅgāraka is generally picturised as ruddy in complexion and

dressed in red and fierce-eyed. Dīkshitar too describes him as Raktāṅgaṁ, Raktāmbarādidaraṁ and Raktanētraṁ. As a martial planet, he is said to wear Shakti and Śūla (Śakti śūladharam).

4. BUDHA

The kṛiti on the fourth planet Budha starts with the words 'Budhamāśrayāmi' and is set to Nāṭakurañji rāga and Jhampa tāḷa the fourth among the Sūlādi-sapta-tāḷas. It is replete with numerous soft terms and the mood of the rakti rāga Nāṭakurañji admirably suits its diction.

5. BṚIHASPATI (Guru) :

The kṛiti on the fifth planet, Bṛihaspati, starts with the words 'Bṛihaspate Tārāpathe' and is set to Aṭhāṇa rāga and Tripuṭa tāḷa the next in Sūlādi-saptatāḷa-series. Astrologically Guru is considered a very beneficial planet capable of getting rid of all dōshas and ending all miseries while Aṭhāṇa itself means getting free from imprisonment or in other words getting rid of the fetters of Saṁsāra. This rāga portrays adbhuta and vīra rasas. The choice of this rāga admirably suits singing such sāhitya phrases as Mahābalavibhō, Gīshpate, Jagatraya gurō, etc.

In praising Guru, Dīkshitar has employed such expressions as Mahābalo vibhō (of great strength), Jagatraya gurō (preceptor of the three worlds), Subha lakshaṇa (handsome) and Jarādi varjita (young). Dīkshitar also hails him as surāchārya (teacher of the Dēvas) adored by Dēvēndra himself. (Mahēndrādyupāsitakrite) and praised by Vishṇu (Mādhavādi vinuta).

6. ŚUKRA :

The kṛiti on the sixth planet, Śukra starts with the words Śrī Śukrabhagavantaṁ and is set to Pharaz rāga and Aṭa tāḷa, the sixth among the Sūlādi Sapta tāḷas. The Sāhitya is replete with many astrological terms. Actually Śukra is Rākshasa guru accepted as one of the Navagrahas. The use of pharaz, a dēśiya rakti rāga, has significance. In fact Pharaz is a foreign rāga adopted into the Carnatic music fold. It is highly appropriate that Dīkshitar has employed this rāga for his song on this Graha who is the Rākshasa guru and also karaka for kaḷatra, martial happiness and last, but not the least, for musical abilities.

7. ŚANI :

The kriti on the seventh planet, Śani, starts with the words 'Divākara tanujaṁ' and is set to Yadukulakāṁbōdhi rāga and Ēka tāḷa, the seventh (last) among the Sūlādi Sapta tāḷas. Yadukulakāṁbōdhi is common in the folk music of most countries. Songs in this rāga are invariably sung in viḷaṁba kāla or slow tempo and its mood also fits in well with the notoriously slow movement of the Graha.

8. RAHU and KETU (Chāyā grahà) :

The last two grahas, Rāhu and Kētu are different from the other seven in that they are minor planets or Chāyā grahas as is evident from the fact that unlike the others these two Grahas do not have any days of the week named after them (Bhānuvāra, Sōmavāra, Maṅgaḷavāra, Budhavāra, Guruvāra, Śukravāra and Śanivāra). Nor do they own houses in the Indian astrological system of 12 houses. It is believed that these two Chāyāgrahas do not have any individual status of their own but share the same body. Dīkshitar has chosen a different category of rāgas and a vilakshaṇa tāḷa for his compositions on these two Grahas with a view to pinpointing the variation in their nature.

The songs 'Smarāṁyahaṁ' on Rāhu and 'Mahāsuraṁ' on Kētu are set in two Pratimadhyama rāgas in contrast to the compositions on the other seven grahas which are all in Śuddhamadhyama rāgas. Smarāṁyahaṁ is in Ramāmanōhari (Rāmapriya) rāga and Mahāsuram in Chāmaraṁ (Shaṇmukhapriya) rāga. Pratimadhyama rāgas are not of ancient origin; they have come into vogue only in comparatively recent times. Again the tāḷa of these compositions is Rūpaka which is the vilakshaṇa tāḷa in the Sūlādi sapta tāḷa series, (also used for the Navagraha kṛiti on Aṅgāraka).

It can thus be seen that Muthuswamy Dīkshitar has not only taken pains to choose appropriate ragas for his compositions on each of the nine grahas but also used all the Sūlādi sapta tāḷas enumerated in the well known tala aphorism for his Navagraha kṛitis.

The Navagraha kṛitis belong to a very special category from both the lyrical and musical points of view. While their sāhitya is monumental with frequent glimpses of Hindu religion and philosophy, notably astrology, the musical moiety reveals Dīkshitar's acclaimed excellence as a composer. They stand out as living examples of an original musical tradition which has a bearing at once on both theoretical and practical aspects and are the epitome of melody as well as highly sophisticated musical embellishment.

DĪKSHITAR AND HINDUSTANI MUSIC

Till about the 13th century, there seems to have been only a single system of music spread across the entire length and breadth of the Indian sub-continent. We come across the terms Hindustani Music and Carnatic Music for the first time in Haripāla's work Saṅgīta Sudhākara written sometime between 1309 and 1313 A.D. It should be remembered that the music of South India came to be significantly called Carnatic Music only after the music of North India developed new trends with the advent of the Muslim rulers, imbibing Persian and Arabic styles in large measure.

The adoption of new melodies and their assimilation into the classical musical stock is no new innovation. This has been going on in different nations of the world from times immemorial. So far as Indian Music is concerned, however, this has been largely confined to Hindustani Music. This is due to the fact that North India was exposed to wave after wave of Muslim invasions from the North West. On the other hand, South India remained comparatively insulated from these influences with the result that Carnatic music has been able to preserve its original form almost in its pristine purity. Perhaps the only changes that have come about Carnatic music are the result of the import of some North Indian melodies and the pride of place for introducing Hindustani rāgas or melodic types into Carnatic music goes to one of the Trinity viz. Muthuswāmy Dīkshitar.

Muthuswāmy Dīkshitar has composed more than 500 songs, the vast majority of them being Kṛitis. Besides he has to his credit at least 5 Rāgamālikas, a Padavarṇa and a Daru. All his kṛitis are invariably in Sanskrit except for two pieces (in Karṇāṭaka Kāpi and Śrī Rāga) which are in Maṇipravāḷam - a mixture of Sanskrit, Telugu and Tamil. They are outstanding for their richness of Rāga bhāva, aesthetic excellence as well as spiritual loftiness. Muthuswāmi Dīkshitar stands unique as a composer of Samudāya kritis, the most noteworthy being the Navāvarṇa kṛitis, Pañchaliṅga kṛitis and Navagraha kṛitis. His encyclopedic knowledge of Vedas, Sastra, Āgamas, Ṭantra and Philosophy are profoundly reflected in most of his compositions. Dīkshitar travelled widely visiting temples[1] spread all over the country and sang in praise of the presiding deities. There are few shrines of note in India around which legends and stories have not grown up. It is one of the interesting feature of Dīkshitar's Kshētra Kritis[2] that they enshrine these legends and this makes for their popular appeal as a sort of pilgrims'Bible. When one thinks of his extensive pilgrimages and the detailed and all-pervading manner in which he sang on the numerous deities, one way well hail him as the 64th Nāyanar and 13th Āḻwar.

Muthuswāmy Dīkshitar's father, Rāmaswāmy Dīkshitar had been initiated in the intricacies of the Science of Music by one Vīṇa Veṅkaṭa Vaidyanātha Dīkshitar of Madhyārjunam. Veṅkaṭa Vaidyanātha Dīkshitar hailed from the family of Gōvinda Dīkshitar and Veṅkaṭamakhi. Therefore, as one would expect, his emphasis was on the system of 72 Mēḷakarthas and janya rāgas as propounded by Veṅkaṭamakhi as well as the latter Lakshaṇa Gītas on the numerous Rāgas in vogue during his time, including those imbibed from the Hindustani system. Naturally these also formed the early lessons of Muthuswāmy Dīkshitar when he learnt the rudiments of music from his father during his childhood. As such Dīkshitar was brought up in Veṅkaṭamakhi's tradition. Veṅkaṭamakhi himself was a master of Hindustani music and had several disciples belonging to that school. That could be the compelling reasons for the fact that Hindustani music strongly appealed to Dīkshitar.

As good luck would have it, Muthuswāmy Dīkshitar was blessed, at a very young age with the opportunity of going to North India in the company of his Guru and mentor Śrī Chidambara Nātha Yōgi and spending 5-6 years at Kāśi (Vārāṇasi). It would appear that they also undertook an extensive pilgrimage to temples situated as far apart as Kāṭhmāṇḍu and Bhadriṇāth. During the later part of the 18th century, Hindustani music had attained the acme of its glory, thanks to the patronage extended by a succession of enlightened Mughal rulers who were themselves musicians and musicologists of no mean attainments. Dīkshitar's sojourn in North India for a fairly long period at this juncture provided him excellent opportunities of not only listening to Hindustani music from its foremost exponents but also of learning it in all its authenticity. He devoted most of his leisure time to the practice of music in general and of Hindustani ragas in particular and acquired mastery over them. This exerted a profound influence on Dīkshitar's music as can be seen not only in the handling of Hindustani rāgas in some of his compositions but also in the portrayal in general of all rāgas.

Though the Hindustani and Carnatic systems of music present distinctive features and may strike one at first as alien to each other, the fact is that they are branches of the same system of music. The theory is the same in both the systems and the treatises in which they are expounded are common to both. It is true that each has developed its own individuality but the difference is merely dialectical in character. In the days of Venkatamakhi, these differences had not become so pronounced. After his time, however, owing to the prevailing political conditions the two systems began to lose contact with each other and to develop in independent lines, resulting in accentuation of the differences. For the same reason, the Hindustani rāgas which had earlier been ascribed in the Carnatic system lost, during this period, some of their original features and instead adopted new sañcharas, thereby taking a somewhat different complexion. In the composition of Muthuswamy Dīkshitar, however, they regain their original purity and form. This is because, having learnt these rāgas first and at Varanasi, Dīkshitar was able to present a picture true to the Hindustani version though he was unable wholly to discard some of their accretions in the South. To give an illustration, Rāga Sāraṅg of the Hindustani system had been adopted in Carnatic Music under the name of Brindāvani. According to Veṅkaṭamakhi's Lakshaṇa gīta in this rāga its Ārōhaṇa is Sa, ri, ma, pa, ni, sa and Avarōhaṇa Sa ni pa ma ri sa and it is the same as that of the Carnatic rāga Madhyamāvati except that it also takes Kākali(Tīvra) Nishādha and has some characteristic sañchāras. The lakshaṇa of Brindāvani in this Gīta conforms fully to that of Sāraṅg of the Hindustani system. Subsequent to Veṅkaṭamakhi's time, this rāga, which came to be called Brindāvana Sāraṅga combining the names of both the systems, underwent some changes. There was an occasional use of Sādhāraṇa (Kōmaḷ,Gāndhāra) which was, of course, of not much consequence. But the Kākali Nishāda prayōga with its characteristic Sañchāras came to be dropped and this completely altered the complexion of the raga. All this was set right by Dīkshitar in his several songs in this raga like 'Śrī Raṅgapura Vihāra', 'Soundararājam' and 'Swāmināthēna'. Except for the very slight use of Sādhāraṇa Gāndhāra (which can even be omitted without any detriment to the pieces), Dīkshitar's rendering of this rāga is precisely the same as that of Sāraṅg in Hindustani music.

Passing on to the compositions of Dīkshitar in other Hindustāni rāgas, he has composed pieces like 'Jamboopathe' and 'Nanda gōpāla' in Yamunā Kalyāṇi which corresponds to Ēma or Suddhakalyāṇ on Hindustani music. For sheer richness of Rāga Bhāva and grandeur, they stand unrivalled. The same may be said of pieces like 'Parimaḷa raṅganātham' and 'Purahara Nandana' in Hamīrkalyāṇi which corresponds to the 'Kēdāra' of North Indian music.

Jayajayavanthi is another Hindustani rāga which had been adopted in Carnatic music under the name Dvijāvanti. Dīkshitar's songs 'Chētha śrī Bālakrishṇa' and 'Akhilāṇdēśwari' in this rāga are magnificent edifices giving a full view of the Rāga in all its aspects. Dīkshitar has composed a song 'Vāsudēvaṁ Upāsamahe' in the raga Māḷava-Pañcama. It would appear that this corresponds to the Rāga Basant of the Hindustani system with some changes which it had undergone in the South.

Two other compositions which are of particular interest in the context of Dīkshitar's compositions in Hindustani rāgas are Paśupatīśwaram on the presiding deity of the shrine at Kāṭhmāṇḍu and Śrī Satyanārāyaṇam on the presiding deity of the shrine at Badrinath. Both these songs are cast in the raga Śiva Pantuvarāḷi, which is the 45th Mela in the scheme of Venkatamakhi (now called Śubhapantuvarāḷi) and corresponds to Miyānki-Tōḍi of Hindustani music reputed to have been invented by the great Tansen. In the days of Muthuswāmy Dīkshitar, Śiva Pantuvarāḷi was a rather obscure and neglected Rāga and even now the position has not changed very much. But Miyānki-Tōḍi is one of the major hits of Hindustani system and it is therefore in the fitness of things that Dīkshitar should have used this Rāga in both these compositions. Inded in the kriti on Paśupatīśwara, the Lord has been described as having a liking for Śiva Pantuvarāḷi Rāga. This would suggest that Miyānki-Tōḍi was being used largely in the Bhajans before the Deities at the time of Dīkshitar's visit to these temples during the course of his pilgrimage in North India.

Even in the handling of rāgas other than those adopted from the Hindustani system, the compositions of Dīkshitar bear a strong impress of his knowledge of that system. The vast majority of his compositions are in Vilamba Kāla with Madhyama Kāla Aksharas at the end, as is the general practice in Hindustani music. They are replete with Gamakas and this is due not only to his being a great Vīṇa player but also the influence exerted by Hindustani music. Though Gamakas are common to both the Hindustani and Carnatic systems, the former lays greater emphasis on some of them, as for example Jaru and the compositions of Dīkshitar give far greater preminence to this Gamaka as compared to other compositions in Carnatic music. It may be said in general that certain Gamakas are very appropriate to Vilaṁba kāla music and so it is only to be expected that they would figure largely both in the Alapa of Hindustani Rāgas and in the compositions of Dīkshitar. In the rendering of these Gamakas, Dīkshitar found much that was congenial to him.

A study of Chaturdaṇḍi Prakāśika of Veṅkaṭamakhi would convince anyone that he never adopted the Grāma-mūrchchana system. It would appear that this is due to the fact that a Saṁpūrṇa Rāga has 8 notes (Ashṭaka) in the octave. The Ashṭaka resembles the Maquams of Arabian music. As already pointed out, Arab music exerted great influence on Hindustani music. The first Arab scale corresponds to the Māyāmāḷavagauḷa scale. This might have been a compelling reason for the fact that Dīkshitar saw it fit to compose his first song,'Śrī Nāthādi Guruguhō' in this rāga.

Through his kritis in diverse ragas of Hindustani origin, some of which are in praise of deities in the temples of North India, Dīkshitar has endeavoured to combine, as it were, the two systems of music and spread the divine message of the North in the South. He can therefore be considered to be the foremost musical integrator of India.

NOTES

1. See 'Pallaki Sēva Prabandham' Appendix 1 by Mrs. Gowri Kuppuswamy, 1977, Mysore.

2. Vide. The following article pp. 93-103.

KSHĒTRA KṚITIS OF MUTHUSWĀMI DĪKSHITAR

The second half of the eighteenth century witnessed an important renaissance in the realm of Carnatic music. During this period were born the three composers, collectively known as the Trinity, who were outstanding both for their bhakti and for the aesthetic excellence of their music. They were Sri Tyāgarāja, Śrī Muthuswāmi Dīkshitar and Śrī Syāmā Śāstri. All of them were born at Tiruvārūr in Thañjāvur district. Among them Dīkshitar stayed longest at Tiruvārūr and sang the praise of the sacred shrine for which Tiruvārūr has been justly famous from the dawn of history. It is the tradition of this country to revere its great saints and men of light and culture who have left their footprints of indelible deepness in the sands of time and Sri Muthuswāmi Dīkshitar certainly belongs to this category.

Sri Tyāgarāja created a revival in the bhakti mārga, believing in the efficacy of repeated recital of the name of the Lord as a means of attaining salvation. Dīkshitar reinforced spiritual life by these and other means as well and his work has both a popular and learned phase. The Bhajana paddati of Tyāgarāja makes us adore him as Nārada's own disciple and his poetic outpourings on Lord Rāma make us revere him as Vālmiki's incarnation. Likewise, when we think of the extensive pilgrimages Dīkshitar made and the detailed and all-pervading manner in which he sang on the different deities enshrined at various places, we may well hail him as the 64th Nāyanmār and the 13th Āḷvār.

It is well known that Tyāgarāja expressly voiced forth different aspects of our philosophy in his kṛitis. Such references are not however, common in Dīkshitar's compositions. Dīkshitar has composed songs in Sanskrit, using easy diction and giving prominence to Bhakti. Just like the Nāyanmārs, he has travelled widely and composed songs in praise of a large number of deities at different places. The noteworthy point about these compositions is that they contain a detailed account of the sthala mahātmya including salient aspects of temple architecture, tīrtha, kshētra viśesha, forms of propiation specified at different shrines and the leading episodes pertaining to the different deities.

It is bhakti and bhakti alone that forms the key note of Dīkshitar's songs, for he was born in answer to the prayers of his parents to god Muthukumāraswāmi of Vaidīśvarankoyil on the day of Krittikā nakshatra, the sacred star of Lord Muruga. At a young age he was blessed by Lord Muruga or Guha at Tiruttaṇi and this led him to adopt the mudra Guru Guha in his compositions, since Guha was his preceptor (guru) who initiated him into the intricacies of music and enabled him to become a great vāggeyakāra.

Dīkshitar composed his first song at Tiruttaṇi, which is one of the six famous abodes of Lord Muruga. This song 'Śrī Nādāti guruguhō' is in Māyāmāḷavagaula rāga. It is a point of interest that till the time of Veṅkaṭamakhi (17th century) this rāga was not in vogue, and it was Veṅkaṭamakhi who classified it under the fifteenth mēḷa. We do not come across any composition in this rāga by the composers who flourished prior to his period such as Sri Purandaradāsa, Tallapākkam composers, Bhadrāchala Rāmadās etc. Even Kshētrajña did not handle this raga in his padas. It is note worthy that Dīkshitar was the first to compose a kṛiti in this rāga. This kriti was followed by seven kritis on Guruguha in the seven other Vibhaktis :

'Mānasaguruguha rūpam' in Ānandabhairavi rāga
'Śrī Guruṇā' in Pāḍi rāga
'Guruguhāya' in Sāma rāga
'Guruguhādanyam' in Balahaṁsa rāga
'Guruguhasya' in Pūrvi rāga
'Guruguhaswāmini' in Bhānumati rāga
and 'Sri Guruguhamurte' in Udhayaravichandrika rāga.

The fact that most of these songs are in rare rāgas bear testimony to his versatality as a composer even at an early age.

From Tiruttaṇi Dīkshitar proceeded to Tirupati, where he composed the songs 'Sēshāchalanāyakam' in Varāḷi rāga and 'Śrī Veṅkaṭagirīśam' in Surați rāga in praise of Lord Veṅkatēśvara.

According to the Saivite tradition, Lord Śiva manifests Himself in the form of five elements in five kshētras. In Kāḷahasti His manifestation is as the Vāyu-liṅga. In praise of this linga, Dīkshitar composed the song 'Kāḷahastīśa' in Husēni rāga. This is one of the Pañchabhūta-kritis. He also composed another song 'Jñānaprasūnāmbike' in Kalyāṇi rāga in praise of the goddess at Kāḷahasti.

At Kāñchipuram, where the Lord is believed to manifest Himself in Prithvī-linga, Dīkshitar composed the second of his Pañchabhūta kritis 'Chintayamākanda mūla' in Bhairavi rāga. The other kṛitis Dīkshitar composed at Kāñchipuram in praise of the deities Kāmākshi, Ekāmṛēśvara, Varadarja and Kailāsanātha are the following :

'Kāmākshi mām pāhi' in Śuddhadēśi rāga
'Ēkāmṛēśvaranāyike' in Karṇāṭaka Śuddasāvēri rāga
'Ēkāmṛanātham bhajēham' inGamakakriya rāga
'VaradarājamUpāsamahe' in Sāranga rāga
'Kailāsanāthēna' in Kāmbhōji rāga
'Kailāsānātham' in Vēgavāhini rāga

Upanishad Brahma Yōgin of Kāñchi taught Dīkshitar Vedanta philosophy and inculcated to him a strong devotion towards Rāma. His influence is clearly reflected in many of Dīkshitar's songs on Lord Rāma. In the kriti 'Rāmachandrēṇa samrakshitōham' in Māñji rāga, Rāma is described as the embodiment of the Trimūrti.

Reaching the shrine at Tiruvoṭṭṛiyūr, he composed the kṛiti 'Ādipurīśvaram' in Ārabhi rāga in praise of thepresiding deity 'Ādipurīśvara' and another song 'Tripura sundari' in Sāma rāga in praise of the goddess of the place.

At Madras, the kriti'Pārthasārathy' in Suddha dhanyāsi rāga in praise of God Pārthasārathi was composed by Dīkshitar. At Tirukkaḷukkunṛam, he composed the song 'Vēdapurīśvaram' in Dhanyāsi rāga in praise of Vēdapurīśvara of the temple at that place.

At Tirvaṇṇāmalai where the manifestation of Lord Śiva is as the Tējo linga, Dīkshitar composed another of his Pañchabhūta kṛitis 'Aruṇāchalanātam' in Sāranga rāga.

At Chidambaram, where the Lord manifests Himself as the Ākāśa linga, Dīkshitar composed his next Pañchabhūta kṛiti 'Ānanda naṭana prakāśam' in Kēdāra rāga. Other songs composed by him at Chidambaram include :

'Śivakāmēśvariṁ' in Kalyāṇi rāga
'Śivakāmēśvaraṁ' in Ārabhi rāga
'Kanakasabhāpatiṁ' in Māḷavaśrī rāga
'Gōvindarājaṁ' in Mukhāri rāga
'Gōvindarājēṇa' in Mēchabhauḷi rāga

Crossing the Coleroon, Dīkshitar reached Vaidīśvaran koyil. In this shrine the presentation of Śaktivēl to Muruga by goddess Pārvati is observed as an important festial. In the famous Kāmbhōji rāga kṛiti 'Śrī Subramaṇyāya' and in 'Śaravaṇabhava guruguham' in Rēvagupti rāga, the references 'Śaktyāyudhadhare' and 'Śaktyāyudha dharakaraṁ' respectively may be noted. In praise of goddess Bālāmbika and god Vaidyanātha of the same temple, Dīkshitar composed the kṛitis 'Bhajarē rēchitta' in Kalyāṇi rāga and 'Vaidyanāthaṁ' in Aṭāṇa rāga.

Dīkshitar's sojourn at Māyavaram would appear to be comparatively long. In praise of goddess Abhayāmba he has composed kritis in different <u>vibhaktis</u> known as Abhayāmbā Navāvarṇa kṛitis . They are :

'Abhayāmbā jagadamba' in Kalyaṇi rāga
'Abhayāmbā mām' in Bhairavi rāga
'Girijayā Ajaya' in Śankarābharaṇa rāga
'Abhayāmbikāyai' in Yadukulakāmbōji rāga
'Abhayāmbikāyāḥ' in Kēdāragauḷa rāga
'Ambikāyāḥ abhayambikayah' in Kēdāra rāga
'Abhayāmbikayāṃ' inSāhāna rāga
'Dākshāyaṇi' in Tōdi rāga

There is also a kriti in Śrī rāga, 'Abhāyambā ninnu' in <u>Maṇipravāḷa</u> i.e., a mixture of Sanskrit, Telugu and Tamil. In particular these kritis reveal Dīkshitar's extraordinary talent and skill in both the tantric and mantric doctrines. He composed another kriti 'Māyūranātam' in Dhanyāsi rāga in praise of Lord Māyūraṇātha of the same temple.

Dīkshitar also visited a nearby shrine at Vaḷḷaḷarkōyil and sang 'Vadānyēśvaraṁ bhajēhaṁ' in Dēvagāndhāri rāga in praise of Lord Vadanyēśvara.

At Tiruvārūr, his birth place, he stayed for many years. He

has composed three groups of vibhakti kṛitis on the deities of the Tiruvārūr temple. The most famous of these vibhakti kṛitis are the **Kamalāṁbā navāvarṇa kṛitis. They are :**

'Kamalāṁbikē' inTodi raga
'Kamalāṁbā saṁrakshatu' in Ānandabhairavi rāga
'Kamalāṁbāṁ bhajarē' in Kalyāṇi raga
'Śrī Kamalāṁbikayā' in Śaṅkarābharaṇa rāga
'Kamalāṁbikāyai' in Kāṁbōji rāga
'Śrī Kamalāṁbikayāḥ' in Bhairavi rāga
'Kamalāṁbikāyāstava' in Punnāgavarāḷi rāga
'Śrī Kamalāṁbikāyāṁ bhaktim' in Śahāna rāga
'Śrī Kamalāṁbikē ava ava' in Ghaṇṭa rāga
'Śrī Kamalāṁbā jayati' in Āhiri rāga
'Śrī Kamalāṁbikē' in Śrī rāga

The second group of vibhakti kṛitis is in praise of Lord Tyāgarāja, the presiding deity of kthe Tiruvārūr temple. They are :

'Tyāgarājō virājate' in Aṭhāṇa rāga
'Tyāgarājaṁ bhajare' in Yadukulakāṁbōji rāga
'Tyāgarājēṇa Saṁrakshitōhaṁ' in Sālagabhiravi rāga
'Tyāgarājāya namastē' in Bēgaḍa rāga
'Tyāgarājōdanyaṁ' in Darbār rāga
'Sri Tyāgarājasya bhaktō' in Rudrapriya rāga
'Tyāgarāje krityā kritiṁ' in Sāraṅga rāga
'Vīravasanta Tyāgarāja' in Vīravasanta rāga

The third group of vibhakti kṛitis is in praise of goddess Nīlōtpalāṁbā of the same temple and they are :

'Nīlōtpalāṁbā jayati' in Nārāyaṇagauḷa rāga
'Nīlōtpalāṁbāṁ bhajare' in Rītigauḷa rāga
'Nīlōtpalāṁbikayā' in Kannaḍagauḷa rāga
'Nīlōtpalāṁbikayi' in Kēdāragauḷa rāga
'Nīlōtpalāṁbikayāḥ' in Gauḷa rāga
'Nīlōtpalāṁbaya stava' in Māyamāḷavagauḷa rāga
'Nīlōtpalāṁbikāyāṁ' in Pūrvagauḷa rāga
'Śrī Nīlōtpalāṁbikē' in Chhāyāgauḷa rāga

It may be observed that all the eight rāgas employed here belong to the Gauḷa family.

Dīkshitar has composed three more songs in praise of Lord Tyāgarāja. They are : 'Tyāgarāja pālāyāsumām' in Gauḷa rāga, 'Tyāgarājayōga vaibhavaṁ' in Ānandabhairavi rāga and 'Tyāgarāja mahādvajārōhaṁ' in Śrī rāga.

Another group of kritis are on five Śiva _liṅgas_ in the temple. They are :

'Achalēśvara' in Bhūpāḷa rāga
'Hāṭakēśvara' in Bilahari rāga
'Valmīkēśvara' in Kāmbōji rāga
'Ānandēśvara' in Ānandabhairavi rāga
'Siddhēśvara'in Nīlāmbari rāga

By some arrangement of openings in the sanctum structure there is always a beam of sunlight on the Achalesvara _liṅgam_. According to the _Kamalālaya Mahātmya_ of Skanda, it was to bless the king Chamatkāra, who constantly worshipped Him that god Achalēśvara manifested thisconstant light on His form and hence came to be known as Achala.

While at Tiruvārūr, Dīkshitar conceived the idea that it would be useful to compose a group of songs in praise of the different planets that could be sung with benefit by all mankind. The result was his famous _Navagraha Kṛitis_[1] and they are :

'Sūryamurtē' in Saurāshṭra rāga (Sun)
'Chandraṁ bhaja'inAsāvēri rāga (Moon)
'Aṅgārakaṁ' in Suraṭi rāga (Mars)
'Budhamāśrayāmi' in Nāṭakuruñji raga (Mercury)
'Bṛihaspatē' in Aṭāṇa rāga (Jupiter)
'Śrī Śukrabhagavantaṁ' in Pharaz rāga (Venus)
'Dīvākaratanujaṁ' in Yadukulakāmbōji rāga (Saturn)
'Smarāmyahaṁ' in Ramāmanōhari rāga (Rāhu)
'Mahāsuraṁ' inChāmaraṁ rāga (Kētu)

Dīkshitar has also composed kritis on the sixteen manifestations of Ganesa in the Tiruvārūr temple known as Shōḍasa Gaṇapatis.[2] Some of these are :

'Mahāgaṇapatiṁ manasā' in Nāṭa rāga
'Śrī Mahāgaṇapati' in gauḷa rāga

'Vātāpigaṇapatiṁ' in Haṁsadhvani rāga
'Mūlādhāra chakravināyakạ' in Śrī rāga
'Pañchamātaṅga mukha' in Malahari rāga
'Karikaḷabhamukham' in Sāvēri rāga
'Uchchishṭagaṇapati' in Dēśi Rāmakriya rāga

All the above songs on Lord Gaṇēśa are composed followed by the Dhyānaślōkas describing the different aspects of Gaṇēśa. For example in the song 'Pañchamātaṅga mukha', the substance of Dhyānaślōka of the five faced Hēramba Gaṇapati is noticeable.

The songs composed by Dīkshitar at Tiruvārūr in praise of goddess Rēṇukā Dēvi and god Sundaramūrti are 'Rēṇukā Dēvi' in Kannaḍabaṅgāḷa rāga and 'Sundaramūrtim' in Ṭakka rāga.

At Mannārguḍi, Dīkshitar composed three songs in praise of Rājagōpāla and two songs in praise of Bālagōpāla. They are :

'Rājagōpālaṁ' in Mōhana rāga
'Śrī Rājagōpāla'inSāvēri rāga
'Śrī vidyā Rājagōpālaṁ' in Jaganmōhini rāga
'Chētaḥśrī Bālakṛishṇam' in Dvijāvanti rāga
'Bālagōpāla pālayāśumāṁ' in Bhairavi rāga

At Tiruviḍaimarudūr, Dīkshitar composed three songs in praise of god Mahāliṅga and they are :

'Mahāliṅgēśvarāya' in Aṭhāṇa rāga
'Chintayē Mahāliṅgamūrtiṁ' in Pharaz rāga
'Mahāliṅgēśvaraṁ' in Pharaz rāga

He also composed the song 'Paradēvata' in Dhanyāsi rāga of goddess Bṛihatkuchāmbāḷ of the same place.

At Kumbakonam, Dīkshitar composed the song 'Kuṁbēśvarāya' in Kalyāṇi rāga in praise of Kuṁbēśvara.

Dīkshitar composed his famous Chaturdaśa Rāgamālika 'Śrī Viśvanāthaṁ bhājehaṁ' in praise of the god Viśvanātha at Kuḻikkarai. other songs he composed at this place include 'Annapūrṇe viśālākshi' in Sāma rāga and 'Kāśi Viśvēśvarāya' in Kāmbōji rāga. These compositions remind us of his stay at Banaras as youth.

Svāmimalai is another of the six important shrines of Lord Subrahmaṇya. There Dīkshitar composed the kṛiti 'Svāmināta' in Nāṭa rāga and 'Śrī Bālasubrahmaṇya' in Bilahari rāga.

At Kīvaḷūr, the doors of the sanctum sanctorium in the Śiva temple were closed for worship, when Dīkshitar reached the place and in great emotion he composed and sang 'Akshayaliṅgavibhō' in Śaṅkarābharaṇa rāga. At the end of the song the doors opened of their own accord. This incident reminds us of the similar episode in the life of Saint Tyāgarāja which inspired the latter to compose the kṛiti 'Teradīyaga rādā' in Gauḷipantu rāga at Tirupati.

Proceeding to Śikkil, Dīkshitar composed the song 'Śriṅgāra śaktyāyudhadhara' in Ramāmanōhari rāga in praise of Lord Subrahmaṇya. Some of the kṛitis composed by Dīkshitar at Nāgapaṭṭaṇam are :

'Śivakāyārōhaṇāya' in Rudrapriya rāga
'Kāyārōhaṇēśam' in Dēvagāndhāraṁ rāga
'Soundarajam' in Brindāvanasāraṅga rāga
'Aṁbā nīlāyatākshi' in Nīlāṁbari rāga

At Vēdaraṇyam he composed the kriti, 'Vēdāraṇyēśvarāya' in Tōḍi rāga in praise of the deity Vēdāraṇyaśvara. At Pulivalam, he composed the popular Maṇipravāḷa-kṛiti 'Veṅkaṭāchalapatē' in Karṇāṭaka Kāpi rāga.

At Tiruvaiyāru he had the opportunity of meeting the Saint Tyāgarāja on the occasion of the celebration of the festival of Śrī Rāma Paṭṭābhishēka in the latter's house. To mark the occasion Dīkshitar appropriately rendered the famous piece 'Māmava Paṭṭābhirāma' in Maṇiraṅgu rāga. The description of Śrī Rāma, his brothers, Sīta, Hanumān, etc., in this kriti is similar to that found in the Tatva Saṁgraha Rāmāyaṇa.

It is noteworthy that the kṛitis composed by Dīkshitar at Thañjāvur in praise of different deities are mostly in vivādi mēlas with samashṭi charaṇas. This was mainly for the purpose of acquainting his disciples Ponniah, Chinniah, Sivānandam and Vaḍivēlu (the famous Tanjore Quartette) with the scheme of 72 mēlas of Veṅkaṭamakhi. Some of these are in praise of goddess Bṛihadīśvari. They are :

'Santānamañjari' in Santānamañjari rāga
'Parañjyōtishmati' in Jyōtiswarūpiṇi rāga
'Himagirikumāri' Ravikṛiya rāga
'Nabhōmaṇi chandragirinayanaṁ' in Nabhōmaṇi rāga

In the Nabhōmaṇi rāga kṛiti, an indirect reference is made to king Sarafoji of Tañjāvur in this manner 'Śarabhēndra Saṁsēvitha Charaṇam'. Other songs composed by Dīkshitar at Tañjāvur are : 'Brihadaṁbikā', in Vasanta rāga and 'Pālayamāṁ brihadīśvari' in Tōḍi rāga, both in praise of goddess Brihadīśvari and 'Śriṅgāra Rasamañjarīṁ' in Rasamañjari rāga in praise of goddess Baṅgāru Kāmākshi.

At Tiruvānaikkāval, where the Lord manifests Himself as Appu liṅga, Dīkshitar composed the last of his pañchabhūta kṛitis 'Jaṁbūpate' in Yamunākalyāṇi rāga. Other songs composed by him are : 'Śrī mātaḥ śiva vāmāṅke' in Bēgaḍa rāga and 'Akhilāṇḍēśvari' in Dvijāvanti rāga.

At Tiruchirapaḷḷi, Dīkshitar composed the kṛiti, 'Śrī Mātṛubhūtaṁ' in Kannaḍa rāga in praise of god Mātṛubūta. Proceeding to Śrīraṅgam, he composed songs in praise of god Raṅganātha. They are 'Raṅganāyakaṁ' in Nāyaki rāga and 'Raṅganāthāya' in Dhanyāsi rāga.

Another holy place Dīkshitar visited is Rāmēśvaram where he composed the popular kṛiti 'Rāmanātam bhajēham' in Kāmavardhani rāga and 'Parvatavardhani' in Sāma rāga in praise respectively of the god and goddess of the temple there. In the nearby shrine at Darbhaśayanaṁ, he composed the song 'Śrī Rāmaṁ ravikulābdhi' in Nārāyaṇagauḷa rāga.

At Tirunelveli Dīkshitar composed three songs in praise of the goddess Kāntimati and gods Gaṇēśa and Śālivatīśvara. They are :

'Śrī Kāntimatiṁ' in Siṁhārava rāga
'Laṁbōdarāya' in Varāḷi rāga
'Śālivaṭīśvaraṁ' in Dēvagāndhāri rāga

He also visited Kalladakuruchi and composed the kṛiti 'Śrī Lakshmi varāhaṁ' in Ābhōgi rāga in praise of the deity there. At Kaḷugamalai he composed the song 'Subrahmaṇyēna rakshitōhaṁ' in Śuddhadhanyāsi rāga and at Tiruchendūr, the song 'Śrī Subrahmaṇyō māṁ rakshatu' in Tōḍi rāga.

The places Dīkshitar visited in Kerala were Trivandrum, where he composed the song 'Pannagaśayana' in Madhyamāvati rāga; Śabarimalai, where he composed the song 'Hariharaputram' in Vasanta rāga and Guruvāyūr, where he composed the song 'Śrīkrishnam bhaja' in Tōdi rāga.

Dīkshitar has composed a number of songs on different manifestations of Lord Gaṇēśa at the temple at Tiruvārūr, but the song 'Raktagaṇapatim' in Mōhana rāga does not belong to this group. The word 'Paraśurāmakshētra prabhāvam' in this song would indicate that it is in praise of Gaṇēśa in one of the temples of Kerala, but this temple has not yet been identified. It is worthy of note that there is reference in the song to pāyasānna offering and it is well known that the offering of the dish pāyasānna or rice cooked in milk (popularly known as pālpāyasa) to the deity is a distinctive feature in Kerala temples.

Another important place Dīkshitar visited was Madurai. He composed quite a number of kṛitis there on goddess Mīnakshī. They are :

'Mīnākshī mēmudam' in Gamakakriya rāga
'Māmava mīnākshī' inVarāḷi rāga
'Śrī Mīnākshī' in Gaurī rāga
'Śrī Madhurāpuri' in Bilahari rāga
'Kādambarī priyāyai' in Mōhana rāga

Some of the Vibhakti-kritis on goddess Madhurāmba are :

'Madhurāmba saṁrakshatu' in Dēvakṛiya rāga
'Madhurāmbām bhajarē' in Stavarāja rāga
'Śrī Madhurāmbikayā' in Aṭāṇa rāga
'Śrī Madhurāmbikāyai' in Kalyāṇi rāga
'Madhurāmbāya' in Bēgaḍa rāga
'Madhurāmbikayām' in Dēśi Simhārava rāga
'Madhurāmbā jayati' in Pharaz rāga

In Madurai he also composed a kṛiti on Pārvati 'Pahimām Pārvati' in Mōhana rāga; on Hālasyanāta (or Sundarēśvara) 'Hālasyanātam' in Darbār rāga and on Sundarēśvara, Sōmasundarēśvaram, in Śuddhavasanta rāga and 'Sundarēśvarāya' in Śankarābharaṇa rāga.

From Madurai Dīkshitar proceeded to Aḻagarkōyil where he composed the song 'Sundararājam' in Rāmakṛiya rāga in praise of the deity Sundararāja there. On his way to Eṭṭayāpuram he stayed for a while at Sāthūr where he composed a kṛiti on 'Veṅkaṭēśvara' in Mēgharañjani rāga. The Zamindar of Eṭṭayāpuram, Veṅkaṭēśvara Eḍḍappa Bhūpati become a patron of Dīkshitar and Dīkshitar spent his last years with him. In the above mentioned Mēgharañjani rāga kṛiti an exceptional reference to Veṅkaṭēśvara Eḍḍappa is made. At Eṭṭayapuram Dīkshitar composed his last kriti 'Ēhi Annapūrṇe' in Punnāgavarāḷi rāga.

Dīkshitar seems to have entertained a special liking for his kriti 'Mīnākshī mēmudaṁ' in Gamakakṛiya rāga as can be seen from the fact that he had it rendered to him by his pupils at the time of his death in 1835.

The basis of all Dīkshitar's kritis is the deep bhakti, bhagavadsvarūpa dhyāna, bhagavad-guṇānu santāna and bhagavadbhajana. If one sings his kshētra kṛitis, one may get the puṇya of visiting the different temples in person and worshipping the various deities enshrined there.

NOTES

1. Vide article on 'Navagraha Kṛitis' in the present book, pp. 77-87.

2. Ibid., pp. 104-116.

SHŌḌASA GAṆAPATI KṚITIS OF DĪKSHITAR

Gaṇēśa holds a unique place of hour in the Hindu Pantheon of Gods. Gaṇēśa's origin is well described by two Nāmāvalis in the Lalitha Sahasranāma - 'Kāmēśvara Mahālōka kalpathaśrī Gaṇēśvara' and 'Mahāgaṇēśa nirbinna vigna yantra prakarshita'. According to the Sowbhāgya Bhāskara commentary on Lalithā Sahasranāma by Bhaskarāchārya these have the following meaning : "seeing the Dēvas fettered by the magical figures set up by the Asuras, the auspicious mother Dēvi Lalitā produced Gaṇēśa merely through looking at the face of Lord Śiva; and She was delighted on seeing Gaṇēśa breaking the obstacles posed by these magic figures and subsequent to their destruction releasing the Dēvas from their fettering influence". This is also the genesis of the concept of Gaṇēśa being the Lord of impediments - Vignarāya or Vignēśvara. However just on the basis of His origin as the off-spring of Dēvi Lalitha and Lord Śiva, Gaṇēśa cannot be regarded as a mere Saivaite Deity. Verily He is a universal and cosmopolitan God revered by all sections of the Hindus. Even staunch Vaishnavaites worship Him as the remover of obstacles under the name of Viśwaksēna. This is brought out by Muthuswāmi Dīkshitar in his Nāyaki kriti 'Raṅganāyakaṁ' on the prominent Vaishnavaite Deity Śrī Raṅganātha of Śrīraṅgam in the lines 'Gaṇapati Samāna Viśwaksēnaṁ'.

Gaṇēśa is an extremely popular and favourite Deity particularly in South India as well as Mahārashtra. Every village in South India, however small, has a Vignēśvara idol with or without a temple to house it. It is said that shrines for Lord Subramaṇya are relatively very common in South India but those for Vignēśvara are even more numerous. Apart from being a universal Hindu God, He is also a truly internation Deity. As early as 3rd century B.C. King Aśōka's daughter Saṅgamitra is reported to have taken a Gaṇapathi idol to Nepal. Even in many countries where the majority of the population profess religions other than Hinduism, Gaṇapathi is quite popular. He was known as "King-Hsein" in ancient China and as "Ko-Kitten" in Japan. Janus of Romans is similar to our Dvi-mukha or double faced Gaṇapathi while Dionysus, the Greek God of theatre, resembles closely our Nṛithya Gaṇapathi. Ganapathi or his close variations are also worshipped in many South East Asian countries like Sumathra, Bali, Java, Barnes, Philippines, Cambodia, Thailand, Malaya and Burma as well as Ceylon.

The emergence of Gaṇēśa worship in India is traced to the hordes of early primitive Aryans who, after descending upon Bhāratavarsha from Central Asia, were wonder-struck on seeing the elephants for the first time by their tremendous strength, massive structure and superior intelligence. In the Śānthi Parva of Mahābhārata, there is a reference to one of these early primitive Aryan tribes - known as Gaṇās - as inhibiting regions like forests and mountains which also formed the natural habitat of the wild elephants. Presumably these Gaṇās began worshipping the elephant as their guardian Deity and this is the genesis of Gaṇēśa worship. This theory is also corroborated by the fact that as given in many Saivagamaic and Tantric texts, the cult of Gāṇapathya (Gaṇēśa worship) spread rapidly in the South Western and Southern regions of India where elephants also abound. Again, as we shall see later from a scrutiny of different music compositions on Gaṇēśa, while some weapons (Āyudhas) associated with this Deity are just the club and axe which were also the first weapons invented by these primitive Aryans for agriculture, others are the Aṅkuśa or goad employed for goading the elephants and the Pāśa or rope used for taming and binding them. Further the chief food materials listed in the sāhitya of these kṛitis are sugarcane and fruits of diverse types which are also the special favourites of the elephant.

There is also a reference in the Ṛig Vēda to Gaṇapathi who is equated with Bṛihaspathi or Brāhmaṇapathi, the Deity of intellect and wisdom. The Mantra therein pointing to the universal nature of Gaṇapathi runs as

"Gaṇānām tvā gaṇapathim havāmahe kavim kavīnām upamaśra
vasthamām jēshṭarājam brāhmṇam brāhmaṇāspata
A nasuṛnvan nuthibhih sītasadhanam"

A similar mantra starting with identical words also figures in the Yajur Veda.

"Gaṇānām tvā gaṇapathim havāmahē priyānantva priyāpati
havāmahe vasi mama ahamajani garbhadhamatvamjasi garbha-
tama".

Though there is no reference to Gaṇapathi in the Rāmayāṇa or Bharata's Nāṭyaśāstra, He finds mention in the latter Smṛithis like

Yagñavalkya. The first reference to Gaṇapathi as a deity in classical Sanskrit literature is met with in Bhavabhūthi's Mālathimādhavaṁ. The development of the Gaṇapathi form seems to have been accomplished during the Gupta period as revealed by the red standstone figure of this Deity at Mutthra which is ascribed to this era. Gāṇāpathya or the Gaṇapathi cult started spreading from the 6th century A.D. and became quite potent during 10th century A.D. by which time it had extended to all parts of the country.

Gaṇēśa represents one of the basic concepts of Hindu mythological symbolism - the identity of microcasm and macrocasm on the tenet that man is the image of God. The elephant represents macrocasm - the Great Being and man, microcasm - the small universe. This identity of microcasm and macrocasm is observed in the permanance of certain relations in nature which can be expressed on the basis of numbers. Everything which our senses can perceive or our minds can grasp can be expressed in terms of quantity or numbers. All that can be counted is quantity or number of Gaṇa (Gaṇayanti budhadhyānte tē gaṇaḥ). Gaṇapathi is the Lord of all that can be quantified in terms of numbers - Gaṇānaṁ pati gaṇapathi. This number principle is the essence of Gaṇapathi's nature. The term Gaṇa connotes several other things also. As the off-spring of Śiva and Pārvathi Gaṇapathi is the head of the Śiva gaṇas. Gaṇa also means the five breath elements viz., Prāṇa, Apana, Udhāna, Samāna and Vyāna and as their Lord Gaṇapathi helps to keep in force the courses of life of all living beings. Gaṇa also denotes the five fundamental elements - earth, water, fire, wind and ether; in this sense Gaṇapathi stands for the supreme power over the efficient course of the Universe and He is called Bhūthagaṇādhi sēvitaṁ.

Symbolically Gaṇapathi can be represented by icon, Yantra or Mantra. The iconic symbol is the stone svarṇapathra. The graphic symbol or Yantra is the Swastika. The sacred Mantra which cannotes Gaṇapathi is AUM or OM representing Tatvamasi - 'Tvamēva pratyakshamasi' - Thou art the visibe of That (Sanapathi Upanishad). It is worthy of note that in this the principle Tvaṁ has the shape of man and Tat has the shape of elephant. As Ōmkārasvarūpi Gaṇapathi is also worshipped as the presiding deity of intuition. According to Upanishads OM is the first and foremost articulate sound denoting the supreme truth. In its sacred sense it stands for the will of Parabrahman both in His Saguṇa and Nirguṇa aspects.

Though this Mantra is referred to as Ēkākshari, it can be split into the three letters A, U and M. Here A stands for Vishṇu, U for Śiva and M for Brahma who represent the three aspects of primordial power respectively sustenance, dissolution and creation. According to Kāḷidāsa ŌM symbolizes the Universal parents Paraśiva and Parāśakti or Purusha and Prākriti and as such also connotes Gaṇēśa who is the product of their union. It also stands for the Trinity of energies - Jñāna śakti, Icchā śakti and Kriyā śakti and it is termed the wish-yielding Mantra.

The ubiquitous influence or omnipresence of Gaṇapathi is felt uniquely in classical Carnatic music. The first song that a beginner learns is the piḷḷāri Geeta 'Lambōdhara lakumikara' in praise of this Deity by Saṅgītapitāmaha Purandaradāsa. Gaṇēśa is reported to have played on the Mṛidaṅgam during the celestial Nṛithya when Mahādēva danced in ecstacy before Lord Vishṇu. There is a ślōka in Gaṇēśāshṭakaṁ.

"Saratna hēma ghaṇṭimaṇi tadā nūpuragaṇaih mṛidaṅga tāḷa
nādabhēda sādhanānu rūpataḥ dhimidhimitta tattōṅgaṇatta
bhīpadho vināyakaḥ mamāṅga mēgharāgarathō brindayati".

It is said that some tāḷas in our music bear a connection with Brahma and Vishṇu - as for instance Brahma tāḷa and Śiva tāḷa. Similarly certain phrases characteristic of mṛidaṅgam playing such as Gaṇa pharan and Gaṇēśa pharan are associated with Lord Gaṇēśa.

Among the seven animal cries to which the seven notes or Saptasvaras of Carnatic music correspond, the seventh note Nishāda has its analogue in the elephants cry (or trumpeting). Also Gāndhāra and Nishāda are mutually consonant or Saṁvādi notes. The initial syllables of the names of these two svaras together reads as a gaṇā or the Lord of the art of singing. In fact in one set of Gaṇapathi Sahasranāma, quite a large number of Nāmāvaḷis read as Gaṇapathi. The Brahmavaivartha Purāṇa asserts that the Ga in the name of Gaṇapathi stands for Vivēka or wisdom and Nā stands for Mōksha or salvation. But according to the Gaṇapathi Atharvashīrsha Upanishad, the Ga denotes Brahman or Manas and Na signifies voice or sound. This again emphasizes the close affinity of Gaṇapathi to music.

Right from the time of Bharata and Mataṅga, both the theory and practice of Indian music received an occult orientation. The saptasvaras acquired a Tantric, theistic or iconic symbolism. Among the seven notes Dhaivata has Gaṇeśa for its presiding deity - the presiding deities for the other six svaras being Agni, Brahmā, Sarasvati, Śiva, Vishṇu and Sūrya. This has a yogic significance with a physiological correspondence. Dhaivata is said to be born out of the region of the forehead in the human body. In the forehead, among the nine Yogic centres or Chakras, the two-petalled Ajña chakra is situated. This is the site of the union of Bindu, Nāda and Kalā where śakti and Śiva reside as one single entity. Praṇava is the Bījamantra of this chakra. It is significant that as already pointed out Gaṇapathi is also Praṇavasvarūpi or Ōmkārasvarūpi. Gaṇapathi himself is the Lord of the Mūlādhāra Chakra which is the seat of Kuṇḍalini Śakti and symbolises Prithvi tatva with Ga or Gam as its Bīja Mantra. This Lordship of the Mūlādhara chakra is repeatedly emphasised in many of Dīkshitar's kṛitis on Gaṇapati as we shall see presently. Now Shaḍja is the svara which is said to emanate from the Mūlādhāra chakra. This has great significance because Shaḍja is the basic note which gives rise to the other six notes - Shaḍja. This again pinpoints Gaṇapathi's importance in the context of music.

According to the anecdote in Skānda and Mauḍgala purāṇas, Indra, getting enraged at King Abhinandana who started performing a Yagña for the purpose of dispossessing him of his Indra Padavi called upon Yamā to destroy the Yāga. Yamā accomplished this by assuming the garb of Vignēśura and in the process also killed the king. When the sages and Ṛishis approached Brahma with the plea that the Asura should be destroyed Brahma advised them to pray to Lord Gaṇēsa. Thereupon Gaṇēsa vanquished Vignāsura and earned the title of Vignanāyaka. As Vignanāyaka, Vignēśvara or Vignahartha, Lord Gaṇēsa is the (Lord and) remover of obstancles. Gaṇēśa forges ahead through the obstacles even as the elephant runs through the jungle treading shrubs, bending and uprooting trees and easily forging rivers and lakes. The rat or Mūshika, despite being a physically incongruous mount for the gigantic pot-bellied Divinity with the Elephant head, is equally capable of overcoming obstacles and gaining access to the granary. The two - elephant and Mūshika - together represent the power of the God to vanquish all obstacles in the way and fulfilling all desires. As Vignēśvara He is the deity whom the pious Hindu invokes when he begins all religious ceremonies, all addresses to even superior Gods, all serious compositions in writing and all wordly affairs of importance. Every auspicious function - whether it be Vidyāramba or Vivāha - always commences with Vināyakastuti for unimpeded progress. So also a carnatic music concert invariably starts with an invocatory song in praise of Gaṇapati. Composers from very early times have paid obeisance to Gaṇēśa through the medium of music. Early composers whose songs on Gaṇapathi are available to us include Annamācharya, Haridāsas like Purandaradāsa and Gōpāladāsa, Kshētragña, Nārāyana Tīrtha, King Shāhaji and Melaṭṭur Veṅkaṭarāma Śāstri. However, it was only during the era of the Musical Trinity that there was a spurt in music compositions onGaṇapathi. Among the Trinity, Śyāma Śāstri is not known to have composed any song on Gaṇapathi whereas Tyāgarāja has just a few kritis on this Deity to his credit. On the other hand Muthuswāmi Dīkshitar was a prodigious composer of Gaṇapathi kritis. At present we have access to as many as 25 of these kritis. This is not at all surprising because, as we have already seen, Gaṇapathi has profound Yogic, Mantric and Tantric significance and Dīkshitar was highly proficient in these fields. Dīkshitar's compositions on Gaṇapathi are a veritable confluence of Jñāna, Bhakti and Āgamas. They draw richly from Yoga, Mantra and Tantra Sastras and reveal their common fulfillment in Advaita Siddhi which the composer actually experienced.

Now we shall pass on to a consideration of the different forms of Gaṇapati. Iconic representations of nearly a hundred forms of Gaṇapati are available in sculpture in different parts of the country. Among these Hēramba Gaṇapathi at the Tiruvānaikkāval Akhilāṇḍēśvari temple, Lakshmī Gaṇapathi at the Teṅkāsi Viśvanātha temple and Nṛitta Gaṇapathi at the Hoyśālēśvara temple at Halebid are quite well-known. The aspect of Nṛitya Gaṇapati merits some elucidation. Gaṇapathi has a vital role to play not only in the field of music but in dance as well. Being the off-spring of Naṭarāja himself, Gaṇēśa is an adept in the art of dancing. Śiva is the presiding deity of Tāṇḍava Nṛitya and Pārvati of Lāsya. Gaṇēśa's dance is a beautiful synthesis of both these dance forms. On both sides of the Halebid Nṛitya Gaṇēśa, we see images of musicians playing on the Mṛidaṅga. According to the tenets of Hindu iconography, the image of dancing Ganēśa has eight hands, in seven of which are held the Pāśa (rope), ankuśa (gaod), mōdakas (cakes), the kundara (a kind of axe), the dante (cone), the valaya (circular band) and the angalya (ring) with the eighth hand remaining free so as to be helpful in the various dance movements and also for proclaiming abhaya to the devotees. This description is in line with Dhyāna ślōkas on the Deity and also Dīkshitar's picture of the Deity in some of his kritis. The Śākta cult of Gāṇāpathya prescribed the worship of Gaṇapathi in 32 forms as described in the Madgala Purāṇa. The Śrītattvanidhi compiled by Mahārāja Mummaḍi Krishṇarāja Woḍeyār preserved in the Mysore Oriental Research Institute contains beautiful colour paintings in the old traditional Mysore School of the 32 Gaṇapathi forms drawn from authentic Silpa sources. The outerprakara wall of the Nañjangūd Śrīkanthēśvara temple has stucco representations on the top of the southern wall of 32 varieties of Gaṇapathi, the names of which have been given in the respective pedestals. Mantra Śāstras and Āgamas refer to 16 forms of Gaṇapati known as Shōḍasa Gaṇapathis which are also reputed to be enshrined in the Tiruvārūr Tyāgarāja temple. According to tradition, Muthuswāmi Dīkshitar is said to have composed a kriti on each of these forms making up his Shōḍasa Gaṇapathi group kritis. According to different versions, various sets of Gaṇapathis are stated to form this Shōḍaśa Gaṇapati group. In fact there are more than 16 Gaṇapati idols installed in the Tiruvārūr Tyāgarāja temple and also more than 16 kritis on Gaṇapati to Muthuswāmi Dīkshitar's credit. As such it is difficult to pinpoint definitely which combination of Gaṇapati forms Dīkshitar had in mind while composing his Shōḍasa Gaṇapathi group kritis. At the direction of Śrī Śankarāchārya of Kāñchi Kāmakōtipeeṭam, sixteen Gaṇapati forms have been installed - two to each corner - in the octogonal Maṇḍapa of Chariot shape in the Śankara Nilaya at Rāmēśvaram. These 16 forms are Mahā, Bala, Taruṇa, Bhakta, Siddhi, Ucchishṭa, Vīra, Lakshmī, Nṛitta, Tripta, Śakti, Dhvaja, Vignarāja, Hēramba, Bhuvanēśa and Ūrdhva. However, not all forms in the above list correspond to Dīkshitar's Gaṇapati kritis. Another list given by Sri K.R. Rajagopalan seems to be quite appropriate in this context. This comprises Vāthāpi, Pañchamātanga, Mulādhāra, Mahā, Śakthi, Ucchchisṭha, Gaṇanāyaka, Śvēta, Rakta, Gaṇanātha and Hastivadana. Let us now briefly look into the significance of each of these kṛitis.

VĀTHĀPI GAṆAPATHIṀ (Haṁsadhvani rāga - Ādi tāḷa) :

This kṛiti is in Haṁsadhvani rāga - a rāga invented by Muthuswāmi Dīkshitar's father Rāmaswāmi Dīkshitar. It is not only by far the most popular Gaṇapati kriti but even the most well known composition in the entire gamut of Carnatic music so much so that as any Gaṇapati song itself has come to be associated with this rāga. This is borne out by the fact that many Vāggēyakāras who came after Dīkshitar have composed many Gaṇapati kṛitis in this rāga - as for instance Vināyaka Ninnuviną by Vīna Kuppayyar, Namāmi Vigna Vināyaka by Krishṇaswāmi Ayya, Gaṁ Gaṇapathe by Muthiah Bhāgavatar, Vandēnishamahaṁ by Vāsudēvāchārya etc. These are only a few examples and many more such Gaṇapathi songs in Haṁsadhvani are there.

Mahā Vaidyanātha Iyer is reputed to have standardized the present chiṭṭai and saṅgatis in this song and popularised it in his concerts. From that time onwards it has become the most favoured invocatory song in Carnatic music concerts. It is said that when Aman Ali Khan, son and disciple of Chejju Khan heard this song played on the Vina by Mysore Vīṇa Sēshaṇṇa, he was inspired so much that he composed the famous Khyal 'Lāgilā Gaṇapati Sāh' with a similar dhātu in this rāga.

This Gaṇapati form (Vātāpi Gaṇapati) has a historical and geographical significance. After winning the battle over the Chālukya in the 7th century A.D., the Pallava monarch Narasiṁhavarman is reported to have brought this idol from Vātāpi, the capital of the Chālukyan Kingdom. As such it represents an early gift from Karnataka to Tamilnadu.

The significant terms in the sāhitya of this kṛiti are Mūlādhāra Kshētra Sthitham (Lord or resider of Mūlādhāra chakra) Parādi Chathvāri vāgāthmakaṁ (embodiment of 4 types ofsound - Parā, Paśyanthi, Madhyama and Vaikari) and Pranavasvarūpa vakratuṇḍaṁ (Praṇavasvarūpi with the crooked tusk).

PAÑCHAMĀTAṄGA MUKHA GAṆAPATHINĀ (Malahari rāga - Rūpaka tāḷa) :

The second shōḍasa Gaṇapathi form is Pañchamātaṅga mukha and Dīkshitar's song on this form is set to Malahari rāga and rūpaka tāḷa. Composing the Gaṇapathi sthuthi in this rāga reflects

Dīkshitar's love and respect for tradition in adopting the same rāga as employed by Saṅgīta Pitāmahā Purandaradāsa for his Piḷḷāri Gītam (already referred to). It is significant that some post-Dīkshitar composers have also used this rāga for their songs on Gaṇapathi - as for example Muthiāh Bhāgavatar's 'Śrī Mahāgaṇapate Dēhi'.

The gist of the sāhitya is that Pañchamātaṅga Mukha Gaṇapati also known as sumukha who has five faces is himself the son of Lord Śiva who also possesses five faces and is the protector of the world made up of the Pañchabhūtas or five elements. His hand poses Abhaya Mudra and the articles he holds like Pāśa, Aṅkuśa, Bālāyudha, Dhanta, Mōdaka, Mudkara weapon, Akshamāla (Japamāla) etc., give a picture of Gaṇapati in line with the description of Nṛitya Gaṇapathi already referred to.

ŚRĪ MŪLĀDHĀRA CHAKRA VINĀYAKA (Śrī rāga - Ādi tāḷa) :

The third shōḍasa Gaṇapathi form is Śrī Mūlādhāra and the corresponding Kriti Śrī Mūlādhāra Chakra Vināyaka is set to Śrī Rāga and Ādi tāḷa. This kṛiti bears eloquent testimony to Dīkshitar's profound knowledge of Tantric and Yogic cults. It is significant that the idol of this Gaṇapathi form is situated in the sanctorum of the Tiruvārūr Tyāgarāja temple enclosed in the icon of a serpant. The opening words themselves proclaim that Gaṇapathi is Lord of the Mūlādhārachakra. Other noteworthy phrases in the Sāhitya are Mūlagaṇanā śōka vināśaka (dispeller of basic Agñāna and sorrow) Prakaṭikrita vaikārisvabhāva (bestower of Vaikāri, the power of speech) and Vikaṭa shatśata svāsādhikāra(who presides over 600 vayas breaths mentioned in the Yōga Sastras).

MAHĀGAṆAPATHĒ PĀLAYĀŚUMĀM (Naṭanārāyaṇi rāga - Ādi tāḷa) :

The fourth shōḍasa Gaṇapathi form is Mahāgaṇapathi. Now four kṛitis of Dīkshitar on this form are available - Śrī Mahāgaṇapathiravathumām in Gowḷa, Mahāgaṇapathim in Naṭa, Mahāgaṇapathim in Tōḍi and Mahāgaṇapathē pālayāśumām in Naṭanānāyaṇi. From among these the last kṛiti has been selected out of two considerations. In the first place it is set to a very rāre rāga not so far handled by any other composer. Secondly it is a Samashṭi Charaṇa kṛiti or short musical form with only Pallavi and Charaṇa which again is Dīkshitar's exclusive contribution to our music. The sāhitya contains references to Gaṇapati being the Lord of Māyāsvarūpiṇi Vallabha and also to Śrī Krishṇa having paid obeisance to Gaṇapati (Anecdote of Syāmantakōpākhyāna).

ŚAKTI SAHITA GAṆAPATHIṀ (Śaṅkarābharaṇa rāga - Tisra Ēka tala) :

The fifth Shōḍasa Gaṇapathi form is Śakti Gaṇapati which portrays Gaṇapathi with red-coloured feet as being associated with another consort - Śakti. The musical form of this composition is Noṭṭusvara Sāhitya or Noṭṭusvara or simply Noṭṭu. This is another of Dīkshitar's exclusive creations. 39 Noṭṭusvaras of Dīkshitar are available to us and all of them are in Śaṅkarābharaṇa rāga. Each comprises one section only with no division intoPallavi, Anupallavi and Charaṇam. Dīkshitar was inspired to compose these Noṭṭus on the lines of the English Band at Fort St. George based on Western music. The Noṭṭu Śakti sāhitya Gaṇapatiṁ is based on a French tune.

UCHCHISHṬA GAṆAPATAU (Kāśirāmakrityā rāga - Ādi tāla) :

The sixth Gaṇapati form is Uchchisṭagaṇapati and the corresponding kṛiti Uchchisṭagaṇapatu is set to Kāśirāmakriya or Pantuvarāḷi rāga. Being a Vāmāchāra form associated with Śrīvidya Upāsana, this has profound Tantric significance. Dīkshitar would appear to have been inspired by the Gaṇapati idol in the Nāgēśvarasvāmi temple at Kumbhakōṇam in composing this kṛiti. The Dhyāna Ślōka of this Gaṇapati form reads as Nārī Yōni Mukasvāda lōlupaṁ kāma mōhitaṁ and the first half of this Dhyāna ślōka figures in the charaṇa of this kṛiti. Gaṇapati is also described here as engaged in playing diverse musical instruments like Bhēri, Vīṇa and Vēṇu.

GAṆANĀYAKAṀ (Pūrṇashadjaṁ rāga - Ādi tāḷa) :

The seventh Shōḍasa Gaṇapati form is Gaṇanāyaka and Dīkshitar's kṛiti on this form is set to Rudrapriyạ rāga, though the current practice is to sing it in Pūrṇashaḍjam. Gaṇapati is described in this kṛiti as the leader of Gaṇas and is being capable of bestowing the Ashṭasiddhis like 'Aṇimā' etc.

ŚVĒTA GAṆAPATIṀ (Rāgachūḍāmaṇi rāga - Tripuṭa tāla) :

The eighth Shōḍasa Gaṇapati form is Svētaganapathi or white coloured Gaṇapati and the corresponding song is set to rāgachūḍāmaṇi rāga which in the Sampoorṇa Mēlapaddhati is the equivalent of the 32nd Mēḷakarta Rāgachūḍāmaṇi. According to tradition this idol form was installed in Tiruvalañjuḷi near Swāmimalai by Indra out of sea foam. This has also been identified by the late Dr. V. Raghavan as the form installed in the east market gate shrine at Tanjore. Dīkshitar states in this kṛiti that Gaṇapati is without beginning or end and is the Lord of Vallabha.

RAKTA GAṆAPATIṀ (Mōhana rāga - Ādi tāḷa) :

The ninth Shōḍasa Gaṇapati form is Rakta Gaṇapati and the kṛiti Raktagaṇapatiṁ is set to Mōhana rāga. Dīkshitar states in the sāhitya that in this form Gaṇapati wears red clothes and seated on a rathna simhāsana. The following ślōka on Gaṇapati comes to one's mind in this context.

"Raktaṁ lambōdaraṁ sarpakarṇakaṁ vāsasaṁ
Raktagandhānulystāṅgaṁ raktapushpaiḥi supūjitaṁ".

The word Raktam in the Gaṇēsatavaśirṣa stands for red and lovely as well.

Dīkshitar states in this kṛiti that Rakta Gaṇapati is popularly worshipped in Paraśurāmakshētra and reveals in Hōma with Pāyasa (Paraśurāma kshētra prabhāvaṁ .. pāyasānna hōmādi vaibhavaṁ). This would point to the Kerala origin of this form of Gaṇapati because Paraśurāma kshētra denotes Kerala and Pāyasa is also comparatively very popular there.

GAṆARĀJĒNA (Ārabhi rāga - Khaṇḍa chāpu tāḷa) :

The tenth Shōḍasa Gaṇapati form is Gaṇarāja and the corresponding kṛiti is set to Ārabhi rāga. Dīkshitar states in this kṛiti that Gaṇapati who is capable of bestowing Ashṭasiddhis like 'Aṇimā' etc., is worshipped by Mantriṇi and lives in the forest as a Brahmachāri.

SIDDHI VINĀYAKAṀ (Chāmaram rāga - Rūpakaṁ tāḷa) :

The eleventh Shōḍasa Gaṇapati form is Siddhi and the corresponding Kṛiti is set to Chāmaraṁ or Shaṇmukhapriya rāga. The phrase 'Mūla paṅkaja madhyasthaṁ' again pinpoints that Gaṇapati is the Lord of Mūlādhāra kshētra. 'Bhādrapada māsa chaturthyāṁ Brāhmaṇādi pūjitam' refers to the well-known Vināyaka chaturthi festival celebrated on the śukhlapaksha chaturthi day of Bhādrapada or Āvaṇi month.

GAJĀNANAYUTAM (Vēgavāhini rāga - Ēka tāḷa) :

The twelfth Shōḍasa Gaṇapati form is Gajānana and the corresponding kṛiti is set to Vēgavāhini or Chakravāka rāga. Dīkshitar refers in this kṛiti to Gaṇapati being Praṇavasvarūpi and his destroying Kuñjarasura. There is an anecdote behind the phrase Ajēndrapūjita or worshipped by Brahma. In the Skānda Purāṇa (Nandikēśvara-Sanatkumāra Saṁvāda) an incident is narrated that following Gaṇapati's marriage to the eight Siddhis (Aṇimā, Mahimā, etc.) Lord Brahma prayed to Gaṇapati that even as through the latter's favour, Lord Vishṇu protects the world and Lord Rudra destroys it. He (Brahma) too would seek Lord Gaṇapati's blessings for carrying on his creation work unimpeded. Pleased with Brahma's prayers, Gaṇapati granted him the book for carrying on his work successfully.

VALLABHA NĀYAKASYA (Bēgaḍa rāga - Rūpaka tāḷa) :

The thirteenth Shōḍasa Gaṇapati form is Vallabha Gaṇapati and the corresponding kṛiti is set to Bēgaḍa rāga. The commencing word of the song itself emphasises that Gaṇapati is the Lord of Vallabha. According to the Tiruttaṇi sthala Purāṇa Gaṇapati helped his brother Subrahmaṇya to encounter Vaḷḷi, whom he wished to marry, by chasing her in the form of an elephant whereupon Subrḥmaṇya came to her rescue and saved her. Thus Gaṇapati engineered the meeting of his brother with Vaḷḷi and was thereby responsible for their wedding. This is brought out by them 'Vallivivāha kāraṇasya'.

LAMBŌDARĀYA (Varāḷi rāga - Khaṇḍa chāpu tāḷa) :

The fourteenth Shōḍasa Gaṇapati form is Lambōdara and the corresponding kṛiti is set to Varāḷi rāga. Dīkshitar states here that Gaṇapati is worshipped by Agastya and Brahma.

ŚRĪ GAṆANĀTHAM BHAJARĒ (Īśamanōhari rāga - Ādi tāḷa) :

The fifteenth Shōḍasa Gaṇapati form is Gaṇanātha and the corresponding kṛiti is set to Īśamanohari rāga. According to Dīkshitar this Gaṇapati form is seated in Ādhāra lotus (Chinmūlakamala sthitham) wears serpents as sacred thread (nāgayagña sūtra-dharam) and gives pleasure through Nāda and Laya i.e. music (Nādalayānanda karam).

HASTI VADANĀYA (Navarōj rāga - Miśra chāpu tāḷa) :

The sixteenth and last Shōḍasa Gaṇapati form is Hasitavadana. The corresponding kṛiti Hastivadanāya is set to Navarōj rāga. The picture that Dīkshitar gives in this Shōḍasa Gaṇapati kṛitis of the different forms of Gaṇapati closely resembles the Dhyāna ślōkas of the Deity in the ancient texts. Dīkshitar describes this Gaṇapati form with spouse (embraced by his consort Māya) as having ten hands each holding lotus, lilly, pāśa (noose), śaṅka (conch), chakra (discus), Ikshukārmukha (sugar-cane bow) paddy shoots, tusk, mace, pomogranate fruit and bejewelled water pot. This description is in line with Rāghava Chaitanyas Gaṇapati Dhyāna ślōka.

"Bīja pūraka tēkshu kār mukha
ruja chakrābja pāśōtpala vrih
yakra svavishāṇa ratna kalaśa
prōdyat karāmbōruhaḥ"

It can be thus seen that Muthuswami Dīkshitar's Shōḍasa Gaṇapati kṛitis are without parallel in the field of Carnatic music. They are painted on majestic and lovely lines and colour around a verbal theme of concentrated and multi-dimensional symbolism embracing the sphere of Yōga, Mantra and Tantra sastras.

PADAVARṆĀS OF SWĀTI TIRUNĀḶ

Varṇās are a class of compositions which present the form of a rāga through musical phrases distributed within a set frame work in two parts - the Pūrvāṅga (consisting of Pallavi, Anupallavi and Muktāyiswara) and the Uttarāṅga (consisting of Charaṇa-pallavi and Ethukkaḍa swaras).

Varṇas fall into two types - Tāna varṇa and Chaukka varṇas. The former are in medium tempo and the latter, in slow tempo. The slow tempo of the Chaukka varṇas, which also contain svara sāhitya, affords facility to the dancer to present these pieces in appropriate gestures. The sāhitya of this class of varṇas is based on the Nāyaka-Nāyikā bhāva and steeped in eroticism and in this respect they closely resemble Padas. For this reason Chaukka varṇas are also known as Padavarṇas.

Mahārāja Swāti Tirunāḷ is a versatile composer of diverse musical forms. In composing dance forms of music, he drew inspiration from the reputed dance master and choreographer Vaḍivēlu, who was a member of the reputed Tanjore Quartette. Vaḍivēlu served for some time as the Mahārāja's court musician and he was a gifted and well known composer of dance forms too. Besides innumerable Padas and a few Jāvaḷis and seven Tāna varṇas, Swāti Tirunāḷ has also composed eighteen Padavarṇas. This is a remarkably large number considering the intricate skill and deep imagination demanded by this class ofcompositions. No other composer can lay claim to such a variety and bulk of Padavarṇas. But even this list may not be exhaustive and it is possible that a diligent search may enable us to unearth more of these compositions by Swāti Tirunāḷ.

Swāti Tirunāḷ's Padavarṇas can be classified into Sthava varṇas and Śriṅgāra varṇas. The Sthava varṇas are mere doxologies; in other words, their themes are restricted to the praise and glorification of various deities. On the other hand the Śriṅgāra Padavarṇas are based on Madhura bhakti which deals with dignified divine love symbolising the yearning of the individual self (jeevathma) for union with the supreme soul (paramāthma). The idea of conceiving God as the Nāyaka and the human soul as the Nāyika is quite ancient. This concept of Nāyaka-Nāyika bhāva with dual significance of spiritual and mundane love pervades the entire canvas of Swāti Tirunāḷ's śriṅgāra varṇas and the royal composer has eminently succeeded in portraying this erotic mysticism coupled with Bhakti in these compositions. The three main characters in his śringāra varṇas are the Nāyaka, Nāyika and Sakhi, they are respectively the Paramātha, the devotee (Jīvāthma) and Guru, who leads the devotee on the path of mukti or salvation. The important themes covered in these śringāra varṇas are the following : (a) Nāyika prays to the Lord directly imploring His love and mercy; (b) the Nāyika overtly complains about the unfaithfulness of the Nāyaka in showing greater attachment and favours to her rival; (c) the Nāyika persuades the Sakhi to go to the Nāyaka and appraise Him of her anguish and fetch Him to alleviate her sufferings; and (d) the Sakhi describes the Nāyaka's love stricken condition and remorse to the Nāyaka, conveys Him her message and seeks His mercy in getting rid of the Nāyaka's agony. These different facets of the Nāyaka-Nāyika relationship have been admirably brought out by Swāti Tirunāḷ in his Padavarṇas.

Swāti Tirunaḷ's eighteen known Padavarṇas are as follows :

<u>Sthava varṇas</u> :

1. Saridīśarvasa	Tōḍi	Aṭa	Krishṇa
2. Jagadīśa Śrījāne	Śuddhasāvēri	Aṭa	Narasiṁha
3. Hā Hantavañchitāhaṁ	Dhanyāsi	Ādi	Bṛihadīśvara
4. Sādhu vibhāta	Bhūpāḷa	Ādi	Padmanābha
5. Sāvēriha tanūja	Sāvēri	Ādi	Pārvati
6. Chapala saṁpad	Bhairavi	Ādi	Padmanābha
7. Sādaramiha bhajē	Madhyamāvati	Ādi	Padmanābha
8. Pālayamām dēva	Pūrṇachandrika	Ādi	Śiva
9. Rāma Akhilaripu	Bēgaḍa	Aṭa	Rāma

<u>Śringāra</u> <u>varṇas</u> :

10. Dāni Sāmajēndra	Tōḍi	Ādi
11. Paramakula hṛidayāṁ	Saurāshṭra	Rūpaka
12. Sāturā kāmini	Kalyāṇi	Ādi
13. Sāmi ninnē	Yadukula-Kāṁbhōji	Ādi
14. Sārasa mridupada	Kāṁbhōji	Ādi
15. Sā vāmā rusha	Khamās	Ādi
16. Sarasijanābha kiṁ	Aṭhāṇa	Ādi
17. Sārasasundara	Nīlāṁbari	Ādi
18. Sā Paramavivaśa	Ghaṇṭa	Ādi

Only two of the Padavarṇas are in the same rāga viz., Tōḍi. He has employed seventeen different rāgas for these padavarṇas - Tōḍi, Śuddhasāvēri, Saurāshṭra, Kalyāṇi, Dhanyāsi, Bhūpāḷa, Sāvēri, Bhairavi, Madhyamāvati, Yadukulakāmbhōji, Kāmbhōji, Khamās, Aṭhāṇa, Pūrṇachandrika, Nīlāmbari, Ghaṇṭa and Bēgaḍa. While the vast majority of these compositions are set to Ādi tāḷa three are in Khaṇḍa jāti Aṭa tāḷa and only one on Rūpaka tāḷa. Four of these padavarṇas have sāhitya in Telugu and the rest in Sanskrit. It is worthy of mention that Swāti Tirunāḷ was the first composer to adopt Sanskrit for Padavarṇas.

It is but natural that many of Swāti Tirunaḷ's Padavarṇas are dedicated to his family deity, Lord Padmanābha, but there are also a few on other deities like Rāma, Krishṇa, Narasiṁha, Śiva and Pārvati. This bears testimony to his catholicity of outlook. Among his Sthava Padavarṇas, Saridaiśavāsa (Tōḍi), Jagadīśa śrījāne (Śuddhasāvēri), Hā hantavañchitāhaṁ (Dhanyāsi), Pālayamāmdēva (Purṇachandrika), Sāveriha tanūja (Sāvēri) and Rāmākhila (Bēgaḍa) are on Lord Krishṇa, Narasiṁha, Brihadīśvara, Śiva, Pārvati and Rāma respectively, while Sādhuvibhāta (Bhūpāḷa), Chapalasaṁpad (Bhairavi) and Sādaramiha bhajē (Madhyamāvati) are on Lord Padmanābha.

Three conspicuous features about Swāti Tirunaḷ's Padavarṇās are (i) their rhetorical beauties, (ii) their general format; and (iii) their rhythmic structures.

(i) Rhetorical beauties :

Rhetorical beauties met within these padavarṇas are of three types viz., instances of Swarākshara, instances of Yati patterns of prāsa. The padavarṇas in Tōḍi, Khamās, Aṭhāṇa and Saurāshṭra rāgas contain instances of Swarāksharas.

For example in Tōḍi rāga Padavarṇa 'Saridīśavāsa'

(1) S R D; d n s n S;;; d n s s n d (2) p d n p d p m p d m
Saridī - - - - śa - - - - - - Pā- - - - - - - - hi-

(3) G R M; p m g m
Garimā - - - -

Coming to Yati patterns, one can cite the instances of the Padavarṇas in Tōḍi (Dānisāmajēndra), Nīlāmbari, Bhūpāḷa, Saurāshṭra and Sāvēri rāgas.

For example the occurance of Mṛidaṅga yati in Tōḍi Padavarṇa (Dānisāmajēndra) the 3rd ettukkaḍai swara after Charaṇa :

m g r S p m g r s d m g r S n d m g r s
madhurasa madhurimasa drusávacasa madimrduhasa

s n d m g r s r s r
mayimayi sarasamihahi

Another example on the occurance of Prāsayati in the Saurāshṭra Padavarṇa Paramakulā hriḍayām is as follows :

Tāpasanuta vasudhāpapatanata sudhāpāvaranijavi-
dhāparimitavibhudhāpada gakulisatāpamapagamaya - 3rd etthukkaḍai swara.

The beauties of prāsa are innumerable in these Padavarṇas. Eloquent examples are the varṇas in Tōḍi, Nīlāmbari and Kalyāṇi. An example of Antyaprāsa in Tōḍi (Dānisāmajēndra) is unique :

Dānisāmajēndra gāmini Tapāmiha kāmini
Mānini chari dināni Mānanīya śrīpadmanbhadhutāni
māmatu mōghāni

Another example of Anuprāsa can be seen in the Kalyāṇi (Sāturākāmini) varṇa :

Nīlatara rajanī ramaṇa kamanīya mukha bhajanīyapadayuga
Nīraruhatapanīya ruchivasanīya bahu mahanīya gatamada : 4th etukkaḍa swaram.

The dvitīyākshara prāsa occurs in the Nīlāmbari Padavarṇa in this manner :

Sārasa śara sundara
Sārasa guṇa nivāsa
Sārada vidhuyuvatām

(ii) General format :

As regards the general format we can see pronounced artistic skill with the Dhātu of many of these Padavarṇas.

(i) The Padavarṇa 'Sā vāmā rushā' (Khamās) is in the nature of the Nāyika's complaint to her divine lover Lord Padmanābha. The lower limit of the rāga sañchāra is Mandra nishāda and there is no descent to the Mandra sthāyi at all. The viśēsha sañchāra Ma Ga Sa occurs in the muktāyi swara while the ārōhaṇa-avarōhaṇa occurs at the close of muktāyi. One meets with the characteristic sañchāra Ma Ni Da frequently. The 3rd ethuakkaḍa swara is divided into four symmetrical parts each resting in Dhaivata.

(ii) The theme of the Padavarṇa 'Dāni sāmajēndra' (tōḍi) centres round the Nāyika's disappointment in love resulting from the Nāyaka's indifference towards her, recounting of her frustration and remorse to the Sakhi and her entreaties to the latter to go and inform the Nāyaka of her plight and bring Him to assuage her suffering.

In the 4th ethukkaḍai we find the following cascade of decent. Pa Da Pa Ma / Ma Pa Ma Ga / Ga Ma Ga Ri / Ri Ga Ri Sa. The 3rd ethukkaḍa has a symmetrical descent in the first avarta : Ma,, Pa Ma, Pa Ma / Ga,, Ma Ga, Ma Ga / Ri,, Ri Ga Ma Ga Ri / Sa,, Ni, Sa Ri Ga. In the next āvarta we can see the phrase with initial swara increments forming a pleasing progression. ma ga ri Sa, / pa ma ga ri sa / da ma ga ri sa, / ni da ma ga ri sa, / sa ni da ma ga ri sa,. In the fifth ethukkaḍai swara one finds Tiśragati in the laghu and first druta of the 3rd āvarta and in both drutams of last āvarta.

(iii) the Padavarṇa 'Sāturākāmini' (Kalyāṇi) commences with the Sakhi straight away telling the Nāyaka about the love-stricken and afflicted state of the Nāyika and suggesting that it is upto Him to remove the latter's suffering. The range of this Padavarṇa is from Mandrasthāyi Pañchama to Tāra sthyāi Gāndhāra. All the sections have swarākshara synchronism at the beginning. One can see in the Muktāyi the beautiful swara cascade : sa ri ga / ni sa ri / da ni sa / pa da ni / ma pa da ri. The charaṇa and the 1st, 2nd, 4th and 5th ethukkaḍa sections end in the full ārōhaṇa merging into Nishāda, the beginning note of the charaṇa. Only the 3rd ethukkaḍa section ends as ni ga ma da. The 2nd ethukkaḍa section has four equivalent phrases with Shaḍja as eḍuppu and nishāda as Nyāsa. Sa, ri ga ri sa ni / Sa, ma ga ri sa ni... The 3rd ethukkaḍa swara has eight equilinear phrases with pañchama as eḍuppu and Madhyama as Nyāsa Pa, ma ga ri ga ma / Pa, da pa ma ga ma... In the 4th ethukkaḍa swara, one can see eight different beautiful phrases ending in Nishāda. Ni, da pa ma pa da / Ni, da ni sa ri sa / Ni, sa ri ga ri sa / Ni, ga ri ga sa ri. This varṇa brings out the rāga bhāva of Kalyāṇi in its entirety.

(iv) In the Padavarṇa Paramakula hridayām (Saurāshṭra) the 3rd ethukkaḍa swara is constituted of a series of permutations with constant graha phrase as follows :

<u>Da pa ma</u> ga ri sa ni <u>Da pa ma</u> pa da ni sa <u>Da pa ma</u> pa da ni sa
<u>Da pa da</u> ri sa ni sa <u>Da pa da</u> ga ri sa ni <u>Da pa ma</u> pa ga ma ga

(v) The range of the Padavarṇa 'Sārasara sundara' in Nīlāmbari is from Mandra nishāda to Tārasthāyi rishabha. The eḍuppu swara of Pallavi is Tara shaḍja, of the anupallavi pañchama, of the muktayi again Tāra shaḍja and of the charaṇa pañchama. Thus theVarṇa is in the shaḍja-pañchama. The dhātu of the beginning of the Charaṇa is identical with that of the first āvarta of the anupallavi. The fine swara cascade in the last ethukaḍa is noteworthy : sa ni pa ma / ni pa ma ga / pa ma ga sa.

(vi) In the muktāyi swara of the Padavarṇa 'Sāvērihatanūja' (Sāvēri) a set of eight phrases begin in the Tāra Shaḍja which is as follows :

<u>Sa ri sa</u> ni da pa da <u>Sa ni da</u> pa ma ga ri <u>Sa</u> ri ga ri sa ni da
<u>Sa</u> ri ri ma ma pa da
<u>Sa</u> ri sa ga ri sa ri <u>Sa</u> ri sa ni da da ri <u>Sa</u> ni da pa ma ga ri
<u>Sa</u> ri ri ma ma pa da

(vii) The third ethukkaḍa section of the padavarṇa 'Sādhuvibhāta' (Bhūpāḷa) is constituted of a series of eight equilinear phrases beginning in Pañchama swara.

Eight of the padavarṇas of Swāti Tirunāḷ contain what is known as the anubandha consisting of an āvarta or two of sāhitya after the last ethukkaḍa swaras. The Anubandha is not, however an innovation introduced by Swāti Tirunāḷ, in this respect he has only followed the earlier tradition.

In the anubandha the names of the rāgas are also coined along with. The following is the sequence of such occurances.

Chapalasampat	- Bhairaviṁ mēm pāpatvim
Sādhu vibhāta	- Bhūpāḷa kanikara
Pālayamāṁ dēva	- Pūrṇachandrikā nibhāṅga
Sārasa mṛidupada	- Kāṁbhōdhi rītirathya
Sā paramavivaśa	- Ghaṇṭākaraṇa sathgati
Sarasijanābha	- Lōkatāraka aṭhāṇa manasa
Sārasarasa sundara	- Nīlāṁbariyasanitya
Sā vāma rusha	- te mukhamājanaya

(iii) Rhythmic structure :

When we consider the rhythmic structure of Swāti Tirunāḷ's padavarṇas, we find some peculiar and unique features. The Pallavi and Anupallavi of the padavarṇa Sarasijanābha in Aṭhāṇa start in the first count of the laghu, while the other aṅgas start at Sama. Ordinarily in Ādi tāḷa varṇas only the Sama eḍuppu is common. But in this varṇa we find the kinds of eḍuppus - Atīta and Sama. His Pūrṇachandrika varṇa set to Ādi tāḷa is a case in point. The whole sections of Pallavi, Anupallavi and Chiṭṭaswaras has each three āvartas - surely an odd number for setting the number of āvartas. According to the original manuscript this varṇa is set to Tiśra gati. It is however worthy of note that Muthiah Bhāgavatar and Raṅganātha Iyer do not agree with its structure in Tiśra gati.

The charaṇa sāhitya for this varṇa is set for 1½ āvartas, followed by ethukkaḍa swaras, each beginning from the middle of an āvarta and ending either at the middle of an āvarta or the close of an āvarta. A most noteworthy feature in respect of these charaṇas is that unless the 3rd and 4th ethukkaḍa swaras are sung twice, the original Tāḷa structure of the charaṇa sāhitya changes.

The fact that Mahārāja Swāti Tirunāḷ was a gifted and versatile artiste in the realm of music can be seen from his numerous Padavarṇas. They form a rich and variegated treasure of dance compositions which he has bequethed to posterity. Through their wide variety, outstanding quality and eloquent appeal of Bhakti, he has established his immortality as a composer.

(This paper was presented at the 175th Jayanti Celebrations of Swati Tirunal Maharaja, Trivandrum, 1988.)

RARE RĀGAS HANDLED BY SWĀTI TIRUNĀḶ

The earliest forms of music extant in Kerala during ancient times have been portrayed in the Śilappadikāram. The Tēvāram, Tiruvāchagam and Divyaprabandham set to pleasing melody and rhythm also had immense influence on the music of the region which played a significant role in the religious, social and cultural life of the people. From early times distinct types of music emerged in Travancore. Diverse varieties, including those of folk and pastoral origin coalesced into devotional music which widely flourished in the temples. This is the genesis of the Sopana style for which Travancore has became famous.

For over 600 years the royal palace of Travancore has ben the favoured abode of music and fine arts. A distinguished lineage of rulers not only extended patronage to the performing arts but some of them were themselves artistes and composers of no mean order. Among a prominent galaxy of Vāggēyakāras including Vīrakēraḷa Varma, Kārtika Tirunāḷ, Aśvati Tirunāḷ, Kuṭṭikuñju Thaṅkachi, Ēṭṭan Tampurān, Āyilyaṁ Tirunāḷ, Kalyāṇi KUṭṭi, Irayimman Tampi, Paramēśvara Bhāgavatar, K.C. Kesava Pillai, etc., Mahārāja Swāti Tirunāḷ (1813-1836) stands as the most prolific and talented personality. His compositions are invariably doxicologies on his family deity Padmanābhaswāmi in which he has poured forth his devotion in full measure. He was also the architect of several innovations in the temple music. Impelled by intense bhakti he systamatised the Nāgasvaram play in the Padmanābhaswāmi temple. He introduced a special service known as Maṅgaḷavādyaṁ on certain occasions corresponding to particular thithis and nakshatras and also composed specific songs in appropriate rāgas to suit these occasions.

Upto Veṅkaṭamakhi's time the music of the south was confined to the four Daṇḍis - Gīta, Rāga, Ṭhāya and Prabandha. One can trace the time-honoured Prasiddha rāgas like Bhairavi, Kāmbōdhi, Śaṅkarābharaṇam, Bēgaḍa etc., to fairly early times. Besides being quite familiar and easily comprehensible by the vast majority of the people, they easily lend themselves to extensive exposition and stir the artistes to unscaled heights in improvisation. But such is not the case with rare or apporva rāgas some of which have become more or less obsolete at the present time. These rare rāgas have however received due attention at the hands of the Musical Trinity - Thyāgarāja, Muthuswāmi Dīkshitar and Śyāmā Śāstri - as well as Mahārāja Swāti Tirunāḷ who were all contemporaries. The lovers of Carnatic music treasure their delectable compositions in the approva rāgas as the sole reliable lakshya for determining their correct ārōhaṇa-avarōhaṇas as well as characteristic svara sañchāras and codifying their authentic lakshaṇas.

The music of the era of the Trinity and Swāti Tirunāḷ extending over the later half of the 18th century and earlier half of the 19th century - was subject to certain general influences. The most important among these was Vēṅkaṭamakhi's Mēḷa scheme which had been formulated during the earlier century. This helped not only to stabilise the rāgas current at that time but resurrect a multitude of ancient rāgas and create new melodies out of fresh combinations of swaras. Based on the Chaturdaṇḍiprakāśika and Saṅgrahachooḍāmaṇi, a large number of Mēḷas as well as Janya rāgas came to be used by these composers.

All these four distinguished contemporary composers possessed different styles and perceptions of their own. While Thyāgarāja's kṛitis are unique in respect of bhāva, Śhyāma Śāstri's compositions are outstanding in rhythmic excellence. The quintessance of Swāti Tirunāḷ's kṛitis is bhakti. And Muthuswāmi Dīkshitar gave the greatest importance to the rāga aspect in his kṛitis.

Coming to the handling of rāgas in their compositions, Dīkshitar was a votary of the Asampoorṇa Mēḷa Paddhati. He was an antiquary, followed faithfully the ancient texts and gave fresh life to a number of obscure ancient rāgas such as Ārdradēśi, Chāyāgauḷa, Māruva, Śuddhavasantham, Mādhavamanōhari etc. Śyāmā Śāstri largely stuck to well known rāgas although he did compose a few pieces in rare rāgas as well like Kalgaḍa and Chitāmaṇi. As a follower of Saṅgrahachooḍāmaṇi, Tyāgarāja was the architect of diverse new rāgas not known till his time such as Naḷinakānti, Navarasakannaḍa, Chechukāmbōdhi, Bindumālini, Kōkiladhvani, etc. As a composer Swāti Tirunāḷ emulated both Dīkshitar and Tyāgarāja. He not only resusicated ancient rāgas like Maṅgaḷakaiśiki, Lalithapañchamaṁ, Gōpikāvasanthaṁ etc., but also ushered in new rāgas not handled earlier such as Śuddhabhairavi, Mōhanakalyāṇi, Haṁsānandi, etc.

In the vast majority of his kṛitis Dīkshitar has introduced the rāga mudra through ingeneously weaving the rāga name in the sahitya fabric. This has served to unequivocally pinpoint the rāga in which the composer intended the piece to be rendered. It has also helped to distinguish between allied rāgas - as for instance Udayaravichandrika and Śuddhadhanyāsi. Swāti Tirunāḷ too has used the rāga mudra in some compositions such as those in Śankarābharaṇam, Mōhanaṁ, Varāḷi, Āhiri, Laḷitapañcham, etc. However the rāga mudra is absent in certain crucial cases. It is therefore a moot question as to whether the authentic rāga of some Swāti Tirunāḷ pieces is Śuddhadhanyāsi or Udayaravichandrika and Karṇāṭaka Kāpi or Hindustani Kāpi.

Swāti Tirunāḷ has handled several rare and apoorva rāgas and he has also to his credit more than one kṛiti in some of them. The following is a comparative list of songs in rare rāgas by the Trinity and Swāti Tirunāḷ along with the commencing words of the sāhitya of one song of each composer, the scale of the rāga as employed in each of these compositions and the number (in brackets) of the parent Māḷakarta.

The ārōhaṇa-avarōhaṇa given against Swāti Tirunāḷ's list of rare rāgas are as found in Dr. Semmangudi Srinivasa Iyer's Swāti Tirunāḷ Kīrtana Māla; that of Muthuswāmi Dīkshitar are found in the Saṅgīta Saṁpradāya Pradarśini of Subbarāma Dīkshitar; that of Śyāmā Śāstri are found in the Śyāma Śāstri Compositions by Smt. Vidya Sankar; that of Thyāgarāja are found in the book Saṅgīta Pravāhaṁ by Dr. M.N. Dandapani and D. Pattammal.

RĀGAS	SWĀTI TIRUNĀL	TYĀGARĀJA	DĪKSHITAR	ŚYĀMĀ ŚĀSTRI
1) Āhiri	Parama purusha (14) srsmgmpdns snDpMgrs	Challare(14) srsgmpdns sndpmgrs	Kusumākara (20) srgmpdns sndpmgrs	Māyamma (14) smgmpdns sNdnDpmgrsRs
2) Bhauḷi	Pārvati nāyaka (15) srgpds - sndpgrs	Mēlūkovayya (15) srgpds - sndpgrs	Śrīpārvati (15) srgpds - sndpgrs	-
3) Bhūshāvati	Gōpanandana (64) srgmpds - sndpmgrs	Tanamīdane (64) srgmpds - sndpmgrs	Bhūshāvatiṁ (64) srgmpdns - sndpmgrs	-
4) Bihāg	Kānhā kab sahi*	-	-	-
5) Bīṁpḷās	Iti samupāgata Snsgmpns-sndpmgrs	-	-	-
6) Darbāri Kānaḍa	Dēvana ke pathi*	-	-	-
7) Dhanāśrī	Viśvēśara darśan*	-	-	-
8) Gaṁbhīranāṭa	Jayadēvaki (36) sgmpns - snpmrs	-	-	-
9) Gōpikāvasantham	Danyōyaṁ (20) rsrgmpdpsns - sndpmgrmgs	-	Bālakrishṇam (20) rsrgmpdpns sndpmgrmgs	-
10) Hamīr Kalyāṇi	Karuṇānidhān* (65) srgmpdns - sndpmgmpms	Mānamulēda (65) srgmpdnpdps sndpgmgrs	Parimaḷaraṅganātham (65) srgmpdns - sndpmgpms	-

11) Haṁsānandi	Śankaraśrīgiri(53) srgmdns - sndmgrs	-	-	-	
12) Jujāvanti	Taruṇī jñān (28) srmgmpds - sndndpmgmrgrs	-	Akhilāṇḍeśvari (28) srgmpdsndns sndpmgrs	-	
13) Kannaḍa	Kalayāmi (29) SgmpmḌns - snsDpmgmrs	Bhajarē rē mānasa (29) sgmpmdns - snsdpmgmrs	Girichakra (28) srgmpdns - sndpmgmrs	-	
14) Karṇāṭaka Kāpi	Kalayāmi (22) srgmpDns-SndpmRgmRs	Jūtāmurāre (22) srgmpdns - sndpmgmrs	Vēṅkaṭāchalapate (22) srgmpmdns sndpmgmrs	Akhilāṇḍeśvari (22) srmpns - sndnpndmpmGgrs	
15) Laḷithapañcha-maṁ	Paramapurushaṁ (15) srgmdns - sndmpmgrs	-	Bṛihadīśvaraṁ (14) sgmdns - sndmpmgrs	-	
16) Malayamārutam	Padmanābha (16) srgpdns - sndpgrs	Manasāyaṭulō (16) srgpdns - sndpgrs	-	-	
17) Maṅgaḷakaiśiki	Śibikaiyil (15) srgmpmgpdns - sndpmgrs	Jayajaya śrī (15) srmgdps sndpmgrs	Śrībhārgavi (15) srgmpds - sndpmgrs	-	
18) Māñji	Harasimudhā (20) sampurna	-	Rāmachandrēṇa (20) sampurna	Brōvavamma (20) sampurna	
19) Mōhanakalyāṇi	Sēvēśrīkāṅtaṁ (65) srgpds - sndpmgrs	-	-	-	

20)	Nāga gāndhāri	Jagadīśa śrījāne(20) nsrgmpds - ndpmgrsn	O Rāma rāma (20) srgmpdn - ndpmgrn	Sarasijanābha (20) srmgmpdn - sndpmgrs	-
21)	Navarasakannaḍa	Vandē sadā (28) Sgmps - sndmgrs	Ninnu vinā (28) sgmps - sndmgrs	-	-
22)	Navarōj	Indirāpati (29) pdnsrgms - pmgrsndp	Nā pāli (29) pdnsrgmp - mgrsndp	Hastivadanāya (29) mpdnsrgmp - pmgrsndp	-
23)	Pharaz	Bhaja bhaja (15) sgmpdns - sndpmdpmgsrs	Varamaina (15) sgmpdns - sndmdpmgrs	Śrīśukrabhaga- (15) sgmpdns - sndpmgrs	Nīlāyatākshi (15) smgmdns - sndpmgrs
24)	Pūrvi	Udhō Suniyo*	-	Guruguhasya	-
25)	Pushpalatika	Bhāvayē (22) srgmpns - snpmgrs	-	-	-
26)	Saindhavi	Iṭu sāhasamula (22) dnsrgmpdn - ndpmgrsnd	-	Saindhavi- rāgapriyē (22) srgmpdns - ndpmgrs	-
27)	Sālaṅganāṭa	Tāpaśamana (15) srmpds - snsdpmgrs	-	Avyājakaruṇā (15) srmpds - sndpmgrs	-
28)	Saurāshṭra	Dinamanu (17) srgmpmdns - sndndpmgrs	Śrīgaṇapatini (17) srmgmpdnds - sndpmgrs	Sūryamūrte (15) srgmpdns - sndpmgrs	-
29)	Sindhubhairavi	Āna Milō*	-	-	-

30) Śrī	Rīna madādhruta (22) srmpns - snpmgrs	Nāmakusuma (22) srmpns - snpdnpmrgrs	Śrīvaralakshmi (22) srmpns - snpdnpmrgrs	Karuṇajūḍu (22) srmpns - snpmrgrs
31) Suddhabhairavi	Vihara mānasa (22) sgmpnds - sndmgrs	-	-	-
32) Suruṭṭi	Sādaramiva (28) Srmpnns - sndpmgpmrs	Bhajanaparula (28) srmpns - sndpmgpmrs	Aṅgārakaṁ (28) srmpns - sndpmgrs	-
33) Yamankalyāṇ	Jai Jai dēvi*	Haridāsulu veḍalu (65) srgmpds - sdpmgrs	Jaṁbūpate (65) srgmpdns - sndpmgmrs	-
34) Śuddhadhanyāsi	Sāmōdaṁ (8) sgmpns - snpmgs	Entanērchina (20) sgmpns - snpmgs	Śrīpārthsārathi (22) sgmpns - snpmgs	

* Hindustani compositions

It can be seen from the above Table that out of the 34 rare rāgas handled by Swāti Tirunāḷ, Dīkshitar alone has composed in 21 rāgas, Tyāgarāja also in 17 rāgas and Śyāmā Śāstri also in just 4 rāgas. There are 10 apoorva rāgas in which Swāti Tirunāḷ is the sōlē composer and 3 in which all the four composers have songs to their credit. Again whereas the number of rare rāgas in which Swāti Tirunāḷ and Dīkshitar alone have composed is 5, the number in which Swāti Tirunāḷ and Tyāgarāja alone have composed is only one rāga. It is worthy of mention that wherever the same rāga has been handled by more than one composer, in the vast majority of cases they do not differ in their parentage (i.e. corresponding Mēḷakarta).

We owe a deep debt of gratitude to Swāti Tirunāḷ for enriching our musical heritage through usering into our repertoire a number of rare rāgas not handled by earliercomposers. In view of the two dominant schools in Carnatic Music - those of Tyāgarāja and Dīkshitar - due care needs to be taken in identifying the allegiance of particular rāgas as handled by Swāti Tirunāḷ to either of the Sampradāyas in perspective. And the appropriate identity in rāga bhava cannot be faithfully portrayed except through bringing intoplay the artiste's manōdharma and faculties of improvisation in the fullest possible measure.

COMPOSITIONS OF TIRUVOṬṚIYŪR TYĀGAYYAR

In any estimate of the worth and contribution of a composer, the cultural environment and tradition to which he was exposed right from birth assume considerable importance. And in the case of Tiruvoṭṛiyūr Tyāgayyar, the persons who wielded the greatest influence in shaping and developing his creative capacities were his own father, Vīṇa Kuppayyar and the latter's Guru, Tyāgarājaswāmi.

Viṇa Kuppayyar was one of the most distinguished among the direct disciples of Tyāgarājaswāmi. The saint composer held Kuppayyar in high regard in view of his rare musical attainments, proficiency in Vīṇa and profound scholarship in Sanskrit and other languages. During the course of his stay for over two decades at Tiruvaiyār, Kuppayyar had the benefit of learning first hand diverse higher aspects of music and the intricacies of musical construction and composition in particular in a manner and to an extent that was not the privilege of any other of the saint composer's direct disciples. Following closely in his mentor's footsteps, Kuppayyar eminently succeeded not only in establishing himself as the most outstanding composer in the Tyāgarāja Śishya Paraṁpara but also in passing on the art to his own son and disciple, Tiruvoṭṛiyūr Tyāgayyar.

Arising from his proficiency and mastery over all aspects of music, Kuppayyar was given the title Gāna Chakravarthi. It was on account of his great reverence to his family diety, Vēṇugōpālaswāmi, that Kuppayyar adopted for his kṛitis the Mudra Gōpāladāsa - a practice which Tyāgayyar also followed for his own compositions.

When in 1837, at the ripe old age of 70, Tyāgarājaswāmi undertook a tour of the northern districts of Tamilnadu at the invitation of Upanishad Brahma Yōgin of Kāñchi, Kuppayyar, who was then the samasthāna vidwān at the court of the Zamindar of Kōvūr, reverentially took upon himself the task of looking after the saint's comforts during his travels. He was also instrumental in arranging Tyāgarājaswāmi's visits to Kuppayyar's native place, Tiruvoṭṛiyūr, as well as Kōvūr and Madras. At the time of his visit to Kuppayyar's residence at Tiruvoṭṛiyūr it was Gōkulāshṭami season and the festival of the family deity, Vēṇugōpālaswāmi, which was in full swing, was being celebrated on a grand scale. It is said that, moved by the spiritually inspiring and artistic atmosphere of the place at that time, the venerable composer sang his Kedaragaula kriti 'Vēṇugānalōluni' to mean that a thousand eyes are need to espy the glorious form of the deity. Since Kuppayyar's third son was born shortly after the saint composer's visit to his residence, the child was named Tyāgayyar in memory of the occasion.

Tyāgayyar was born at Tiruvoṭṭiyūr in 1845 and lived till 1917. He learned the rudiments of music from Fiddle Ponnuswāmy, a senior disciple of Kuppayyar and soon proved to be the worthy son of a worthy father, holding aloft the family tradition of unflinching service to music and dedicating his entire life to the cause of the art. Foremost among all Kuppayyar's disciples, Tyāgayyar turned out to be a delectable composer of tānavarṇas, rāgamālikas and kṛitis.

Many people approached Tyāgayyar, as the most eminent lakshaṇa-lakshya vidvān of the time, to have their doubts regarding both the theory and practice of music clarified. It was said that Tyāgayyar was such an original and creative artist that musicians greatly profited through listening to his performances. Pallavi exposition found a pre-eminent place in his concerts and in singing or playing kalpanāswaras he adopted a very attractive exalted style. Quite a few also learnt music at Tyāgayyar's feet and some became accomplished musicians and performers themselves, the most prominent among them being the late Saṅgeeta Kalānidhi Ponnayya Piḷḷai. Tyāgayyar's house in Muthiālpeṭ or George Town became a centre for music and a veritable place of pilgrimage for musicians and music lovers alike. Many votaries of music derived inspiration by coming into contact with him. Alongwith Kuppayyar, Tyāgayyar was mainly responsible for converting Madras into a seat of musical learning and he was the central figure in the cultural life of the city during the closing decades of the last century and the early decades of this century.

Tyāgayyar continued the tradition of celebrating various festivals like Gōkulāshṭami, Chitrā pourṇami, Vināyaka chaturthi, etc., which his family was engaged in right from his father's time. Contemporary top ranking musicians from all over South India considered it a previlege to come and perform at these festivals, for it was deemed a rare honour for any musician to have an opportunity to perform before Tyāgayyar's circle of musical luminaries who adorned Madras.

Tyāgayyar's compositions do not suffer from artificial or laboured construction. The underlying music is natural and easy flowing. They are replete with sangatis reflecting the diverse facets of the rāga. The rāgabhāva is lustrously presented with the melodic personality of each rāga being portrayed in a picturesque manner.

Like his father Tyāgayyar too was an accomplished Vīṇa player. This has relevance to the fact that both have shone as remarkably successful composers of tānavarṇas. Being Vaiṇikas themselves, they could import the correct tāna style into these compositions. Their tānavarṇas serve as good excercises for the voice as well as instruments. Also Vidwāns feel a delight in singing or rendering these varṇams at the commencement of their concerts since they serve to invoke the appropriate musical atmosphere and build up the tempo. A popular anecdote concerning Tyāgayyar's well known Darbār varṇam 'Chalamēla' is worthy of mention here. Once, at a congregation of Sangīta Vidwans gathered at the residence of Tachūr Singarāchāryulu, a sporting suggestion was made that all the Vidwans present there may compose a varṇam in Darbār rāga and bring it to the assembly. On that occasion, to start with two Vidwāns recited their varṇams one after the other. Then came Tyāgayyar's turn and he sang his varṇam 'Chalamēla' set to Ādi tāḷa. This composition made such an impression on those assembled that all the other Vidwāns tore away the papers on which their respective varnams were written for after listening to Tyāgayyar's varṇam, they decided that their own compositions did not deserve even a hearing.

Tyāgayyar had also a flair for composing rāgamalikas. He has provided Dhātu and Mātu to the rāgamālika 'Śrī Ramaṇa Padmanayana' set in 16 rāgas. He has also recast Nārāyaṇa Tīrtha's well known Tarangam 'Jaya jaya gōkulabāla' originally set to Kurañji rāga into a rāgamālika in 5 rāgas comprising Bhairavi, Aṭhāṇa, Kāmbōdhi, Kalyāṇi and Suraṭi with briliant chittaswaras adorning each section and the Makuṭaswara in Bhairavi having a delicate beauty of its own.

Through his two works - Pallavi svarakalpavali and Sankīrtana ratnāvaḷi, Tyāgayyar has placed the entire music world under a deep debt of gratitude to him. These books, both in Telugu, were published respectively in the years 1900 and 1907 but both have long been out of print. However Pallavi Svarakalpavalli, which contains all Kuppayyar's compositions, but no kṛiti of Tyāgayyar, was republished in Tamil in 1971 by Sangīta Vidwan Thērazandūr V. Ranganāthan with the financial aid of the Central and Tamilnadu State Sangeet Nataka Akademies. This has definitely helped in providing greater access and hence larger exposure and currency to Kuppayyar's kritis. On the other hand the fact that the other work, Sankīrtana ratnāvaḷi, which is the sole repository of Tyāgayyar's kṛitis, has not so far been republished has contributed, in a large measure, to their remaining comparatively obscure and not having received the attention they rightfully deserve.

A remarkable feature of Pallavi swarakalpavalli concerns the portion devoted to svara extemporisation for pallavi exposition giving comprehensive svaraprasthāras in ½, 1, 2, 4, 8 and 16 āvarthanas for different age old Ethukkaḍai pallavis in various rāgas and tāḷas. This work derives its name Pallavi svarakalpavalli from the fact that these pallavi svaraprasthāras are a veritable <u>kalpavṛiksha</u> for the students and learners of music. Of course improvisation becomes a misnomer in the context of committed <u>chiṭṭa</u> but what is done here is to present for guidance illustrative svara amplifications. If one diligently practices the svaraprasthāras given in this book, one can surely imbibe the capacity to sing naturally and systematically kalpanāsvaras for any rāga and tāḷa with accuracy. In addition Palavi svara kalpavalli presents 5 āditāḷa varṇas, 9 aṭatāḷa varṇas and 53 kritis of Kuppayyar including his Kālahastīśa and Venkaṭēśa Pancharatnam groups. As for Tyāgayyar's compositions, it contains 6 āditāḷa varṇas, 5 aṭatāḷa varṇas and the two rāgamālikas already referred to but none of his kṛitis.

Sankīrtana ratnāvaḷi is devoted exclusively to Tyāgayyar's compositions. In addition to 4 tānavarṇas, it contains a group of 108 kṛitis composed by Tyāgayyar in praise of his family deity Vēṇugōpālaswāmy, which is collectively known as 'Ashṭōttara kṛitis'. In such an endeavour, Tyāgayyar must have been inspired by the example of his own father and mentor, Kuppayyar, who has to his credit two sets of group kritis - Kāḷahastīśa and Veṅkaṭēśa Pañcharatnams - and even to a greater extent by Tyāgarājaswāmi himself who was quite a prolific composer of group kritis. However, Tyāgayyar was the first composer in the anals of the history of Carnatic music to have composed Ashṭōttara group kṛitis and only one other composer has so far emulated Tyāgayyar in this regard viz., Saṅgīta Kalānidhi Harikēśanallūr Muthiāh Bhāgavatar, who was Tyāgayyar's junior by a generation. In Saṅkīrtana ratnāvaḷi, the Ashṭōttara group is preceded by 3 benedictory kṛitis - the rather obscure Gaṇēśastuti in Dhanyāsi beginning with the words 'Kāpāḍu Gaṇanātha and then the comparatively better known Sarasvati stuti 'Saraswati Nannepuḍu' in Kalyāṇi and the Gurustuti 'Tyāgarājaswāmi guruni' in Kharaharapriya in which Tyāgayyar pays obeisance to Tyāgarājaswāmi, his grand guru, as his own actual personal guru. The epilogue for the work too comprises 3 compositions. The first of these in Punnāgavarāḷi beginning with the words 'Kashṭamulanu dīrchinanu' features the prabandha mudra 'Ashṭōttara śata kīrtanamarpaṇa jēyuchu' to mean that the composer is dedicating to Almighty his garland of 108 kṛitis. One can see such a prabandha mudra also in Muthiāh Bhāgavatar's Pushpalathikā kṛiti 'Gurunātha' one of the benedictory compositions in the Kannaḍa language forming the prelude to his Chāmuṇḍāmba Ashoṭtara (group) kṛitis; the relevant sāhithya here is 'Chāmuṇḍāmba devi śakthyashṭōṭtara śatanāmagaḷigē'. The Punnāgavarāḷi kṛiti is followed by the Lakshmīstuti 'Ksheerasgara kanyaka' in Aṭhāṇa and finally comes the maṅgaḷaṁ in Madhyamāvati beginning with the words 'Śrī Vēṇugōpālanaku'.

Whereas Tyāgayyar has set 102 kritis of his Ashṭōttara group in Ādi tāḷa, he has used rūpaka tāḷa for only 5 kṛitis and Tripuṭa tāḷa for just one. On the other hand he has not repeated any rāga twice for this Ashṭōttara group. In other words, he has employed 108 different rāgas for them. His choice of these rāgas presents some noteworthy features. The first five songs have been composed in the Prathama Ghana pañchakaṁ (Nāṭa, Gauḷa, Ārabhi, Varāḷi and Śrī) and for the next five songs the Dvitīya Ghana pañchakaṁ (Rītigauḷa, Nārāyaṇagauḷa, Kēdāraṁ, Nāṭakurañji and Bhauḷi) have been used. It may be mentioned here that these are the very rāgas in which Kuppayyar has composed his Navarāgamālika varṇam 'Inta kōpa' with the omission of Nāṭakuruñji in one pāṭāntharaṁ and Bhauli in the other. While many prasiddha rāgas have been used for his Ashtottara group, there is a considerable proportion of apoorva rāgas as well. Tyāgayyar followed the Tyāgarājaswami tradition in adopting the Sampoorṇa Mēḷapaddhati for the rāga nomenclature. Like the saint composer, he has used quite a few Mēḷakarta rāgas for his group kṛitis - 19 in al, 11 from the Śuddha madhyama group and 8 from the Prati madhyama group. Of the rest, 68 are Śuddhamadhyama janya rāgas. 35 of these or nearly one third of the total rāgas employed for the Ashṭōttara group are apoorva rāgas. Among these 15 are absolutely obscure rāgas which have not been used by any other composer before or after Tyāgayyar's time including the Trinity, viz., Gōshiṇi, Siṁhaḷa, Śāradābharaṇam, Haṁsanārāyaṇi, Lōkarañjani, Mēchakāṅgi, Bhūshakalyāṇi, Sēshanādaṁ, Siṁhāravaṁ, Dēśīya Gānavāridhi, Kanakakusumāvaḷi, Ratnabhānu, Ratnakānti, Choorṇikāvinōdini and Haṁsagiri. Only the first three of these are Śuddha madhyama janya rāgas. The other twelve are Prathimadhyama janya rāgas. Two other rare rāgas - Guḍamallār and Vijayanāgari - have also not been handled by any other composer including the Trinity but with the single exception of Muthiāh Bhāgavatar. However the fact that Tyāgayyar was a senior contemporary of Muthiāh Bhagavatar lends credence to the possibility that the latter derived inspiration from Tyāgayyar in introducing to the Carnatic music fold these rāgas which have since attained some popularity.

Apart from these 17 obscure rāgas, there are 18 apoorva rāgas in which apart from Tyāgayyar, Dīkshitar and/or Tyāgarājaswāmi have also composed kṛitis. Let us in the first instance consider rāgas in which Dīkshitar has kṛitis to his credit but not Tyāgarājaswāmi. These are 4 in number - viz., Ārdradēśi, Kannaḍabaṅgāḷa, Gaṅgātaraṅgiṇi and Kuntaḷaṁ. The scales adopted by Tyāgayyar for these rāgas differ to varying extents from those adopted by Dīkshitar though the respective mēḷas are the same except in the case of Kuntaḷaṁ. This rāga as adopted for Dīkshitar's kṛiti 'Śrī Sugandhi Kuntalambike' is in fact a pratimadhyama raga belonging to the 61st mēḷa whereas Tyāgayyar's Kuntaḷaṁ for his kṛiti 'Māṭi Māṭiki Nee Nāmame' is a janya of chakravaka. Only two compositions are available in this rāga which is mentioned in Saṅgīta Ratnākara of Śārṅgadēva.

There are 5 apoorva rāgas in which besides Tyāgayyar, Dīkshitar and Tyāgarājaswāmi have both compositions to their credit viz., Mangaḷakaiśiki, Gunṭakṛiya, Āndhāḷi, Chāyātaranginị and Manōhari. There are considerable differences in the scales of these rāgas as adopted by Tyāgarājaswāmi and Dīkshitar and in the case of Manōhari even the mēḷas are different. Tyāgarājaswāmi's Manōhari for his kṛiti 'Paritāpamu' is a janya of the 22nd mēḷa whereas Dīkshitar's Manōhari for his piece 'Śankaram Abhirāmi Manōharam' is a janya of the 33rd mēḷa. In all these rāgas, Tyāgayyar has faithfully followed the Tyāgarājaswāmi Sampradāya rather than that of Dīkshitar.

Finally there are 9 apoorva rāgas in which in addition to Tyāgayyar, only Tyāgarājaswāmi has composed kṛitis but not Dīkshitar. In Supradeepam, Manjaṛi, Māruvadhanyāsi, Jayantasēna, Kāpinārāyaṇi, Gānavāridhi, Ramāmanōhari and Vijayaśrī there is only a single kṛiti of Tyāgarājaswāmi and in Kōkiladhvani he has composed two kṛitis. These compositions form the sole lakshya for the lakshaṇa of these respective rāgas and Tyāgayyar has implicitly followed the Tyāgarāja sampradāya in his delineation of these rāgas for his own kṛitis.

Tyāgayyar's kṛitis abound in technical beauties. He had the flair for decorating them with beautiful chiṭṭaswaras. As many as 50 compositions of his Ashṭōttara group contain chiṭṭaswaras including the first 10 pieces in the Prathama and Dvitīya Ghana panchakam. They serve to adron these compositions. The madhyama kāla chiṭṭaswaras lend a verve and dignity to his kṛitis. The solfa passages have a gripping interest about them.

Tyāgayyar has spared no pains to use the appropriate words with natural beauty for the sāhitya of his kṛitis replete with arthabhāva. The easy diction employed and the mellifluous nature of the sāhitya are noteworthy. The words blend very well with the tune and give a pleasant impression. In regard to the sāhitya of his kṛitis, Tyāgayyar has taken Tyāgarājaswāmi as his model and attempted to emulate him. This is borne out by the fact that the commencing words of the Pallavis of some of his kṛitis are the same as in some of the saint's compositions. His Kuntaḷam kṛiti 'Māṭi māṭiki' is reminiscent of Tyāgarājaswāmi's Mōhanam kṛiti with the same beginning. Other such instances are the Vakuḷābharaṇam kṛiti

'Dēvādi Dēva' and the saint's Sindhurāmakṛiya kṛiti; the Vijayaśrī kṛiti 'Evaritō' and the saint's Mānavathi kṛiti; the Śrīrāga kṛiti 'Kōrivachchitinayya' and the saint's Bilahari kṛiti; the Dhanyāsi kṛiti 'Evarunnāru' and the saint's Māḷavaśrī kriti; the Gowḷa kṛiti 'Ēla nee dayarādu' and the saint's krit in Aṭhāṇa; the Gowḷipantu kṛiti 'Muddumōmu' and the saint's Sūryakāntaṁ kṛiti; the maṇiraṅgu kṛiti 'Sarsīruhanayana' and the saint's Bilahari kṛiti; the Sāma kṛiti 'Mārubalka' and the saint's Śrīrañjani kṛiti; and the Lōkarañjani kṛiti 'Ennaḍujūchuno' and the saint's Kalāvati kṛiti.

The sāhityas of Tyāgayyar's kṛitis are also replete with diverse rhetorical beauties like Ādiprāsam, Anthyaprāsam, Anuprāsa Yati etc. The phrases like Thali, Vulla, Challa in the charaṇam of the Pantuvarāḷi kṛiti 'Iṭuvanṭi' is an instance of Ādiprāsam. Similarly the phrases 'Nammitini' and 'Brōthuvaṇi' in the Īśamanōhari kṛiti 'Nī pādāmbuja mulanu' and 'Dhyāniñche, brōche' in the anupallavi of 'Sārasadaḷa' (Bilahari kṛiti) typify Anthyapráśa. The phrases 'Thāpamulu, Japamulu, Kripakalu' in the charaṇa of the Kāpinārāyaṇi kṛiti 'Jagadīśabrōva' exemplify anuprāsam. As an example of Yati one may mention the phrases 'Palumāru ninu' and 'Palukulu' in the anupallavi of the Kannaḍabaṅgāḷa kṛiti 'Ilalōna nīku' and the phrases 'Chentha, Chintha' in Pallavi and Antha and Śāntha in Charaṇa in the Haṁsadhvani kṛiti 'Chentajērchi'.

The sāhityas also contain numerous references to anecdotes from the Itihāsas and the Purāṇas. To give only a few instances the Maṇiraṅgu kṛiti 'Sarasīruha nayana' contains references to Gejēndra mōksham and Draupadi Mānasaṁrakshaṇam; the Tōḍi kṛiti 'Prārthinchiti palumāru' refers to Gītōpadēśaṁ; the Chakravāka kṛiti 'Nenarumeeraganu' to Ajāmiḷa's story; and the 'Dharmavati kṛiti 'Dāthavu ṇeevegāka' to Mahābali and Vāmana avatāraṁ.

It can thus be seen that Tiruvoṭṭriyūr Tyāgayyar has composed his Ashṭōttara kṛitis in several rare as well as prasiddha rāgas and many of them are also replete with diverse rhetorical beauties. Quite a few are concert-worthy pieces. No efforts should be spared in ensuring their inclusion in our general repertoire of compositions. They certainly deserve a far wider currency.

(This was presented at the Annual Conference of the Music Academy, Madras in 1986.)

TILLĀNA

Tillāna is one of the Prabandha varieties that came into vogue and attained immense popularity after the time of the Musical Trinity. The Dēśi Prabandhas of the medieval period in the history of our music are the forerunners of all the forms representative of the art, sacred, secular, dance and instrumental music that emerged later and the Tillāna, characterized by a profusion of rhythmic syllables, is no exception. As regards the etymology of the term Prabandha, it is generally believed that it is based on the words Pāda and Bandha. Pādabandha became Prabandha to mean a composition bound by certain rules and regulations relating to structure, theme, etc.

There is a widespread conception that the Tillāna is derived from the North Indian form Taranā. However, there is sufficient evidence in diverse Lakshaṇa treatises to controvert this view notwithstanding the fact that Tillāna got a filip from the plethora of Hindustāni musicians who flocked the Tanjore royal court during the Marāṭha rule and popularised various North Indian musical forms including Taranā.

Our earliest music and dance treatise, Bharata's Nāṭya Śāstra, does not refer to Prabandha as such, but Geetha or Geethi - a composition with rhythmic bias - finds a place there. A type of Geethi called Khanḍika, centred on mystic syllables, was pronounced by Brahma for the proper development of art and Bharata, as His chosen mouth piece, propagated them for the benefit of humanity.

"Jhanthum jhanthum Digi Digi Digi Digi
Jhanthum jagati avali taka macha jhāla
Titi Jhāla Paśupati Digi Digi vadir
Gōgaṇapathi titidhā
Digi taga jhantum jhantum tagu-Digi"

These syllables formed the nucleus for rhythmic solfa. The Tamils seized upon them with alacrity. Successive generations of musicians in the South developed it as a vital branch of the art sparkling with a whole world of fascinating solfa for rhythm.

The popular notion that the Tillāna is exclusively an adaptation from Hindustani compositions of analogous character like **Taranā is ill-founded and Sārṅgadēva's Saṅgīta Ratnākara itself** contains incontrovertible data which can help to correct this misconception. Karaṇa Prabandha is described in this treatise as comprising a mixed medley of Svara, Pada and rhythmic phrases interspersed When Gōpāla Nāyaka was taken away to the north by the Muslims as a prisoner, he endeared himself to his captors through his extraordinary talents and erudition in music. Gōpāla Nāyaka is reputed to have taught Amīr Khusru, among other things, the Karaṇa Prabandha which later flowered as the Tillāna or the Taranā. Drawing inspiration from this Prabandha and using the traditional form of dhruva pada hymns or quatrains and their shortened syllables employed in Indian vocalizing (such as 'tum' 'dar' 'dāni' etc.) in combination with certain words from the Persian which also had abstract connotations, Khusru paved the way for the musical form which came to be known as Taranā. Thus one may regard the Tillāna or Taranā type of composition to be the product of composite North and South Indian intelligence with roots in the Prabandhas.

Prabandha is made up of 4 dhātus or avyayās - Udgaraha, Mēlāpaka, Dhruva and Ābhōga, corresponding respectively to the present day Pallavi, Anupallavi, Charaṇa and concluding portion of Charaṇa. Whether the Prabandha comprises all these four avyayās or only three (tridhātu) or two (dvidhātu), it has in all six aṅgās - Svara and Tāḷa as well as Birunda, Pada, Tēnaka and Pāṭa. Among these, the first two established the Niryukta (Nibaddha) character of the Prabandha ensuring its steady course from Udgaraha to Ābhōga. Diverse musical forms gradually emerged from the Prabandhas depending upon the relative importance of the other four aṅgas in their make up. A form characterised by preponderance of Pāṭa is the Tillāna. It heads the list of Pata-prominent forms of similar nature like Solkaṭṭusvaram, Kaivāra prabandham, Geeta prabandham, Jatisvaram, Daru varṇam, etc.

Pata itself is a term referring in general to Vādyālankāras or instrumental sounds and in course of time came to signify the rhythmical sounds produced by percussion instruments. Muraja Pāṭas are the rhythmic sounds that are born out of the percussion of skin-covered instruments like Mridaṅgam, Maddaḷam, Muraja, etc.

These sounds are denoted by simple syllables like Thā, Naṁ, Ki, Ṭa, Thi, La, Na, Dhōm, Dham, Jham, Nam, Thiru, Tharu, etc. When these individual syllables are grouped together we get compound syllables like Thaka, Thakiṭa, Thakaddhimi, Thakajaṇu, Tharikiṭa, Thiruthiru, Thilāna, etc. This is the genesis of the term Tillāna. These compound syllables belong to the realm of Pāṭa among the Prabandha aṅgas and are also known as jatis. When pronounced as such without admisture with any other aṅga (as for instance svaras) it is termed Kanugōl which is sometimes employed as a Tāḷa accompaniment. On the other hand, when the jatis get interspersed with the Saptasvaras, it becomes a case of Miśrapāṭas called Solkaṭṭusvaras (Solkaṭṭu). This is the essential fabric in the structure of the Tillāna.

Chronologically the term Prabandha is mentioned for the first time in the Brahaddēśi of Mataṅga wherein it is stated that they emerged from the five faces of Lord Śiva. Prabandhas were classified into Nibaddha and Anibaddha depending respectively on whether or not they were set to Tāḷa. The Niryukta prabandhas belonging to the former variety were prescribed to be sung only to certain specific Tāḷas, metres, sentiments, etc. Śārṅgadēva, who draws profusely upon Mataṅga, Sōmēśvara, Jagadēkamalla etc., for his description of the Prabandhas, delineates several of these composition which are rāgamālikas, and tāḷamālikas both under the Alikrama and Viprakīrṇa varieties. Panchatāḷēśvaram was sung in the 5 Mārga tāḷas to the accompaniment of Pāṭaksharas from Paṭaha, Huḍuka, Śaṅkha, Kamsyatāḷa and Muraja respectively in addition to svara exposition. Five varieties of Pāṭas (Nāgabandha, Svastika, Alagna, Śuddha and Sōmāskhalita) are believed to have emanated from the five faces of Śiva as did also the five mārgatāḷas themselves.

Historically compositions with Pāṭas, Svaras and Sāhitya together or separately in diverse aṅgas can be traced to the medieval Prabandhas - particularly the Karaṇa and Kaivāra prabandhas. According to Śārṅgadēva the Prabandhas are classified into three major divisions - Sooda prabandhas, Alikrama prabandhas and Vipra-Keerna prabandhas. Whereas the Karaṇa prabandha is the second among the eight subdivisions of the Sūḍa prabandha, the Kaivāra prabandha is the fourth among the twentyfour subdivisions of the Alikrama prabandha.

Matanga has listed only two Karaṇa Prabandhas - Bhaṇḍa Karaṇa made up of Muraja aksharas and svaras and set to any tāḷa and Pada Karaṇa which is constituted of hasta pāṭās. According to Gōvinda Dīkshitar and Veṅkaṭamakhi, Bhaṇḍa Karaṇa is a variety wherein the Udgaraha and Dhruva contain cleverly interwoven Muraja pāṭās. In the Pāṭākaraṇa, the hasta pāṭās also figure along with svaras in the Udgraha. In the Citrakaraṇa, while the Udgraha consists of svaras and hasta pāṭās, the Dhruva section is made up of Muraja pāṭās and Pada.

In the Kaivāra Prabandha, which may be regarded as another immediate percursor of the Tillāna, the Ūdgraha and Dhruva sections in general comprise Pāṭās while the Ābhōga section includes Pada. Out of the nine prabandhas which figure in Subbarāma Dīkshitar's Sangeeta Sampradāya Pradarśiṇi, only the relatively long Gowri Rāga prabandham is completely bereft of Pāṭa or jati. The lakshya prabandham in Haṁsadhvani rāga (Maṭya), the Śrīraṅgaprabandham in Bhowḷi (Ēka) and the Umātilaka prabandhas in Mēchabhauḷi (Tripuṭa) and in Husēni (Ēka) have comparatively less jātis. On the other hand, jatis are prominent in the framework of Kabhai (Dēśiya) prabandhas in Phraz (Ādi) and Yamunākalyāṇi (Ādi) as also in the Gowḷa rāga prabandham (Jampa). In fact the latter prabandham has been presented as a Kaivāra Prabandham by Harikēśanallūr Subramaniam in his book 'Geetha Prabandha Māla'. Veṅkaṭamakhi's Kaivāra Prabandham in Nārāyaṇa Gauḷa (Maṭya) featured in the Saṅgīta Sampradāya Pradarśini may well serve as the model for the Kaivāra Prabandha. It consists of 4 Khaṇḍas- Pāṭava Khaṇḍam, Jāvada Khaṇḍam, Ālāpa Khaṇḍam and Mudra Khaṇḍam. The first two sections are made up entirely of Pāṭās or jātis. Along with a few words of Sāhitya, the Ālāpa Khaṇḍam comprises esentially vowel extensions preseumably for the purpose of facilitating rāga ālāpa or elaboration. The final Mudra Khaṇḍam which contains the Vāggeyakāra and Prabandha Mudras ends in jatis. The feature of the composition beginning as well as ending in jatis (Pāṭa) is also seen in many other Kaivāra Prabandhas presented in the Geeta Prabandha Māla under reference - those in Nāṭa (Rūpakam), Gowḷa (Jampa) and Śaṅkarābharaṇam (Jampa). This lends unequivocal support to the view that the Tillāna was evolved out of the Kaivāra Prabandhas.

Nārāyaṇa Tīrtha and Ūttukkāḍu Vēṅkaṭasubbier were the earliest Vāggēyakaras to make use of jatis in their compositions.

The former's Krishṇa Leela Taraṅgiṇi contains exquisite Śolkaṭṭus particularly in the context of describing the Rāsakreeḍa and Rādhākṛishṇa episodes. Ūttukāḍu Vénkaṭasubbier's Rāsa Śabda kīrtanas are replete with attractive Chiṭṭaswaras as well as jati passages characterised by a profusion of diverse rhythmic patterns including Tiśram, Miśram, Khaṇḍam and Saṅkīrṇam. A Tillāna in the Puranirmayi Paṇṇ is ascribed to this composer. Melaṭṭur Vīrabhadrayya is credited with being the creator of the musical form Tillāna. His composition Dani Tillilāna in Pantuvarāḷi rāga (Ādi) carries the Achyuta Varada Mudra :

"Dāni tillana thana thamdari
Nādiri dirana thamdari dirana
Tillāna dattillāna tirana daritillāna tirina
. . . .
Elukora jil jil jil
Manachun tamigaḷigēnu idugo sarasunika ippuḍu
Achyuta varadananthu"

Another ancient Tillāna is the one composed by a North Indian musician at the court of Tulajā Mahāraja in Tanjore in praise of his royal patron. Set to Kalyāṇi rāga and Ādi tāḷa it runs as follows :

"Thai thai thai thayim dhattha thinna Digi digi
. . . .
Tulaja rāja chattrapathi chiranjeevi
Tam thaddha digitha thām thaddha digitha
thalāṅgu thagadha thaka thalāṅgu thagadha thaka
thalāṅgu taga taga"

Jatis along with Solkaṭṭusvaras and Chiṭṭasvaras are the major constituents of the Tillāna and Sāhitya is used sparingly merely as the vehicle for Dēvata or Pōshaka stuthi, besides the composer's signature. However, instances are also known of Tillānas with no sāhitya whatsoever as indicated below (Yaman rāga, Tiśra Gathi, Ēka Tāḷa).

Pallavi

Udadana dirināre

Anupallavi

Danadheem danaḍheem dhaṇadheem

Charana

Nādiri diridāni thōm diridirithāni dana īlalō
Thadani dāni ilalo dana dheem dana dheem dana dheem

As a form belonging to once to the spheres of both art and dance music, Tillāna finds a place as indispensable captivating item in music as well as dance concerts. In the former it provides a crisp finale after the heavy dose of Rāgam, Tānaṁ and Pallavi. In the latter it comes as a welcome lively change with its quick tempo music following the leisurely Abhinaya for the long drawn out Padam. Being intended mainly to project the pure Nṛitta aspect of Bharatanāṭyam, the Tillāna enables the dancer to exhibit mastery in this aspect with scintillating footwork and poses. The introduction of cross rhythms with unlimited scope for variations confers additional beauty and charm on this composition. In Harikathā kālakshēpaṁ, Tillāna is traditionally rendered immediately after the introductory Purva-pitika with a view to evolving the proper musical atmosphere. Sometimes the Harikathā performer may also suddenly switch over to a sprightly Tillāna in the midst of his discourse just to relieve the monotony of the audience.

In the sphere of Abhayāsa Gānam too, Tillānas have great value. To the vocalist, singing these compositions would help to impart good training to the tongue since other jatis in the 4th degree or speed have to be rendered with clarity. In the case of instrumentalists Tillānas provide scope for useful training in swift bowing or fast plucking.

The Tillāna comprises three sections (Trikaṇḍa) - Pallavi, Anupallavi and Charaṇam. While the Anupallavi is made up entirely of jatis, the Charaṇa (which scarcely exceeds one in number) carries the composers' signature in its sāhitya besides solfa syllables and jatis. However, instances are also known of Dvikhaṇḍa Tillānas consisting of only Pallavi and Anupallavi or Pallavi and Charaṇam. In the former case the Anupallavi is constituted of jatis, Chiṭṭasvara and Sāhitya.

The Sahitya in the Tillāna is in any one of the South Indian languages besides Sanskrit. The galaxy of prominent Tillāna composer include Swāti Tirunāl, Tanjore Quartette, Mysore Sadāśiva Rao, Kunrakuḍi Krishṇa Iyer, Maha Vaidyanātha Iyer, Paṭnam Subramaṇya Iyer, Pallavi Sēshayyar, Mysore Sēshaṇṇa, Rāmanāḍ Śrīnivāsa Iyengar and Muthiāh Bhāgavathar.

Tillānna is a short and lively composition. Those that figure in music concerts hardly take a few minutes to perform. Most Tillānas are set in Madhyamakāla. As an example of Viḷamba kāla Tillāna may be cited Pallavi Sēshayyar's Vasanta Tillāna 'Jham Jham tarita jham'. Saṅgatis adorn such Tillānas.

Some Tillānas are scholarly compositions. The Kanaḍa Tillāna Gowrī Nāyaka of Mahā Vaidyanātha Iyer in Simhanandana tāḷa belongs to this category as does the Tōḍi Kambarāmāyaṇa Tillāna 'Dani tana tirana' of Kunṛakkuḍi Krishṇa Iyer. Tillāna Daru resembles Tillāna in beginning and ending with jatis but differs in respect of a large proportion of words in its·mātu. Krishṇaswami Ayyā's Tillāna Daru in Suraṭi rāga, Ādi tāḷa, beginning with the jatis 'Nādiri tāni timdari' is an excellent representative of this type of composition.

The vast majority of Tillānas have been composed in Ādi Tāḷa. Tillānas in other tāḷas are very few Apart from Mahāvaidyanātha Iyer's Simahanandana Tāḷa Tillāna already referred to, Rāmanāḍ Śrīnivāsa Iyengār has to his credit a Tillāna, in Lakshmīśa tāḷa - one of the 108 tāḷas.

The early composers employed mostly Ghana rāgas for composing their Tillānas, but with the passage of time there was a noticeable trend towards the adoption of Dēśiya rāgas. Tillānas can be classified intoclassical and light-classical varieties.

During the past few years, there has been a welcome spurt in the composition of Tillānas by many senior performing musicians. Their dhātu are characterised by several catchy and fascinating innovations, while their mātu are replete with pleasing embellishments like prāsa, yati, yamaka, etc. These highly delectable compositions have become extremely popular with students of music, musicians as well as wide cross-sections of music lovers.

DARUS IN CARNATIC MUSIC

Almost all musical forms in the realm of Carnatic music owe their origin to one or other of the medieval Prabandhas and the Daru is no exception. A study of the structure of various musical forms such as Kṛiti, Kīrtana, Varṇam, Padam, Daru, Jāvaḷi, Tillāna, etc., makes it abundantly clear that Carnatic music has been maintaining the ancient tradition of the Prabandhas far more faithfully and rigidly than Hindustani music. As in Carnatic music, so in the Prabandhas strict adherence to the structure of the composition is compulsory. Actually this rigid fidelity to the composition in the case of the Prabandhas was carried to such levels that the repetition of one part turned it altogether into another Prabandha.

The word Prabandha is a generic term which refers to any well-knit composition but in music it meant a particular form where there were several kinds within that prescribed framework. Prabandha finds mention for the first time as early as 7th century A.D. in Mataṅga's Bṛihaddēśi but it is in the Saṅgīta Ratnākara of Śārṅgadēva which appeared five centuries later that it received comprehensive treatment. The Prabandha Adhyāya of this treatise enumerates and describes 260 varieties of Prabandhas, each with minor differences.

The four-fold channel of all musical expression is Gīta, Ālāpa, Ṭhāya and Prabandha as brought out by the concept of Chaturdaṇḍi. 'Prabandhyēti Prabandha' i.e., that which is composed is a Prabandha. However only that composition which is made up of six aṅgas and four dātus is alone entitled to be called a Prabandha. Prabandhas have been broadly classified into 3 varieties - Sūḍa, Ali and Viprakeerna. The first variety Sūḍa Prabandha is of two kinds - Suddha Sūḍa and Sālaga Sūḍa. Again the Sālaga Prabandhas are of 7 types - Dhruva, Maṭṭha, Pratimattha, Nissa, Aḍḍa, Rasa and Ēkatāli. It is this Dhruva Prabandha which is the progenitor of the musical form Daru.

The term Dhruva itself is traceable to the Dhruva or stage songs clearly elucidated in the Nāṭya Śāstra. Bharata devotes a whole chapter, in this earliest of the treatises on our Fine Arts, to these Dhruva songs, describing and illustrating different classes, divisions and sub-divisions of Dhruvas and their uses. They were essentially versified musical compositions which formed an important part of our ancient Sanskrit dramas. According to Bharata these were called Dhruvas in view of the fact that its words, Varṇas, Alaṅkāras and Jātis were regularly (i.e. Dhruvam) connected with one another. Five kinds of Dhruva songs have been described in the Nāṭyaśāstra - Pravēśika, Nisskramika, Prasādita, Akshēpita and Antara, and they were employed in particular scenes and situations in the drama. Many of these Dhruva songs bear a close resemblance to some of the Darus featured in our post-medieval operas and dance-dramas. For instance the Pravēśika of Nāṭya Śāstra which denotes the song heralding the entrance of a particular character on the Stage has its parallel in the Pātrapravēśa Daru of the Bhāgavata Mēḷa and Kuravañji Nāṭakas. Another common feature was that both Dhruvas and Darus were eminently capable of evoking diverse rasas, this being the main function of both in our Gēya Nāṭakas. Prabandha Gīti too possessed not only the Dhātus, Angas and Jatis but also brought out the rasās.

Dhruva Prabandha refers to a special type of composition since the prefix Dhruva signifies an unbending rigidity in the composition. It has two initial sections. The dhātu or the musical setting is the same for both the sections, the Sāhitya, however, being different. Both the sections constitute the Udgraha. Then follows the third section, the dhātu of which employs swaras of higher pitches. This section itself constitutes the Ābhōga and the conclusion of the Udgraha is reckoned as Dhruva. Etymologically the role of Dhruva was repetition. It was a portion which was constant in each part and was repeated after completing the different parts of a composition like the Udgraha and the Mēlāpaka. In modern musical compositions the Dhruva stands for Charaṇa. The relationship of the Dhruva Prabandhas to the Darus in our Nāṭya and Gēya nāṭakas can be gauged from the fact that the latter too have mostly a pallavi followed by a multiplicity of charaṇas, all of which are sung to the same dhātu although there are some Darus also with the Anupallavi section. The fact that the different classes of Dhruva Prabandhas have been dealt with in detail by Raghunātha Nāyaka in his lakshaṇa treatise Sangīta Sudhā cannot be a mere coincidence because it was at the time of the Nāyak rule at

Tanjore that the Daru made its appearance, to start with in the Yakshagāna.

The earliest Yakshagāna that has so far been traced is the Āndhra Yakshagāna 'Sugrīva Vijayamu' by Kandakuru Rudra Kavi who floruished in Krishṇadēvarāya's court. Apart from different types of Ragadēs, its music was set in complicated metrical verses such as Ardhachandrika, Davaḷa, Ēla, etc. By the time of Vijayarāghava Nāyak these bombastic forms came to be discarded and the far more attractive Darus composed in appealing rakti rāgas took their place with only sparing use of verses. Darus gained wide currency and popularity in the multitude of Nāṭya and Gēya Nāṭakas composed during the Marāṭha rule of Tanjore.

The musical form Daru commonly encountered in the Telugu and Tamiḷ dramas and operas of the type of Yakshagāna, Bhāgavata Mēḷa Nāṭakas and Kuravañji Nāṭakas, Therukkoothu etc., belong to the sphere of applied music. Essentially Daru is a story song. In many cases entire dialogues are in the form of Darus. Darus have been composed on historical or puranic themes as also love themes. Sometimes they were also in praise of a patron. A characteristic feature of Darus is the profusion of sāhitya or words therein. The sāhitya is naturally of importance. In form the Darus essentially resemble the Kīrtanas. While a few comprise Pallavi, Anupallavi and Charaṇa, many are made up of only Pallavi and many Charaṇas. The plethora of Charaṇas, all of them being sung to the same music, is their special characteristic. The tempo is usually Madhyamakāla but some are also rendered in Vilamba kāla. Chāputāḷa has been most largely employed in the Gēya Nāṭakas of the Marātha rulers, Bhāgavatha Mēḷa Nāṭakas as well as Tyāgarāja's Nowkā Charitram. Next in frequency of use comes Ādi and Jampa tālas. The music of the Darus is comparatively simple in nature with no elaborate or difficult rāga sañchāras or saṅgatis finding a place. Only rakti rāgas conducive to the expression of various sentiments have been invariably used in the Darus. Sowrāshṭra rāga seems to have been a special favourite of the composers of this musical form. However sometimes a few uncommon rāgas also find a place.

Darus have been classified into various types depending on their functions. Svagadha Daru denotes musical soliloquy with the tune being of a recollective nature. The Pralāpa Daru portrays a sorrowful state of mind. Heccharika Daru is employed for saluting the monarch. Pādavandana Daru refers to approaching the deity's sanctum sanctorum step by step followed by retracing the steps.

The earliest Daru we encounter occurs in Vijayarāghava Nāyak's Yakshagāna 'Vipranārāyaṇa Caritra'. During the Nāyak rule at Tanjore, Darus were composed in plenty for use in musical plays enacted at the Royal court. There are in these plays example like Thendṛal Daru, Veṇṇilā Daru, Manmatha Daru, etc., dealing specifically with the experiences of courtesans in love with the hero who was invariably the king. In fact these Darus on love themes may be considered to be forerunners of Jāvaḷi.

It was however only at the hands of King Shāhaji and his illustrious brother Tulajāji that this musical form attained perfection and prominence. King Shāhaji put together the traditions of the literary Prabandhas and the Yakshagāna tradition and created a fusion of the two in his wonderful Driśya Kāvyas 'Śankara Pallaki Sēva Prabandham' and 'Vishṇu Pallaki Sēva Prabandham'. Both of these are replete with Darus as well as his Yakshagānas 'Sāchi Purandaramu' and 'Sati Dāna Sāramu'. All these Darus contain Shāhaji's signatures, like Tyāgēsabhūpa, Tyāga śowra, Tyāga muraḷi, etc.

King Shāhaji has composed different classes of Darus. One of his pieces is the Svarākshara Daru 'Sarigamapadani'[1] in Rāgamālika in Ādi tāḷa.

Among the special types of Darus composed by Shāhaji, mention may be made of the Salām Daru and the Jakkini Daru belonging to the spere of Dēśi music. Salām is a Marathi word meaning paying obeisance and Shāhaji has composed Salām Darus on the deities enshrined in various kshetras like Chidambaram, Tanjore, Vaitheeśvaran koil, Tiruvārūr, Mannārguḍi, Madurai, Śrīrangam, etc. They are also featured in his Pancharatna Prabandham and Tyāgarāja Vinōda Chitra Prabandham. In his Salām Daru on Padmanābhasvāmi, exquisite Yamakam, like Padmasambhava, Padmālaya, Padmapatra, Padmanābha, etc. occur. In his Kalyāṇi Salām Daru, Ādiprāsam, Dvitīyāksharaprāsam, Antyaprāsam, etc., are featured. The Salām Daru 'Ambanilaya Chidambara' on Tillai Kāḷi in Rāgamālika is a fine piece.

Jakkini Darus may be deemed to be the earlier form of Tillānas and prior to the advent of Tillānas, the last item in Jakkini dance used to be performed to the music of Jakkini Darus. The Māthu of the first section of Jakkini Darus consists entirely of Jatis while the Sāhitya is featured in the second part. Mataṅga is said to be the originator of the Jakkini Dance and King Shāhaji has composed Jakkini Darus as a dance form in his opera Śaṅkara Kāḷi Naṭana Saṁvādam. Jakkini Darus are traced to Jakkulas - a class of Andhra dancers and minstrels who used a variety of drum called Jakki. It is worthy of note that in Jakkini Darus folk terms like 'Ellilām' 'Ellāmale' 'Ellilām lāle' etc. are used profusely. As an example the Jakkini Daru 'Indukalādhara sundara' set to Bilahari rāga and Āditāḷa may be cited.[3]

One of the earliest Kuravañji Nāṭakas known to us is the Tyāgēśa Kuravañji whose author is not known. However the internal evidence available therein confirms that he must have lived during King Shāhaji's time. This Kuravañji contains many Darus in Tamil.

King Tulajāji's 'Śivakāmasundari Pariṇaya' nāṭakam is an exquisite work featuring diverse types of Darus like Varṇana Daru, Saṁvāda Daru, etc. Varṇana Daru is a descriptive piece expatiating on the personality of the character, place, incident, scenery, etc. and King Tulajāji's varṇana Daru 'Bhūlōka Kailāsamenna' set to Kurañji rāga and Chāpu tāḷa is an ideal example.[4]

Saṁvāda Daru denotes a musical dialogue or conversation between two characters with the presumption that a certain conclusion is arrived at. A good example is king Tulajaji's Saṁvāda Daru 'Tāmasuraḷavu Māya'[5] from the same opera set to Nāṭakuruñji rāga and Ādi tāḷa.

The beauty of another of Tulajāji's operas 'Rājamañjana Vidyā Vilāsa' stems from the fact that the royal composer has employed appropriate rāgas in each situation - like Mōhana for indicating the arrival of Mōha or ilustion, Ānandabhairavi for denoting Ānanda's arrival and Śaṅkarābharaṇam for the Daru announcing the Darśan of Lord Śaṅkara. One of Tulajā's court poets, Ghanaśyāma, has composed an allegorical drama entitled 'Navagraha charita' containing Pātrapravēśa Darus beckoning the arrival of various characters.

Kavi Māthrubhūthayya's Yakshagāna 'Parijātapaharaṇa Nāṭakamu' contains Maṇipravāḷa Darus with sāhitya passages in Hindi, Marathi, Kannada, Telugu and Tamil. In the 'Rājamōhana' kuravañji of Girirāja Kavi, King Serfoji'scourt poet, the heroine sends a love message to the King through a parrot in a Daru set in Bhairavi rāga while the advent of the Kuravañji is indicated in a Praveśa daru who reads the heroine's palm and foretells the happy union of the couple.

The famous opera 'Rāmanāṭakaṁ' of Aruṇāchala Kavi contains as many as 200 Darus. Mostly they are quite big pieces, each containing not less than 3 long charaṇas. The tempo of these Darus is mostly Vilaṁba because of the profusion of words. They rank quite high in quality in view of their Yati and Prāsa, loftiness of ideas and musical excellence. Another characteristic feature is that they feature many proverbs like 'Pazham nazhuvi pālil vizhundār pōle', 'Veṇṇaikku pallu muḷaithārppole', 'Pāṁbukku pāl vārkka vārkka', etc.

King Shāhaji has composed an Anulōma Vilōma Daru 'Naguthādiṭṭēdi' in Telugu. Muthuswāmi Dīkshitar's father Rāmaswāmy Dīkshitar has to his credit a similar Daru in Sanskrit, revealing his erudition in this language. This anulōma vilōma Daru 'Sārasadaḷa nayana'[6] is set in Gaṅgātaraṅgiṇi rāga and Rūpaka tāḷa.

Darus are very prominent in the Bhāgavata Mēḷa Nāṭakaṁ of Melaṭṭūr Veṅkaṭarāma Śāstri who was a senior contemporary of the Trinity. He has composed in all 12 dance dramas belonging to this group, the most well known being 'Prahlāda Charitraṁ'. As the play proceeds, each character announces himself with a Pātra Pravēśa Daru. The Kōṇaṅgi Daru is sung at the appearance of the divine clown. This Daru is usually set in Kāṁbōdhi rāga and its tessitura centres round the Tāra Shaḍja.

Among the Trinity, Śyāmāśāstri does not seem to have composed any Darus. Tyāgarāja is said to have composed three operas, but among them only two are now available to us since there is no trace of the 3rd opera 'Sītarāma vijayaṁ'. Prahlāda Bhakti Vijayam comprises only Kīrtanas. However Darus of diverse types figure in the saint's 'Nowkā charitraṁ'. In the Uttara pratyuttara Daru from Nowka charitram 'Indukēmi'[7] set to Varāḷi rāga and Chāpu tāḷa, statements are made alternatively by two characters.

Muthuswāmy Dīkshitar has to his credit the Śrīrañjani Daru 'Nī sari sāṭi'[8] set to rūpaka tāḷa. It is worthy of note that whereas Dīkshitar has composed kṛitis almost exclusively in Sanskrit, this Daru is in Telugu. Anuprāsa is featured in the terms 'Valabu', 'Solabu', 'Kalubu', 'Kolubu', etc. There is allusion to an anecdote pertaining to Śiva Līla in the phrase 'Vāśavādi amarulella Vamṛi svarūpameṭṭhi Vāsudēva Garvamañji'.

None in Tyagaraja's Sishya Parampara seems to have devoted any attention to this musical form. The Kēdāragaula Daru 'Kāmiyiñchinnudira' in praise of his patron, the Zamindar of Uḍayarpāḷayam, is ascribed to Śyāmasāstri's grandson, Annāswāmi Śāstri.

Krishṇaswami Ayyā, who would appear to have been influenced more by Muthuswāmi Dīkshitar, has to his credit a rare piece known as Tillāna Daru set in Suruṭi rāga and Ēka tāḷa.[9] This piece begins with Jatis after the manner of Tillāna followed by Pallavi, Anupallavi and Charaṇa. At the end of the charaṇa a new Jati passage is sung and the piece concludes in the Pallavi.

Among the modern composers Muthiāh Bhāgavatar has composed four Varṇas - two in Kannada and two in Telugu. They contain jatis, svara as well as Sāhitya. Some of them have become popular, the most well-known being the Kannada Daru 'Māthē Malayadhvaja' set to Khamās rāga and Ādi tāḷa.

1

Svarākshara Daru

King : Shāhaji

Rāgamālika Adi tala

Śankarābharaṇa : Sarigamapadhanivīka paiḍika
Taruṇu levvaru dānisarigāri

Kharaharapriya : Alinīla vēṇulu abjanibhāsyulu
Kaḷakanṭhulu dānisarigāri
Jalajadaḷkshulu sarasabimboshṭulu
mēlata levvaru dānisarigāri

Kalyāṇi : Karikumka kujamulukarpura gandhulu
harimadhyālu dānisarigāri
dharaṇithambulu dhāvaḷyahāsalu
dharakanṭulu dānisarigāri

Tōḍi : Prauḍalu bālalu muktalu nātōḍi
Chēḍelevvaru dānisarigāri
Veṭukadō tyāgavṛiddhāchala nī nu
Guḍelevvaru dānisarigāri

Tōḍi : Dpm Pmg Mgr Grs pmG rSn DnsrGr

Kalyāṇi : sRgmpdNsndpmG raGrSn DnsrGr

Kharaharapriya : RGMpdNdpmgr SGrSn DnsrGr (Srigampadani)

2

Salām Daru

Rāgamālika Jati

Rāga : Kalyāṇi Ambanilaya chidambara vilasita
lambōdaraherampa salāmu

Tāḷa : Ādi Ambaramaṇiruchi ḍambaviḍambana
Ambujahitachidambara salāmu

Jati

Rāga : Suruṭṭi
Tāḷa : Aṭa

Sati nirmalamati chakrāṅga
gati suguṇa vatisalāmu

Jati

Raga : Asaveri
Tala : Misrachapu

Nandanandana induvadana
kunda radana gōvinda salāmu
manda hasana mandajōdharaṇa
nandita gōpāla vrindasalāmu

Jati

Raga : Revagupti
Tala : Adi

Vāsavahita kamalēśana kṛita bhṛita
bhāsana sadguṇa bhāsure salāmu
bhōsala dēvate śrī sāhanutō mahi-
shāsura mardini dāsapāle salāmu

Jati

Raga : Pantuvarali
Tala : Misrachapu

Daṇḍita mayakuṇḍali bhūshaṇa
Kandaparaśukaṇḍikaramaṇa
daṇḍitarippmaṇḍalavara vēdānda
dundator daṇḍa khaṇḍana
maṇḍita śaśi khaṇḍanādi jaḍa maṇḍala maṇi
kuṇḍala nuta kaṇḍala hari kandassila kō
daṇḍa tripurahara puṇḍarīkachēla salāmu

3

Jakkini Daru

Raga : Shāhaji
Bilahari

Adi tala

Indukalādhara sundara vadana purandhara vandita śaraṇu rē
Kundaradana aravindansyane sara
nandia sāhēndra nandaru pa

Ellilām ellām le dēvādi dēva
Ellilām ellām lē ellilām ellām le

Jati and Swara passages

Nāyaka bhuvana vidāyaka kēśava
Sāyaka tyāga muktidāyakaśankra
Ellilām ellām lē dēvādi dēva
Ellilām ellām lē ellilām ellām lē

4

Varṇana Daru

Raga : Tulajāji

Kuruñji Miśra Chāpu tāḷa

Pallavi : Bhūlōka kailāsa menna Ī mahādēva
pura mindrapuri kanana minna

Charaṇa : Sala mulaprakiri dalusadana mulu
jaladhikanya samukūdalu

Rāja bnadhu lāsamanulu Ī puramēlē
Rājasīlamulanakhamulu

5

Saṁvāda Daru

Raga : Tulajāji

Vidya : Tamasuralavumayanivu nātho
Taru maru mātalātaka pōve

Maya : Nī mōmujūchina poraluvo vidya
nindhupikarulaiyundurukaṭave

Vidyā : Hayiyōḍati ninnu upāyani vāriki
māyani bratukēlamāyamugatavē

Māya : Gayyalisanamuna garviñchi gūṭalu
kuyyaku nī sempa koṭṭa poyyēne

Vidyā : Sarigāni vārito śaṅkamu chēsite
varusaḍappihani vachchune

Māya : Vēyelane vidya nimatam munanunna
viritulaku guruvu daivamu galada

6

Anulōma Vilōma Daru

Gaṅgārataraṅgiṇi Rūpaka tāḷa

Ramaswami Dikshitar

Pallavi : Sarasanayanasarasā saratara ratasarasa

Anupallavi : māratarātatāramā maṇitamadhyamataṇima
tarapa bhāparata tapitavayavatapita

Charaṇa : Bhārambhatavita bharambhā bhāvarāga
tāḷatāgaravabha
bharatētsvatatērapa sanamatitapatita manasa
baravidhirōdhiviraha havananadana navaha
sasatumēdheme sarasa sakhiveṇkaṭa krishṇasarasa

7

Uttarapratyuttara Daru

Varāḷi Miśra Chāpu tāḷa

Tyāgarāja

Pallavi : Gopi : Indukēmi sētumamma krishṇa
ḍentamātalādēnamma

Charaṇa : Gōpi : maguval anteyintavada māku
maneme prāṇamu gada

Krishṇa : Gusa gusalandemi vachchu chēlulā
Usa runḍe ūru pō vachchu
....

Gōpi : Rajanyayiṭulenchu valatu tyāga
rāja vinuta prēmagaladu

8

Śrīrañjani Rūpaka tāḷa

Muthuswāmi Dīkshitar

Pallavi : Nīsari sāṭi daivamedhu lēdanimarulukonṭira
Nidānarā nannēlarā

Charaṇa : Vasavādyamarulella vaṁṛiśvarūpameṭhṭhi
vāsudēva garvamahachi varusagāna
maruśrīpuravāsadāsachitvilāsa
vallikēsajagadīśa
Nimīdane mikula vaḷapusolapugalupu golupu

manaṁbuto nijaṁbuga bayaluderihoyalumiri
chelimikōri valachinanu birahabahuvaralosaku

9

Tilāna Daru

Suruṭṭi Ēka tāḷa

Krishṇaswāmayya

Nādiru tāni tōṁdiru tāni stara tarana
tanam tam diridiri tamdiri tillilām tillilām
tanam ta taratāni tadiri tom diri nādiri
diridiri
dirididdtilāna dirididitillāna diritillāna

Pallavi	:	Pālaya mām śiva śaṅkari bhaktajananda kari
Anupallavi	:	Bhālachandraśēkhara amba paramēśvarirājēśvari Sulabanējaganmōhini jalajadalāyata lōchane
Charaṇa	:	Kanakōjjvala nāyike Kalyāṇaguṇadambike sanakādimunisannuta śārada trayambike kanskādri nīva- sinikaṇḍike kātyāyainivara dāyike janani śrīkṛishṇārch itē jayasaṅgita sara sasike

Jati and Śoḷḷu

(This paper was presented at the Annual Conference of the Music Academy, Madras in 1985.)

PALLAVI IN SOUTH INDIAN MUSIC

The distinctive feature of our Indian music is Manōdharma Saṅgeeta—an aspect best exmplified in the exposition of Rāga, Tāna and Pallavi which calls for a large measure of spot improvisation in concerts as against compositions like Varṇam, Kṛiti, Padam, Jāvaḷi, Tillāna, etc., which belong to the realm of Kalpita saṅgeeta. In the past there were not only adepts in elaborating particular rāgas for hours together like Tōḍi Sītārāmayya, Śaṅkarābharaṇam Narasayya, etc., but also famous specialists in Pallavi exposition like Pallavi Gōpala Iyer, Pallavi Śēshayyar, Pallavi Doraiswāmy Iyer and Shaṭkāla Gōvinda Mārār. Pallavi Saṁpradāya is to be found only in the Carnatic tradition and our Nāgaswara vidwāns have played a very prominent role in helping it to flourish.

It is said that till the early decades of this century, concerts of Carnatic music used to be invariably of at least 4 hours duration with Rāga, Tāna, Pallavi being the major segment occupying the lion's share of the time, if not the exclusive item. Among the distinguished Pallavi exponents who flourished during the closing decades of the last century and the early years of this century, special mention must be made of Nāmakkal Narasiṁha Iyengār who possessed unsurpassed mastery over rhythm, Neraval and Swaraprasthāraṁ, particularly in Tiśra naḍai. Others who belonged to this galaxy were Rāmanāḍ (Poochi) Śrinivāsa Iyengār, Konērirājapuram Vaidyanātha Iyer, Kallaḍaikuruchi Vēdānta Bhāgavatar, Mazavarāyaṇendal Subbarāma Bhāgavatar, Kāraikkuḍi (Veeṇai) brothers (Subbrāma Iyer and Sāṁbaśiva Iyer) and last but not the least Conjevaram Nāyanā Piḷḷai. The disappearance from the scene of Nāyanā Piḷḷai, who possessed a ramarkable mastery over layā, brought to an end the era of exalted Pallavi exposition. An ever accelerating tempo of life and consequent reluctance on the part of the audience to sit through any concert of more than 2 hours duration, all round dilution and decline of classical values resulting from increasing exposure to cinema and pop music and a perceptible craze for variety in everything not excepting items in concert programmes have paved the way for reducing both the importance and duration of Pallavi in contemporary concerts and in an increasing number of cases, the tendency is to do away with Pallavi altogether. This is indeed a very sorry state of affairs which has somehow to be remedied if Carnatic music is to be restored to the glorious traditions of the past.

Rāga

Rāga represents the culmination of the conscious efforts of our musicians from times immemorial to bring out the different rasā bhāvas which spontaneously sprang out of their inner selves. The diverse rāgas which emerged in this fashion resulting from the emotions experienced by our singers developed in stages during the history of our music and our musicologists prescribed appropriate lakshaṇas to the rāgas to give each one of them a distinctive identity. It should not be forgotten that these lakshaṇas were based only on the lakshyas as prevalent at different periods in the course of the evolution of our music. Right from the times of Bharata and Mataṅga, lakshaṇas like graha, aṁśa, tāra, etc., became essential for the development of Jatis which were later enlarged to include Sanyāsa, Vinyāsa etc. Along with Shuddha, Saṅkīrṇa etc., this blossomed into 18 Jatis. The comparatively ancient rāgas in vogue over a long span of time came to be known as Mārga or Bhāshā rāgas while those of recent origin were called Dēśi rāgas. Depending on the exigencies of time and region, the rāgas underwent considerable changes and came to be classified into Rāgas and Rāgiṇis, Stree-Purusha rāgas as well as Ghana, Naya and Dēśi rāgas. Other divisions include Rāgāṅga, Bhāshāṅga, Kriyāṅga and Upāṅga as well as Sampoorṇa, Shāḍava and Ouḍava sections. Subsequent to the time of Veṇkaṭamakhi, innumerable rāgas came into existence based on the Janaka-Janya system of rāga classification. At present some Vidwans have brought into popularity even many Vivādi rāgas.

Once the rāga has been selected for exposition of the pallavi, its detailed development in the pre-pallavi session is done in three parts—Ākshiptika, Rāgavardhani and Makaraṇi. Ākshiptika connotes the introductory rendering of the rāga and its main purpose is to make distinct beyond the shadow of any doubt the identity of the rāga. Rāgavardhani or the central portion refers to the extensive delienation of the rāga and this is carried out progressively in different stages. The first stage covers Madhyastāyi to Mandrastāyi. The next stage of the ālāpana is mainly in the Madhyastāyi. The sañchāras in the subsequent stage are largely in Tārastāyi. The last stage of Rāgavardhani comprises sañcharas from Mandrastāyi to Tārastāyi in three kālas replete with birgas. The finale of the entire ālāpana is Madhyastāyi shaḍja and this concluding portion is known as Makaraṇi.

Tānam

In the ancient Bandara language Thēna is an auspicious word connoting the esoteric concept 'ŌM TAT SAT OR THATHVAMASI' and it is possible that in course of time this term changed into Thānaṁ. In Mantra shāstra, if we split the word Tānam into the constituent syllables Tha, A, Na and Am, the Thakāra is said to denote Śaṅkara, the Akāra, Brahma; the Nakara, Vishṇu; while the final Bindu Am represents all the three deities together i.e., the Trimūrti.

According to the late Saṅgeeta Kalānidhi Muḍikoṇḍān Veṇkaṭarāma Iyer, in our ancient music texts, the term Tāna refers merely to the diverse permutations and combinations of svaras. In these texts it is mentioned that ragas are Ananta and so are Tāḷas. The word Ananṭa would also refer to Sarvēśvara and as such rāgas are rendered using the syllables which go to make up this term viz. Āa, Naṁ and Taṁ—particularly the Aakāra which is used most profusely. As in the case of Varṇas, one can render rāgas and for that matter Thānaṁ too in 3 kālas—Chaukka, Madhyama and Durita. When the rāga is rendered in Madhyamakāla, the syllables Thā and Nā are used far more frequently in succession along with the Aakāra so as to sound like Thānaṁ and this possibly is the genesis of the Thānaṁ as currently prevalent in the realm of Carnatic music. The optimal kālpramāṇam for Thānaṁ is Madhyamakāla while Duritakāla Thānaṁ is known as Gānaṁ. Two broad classifications of Thānaṁ are Shuddha thānaṁ and Kooṭa thānaṁ. The latter comprises different types like Chakra thānaṁ, Mānava thānaṁ, etc.

Pallavi

In modern parlance, the term pallavi refers to two differnt entities—first the initial portion of a musical composition and secondly the extensive exposition of a line of musical words set to a chosen rāga and an āvarta of tāḷa inclusive of elaborate Neraval or Vinyāsa and Swaraprasthāra. In the view of distinguished musicologists of Karnataka like the late Sangeeta Kalānidhi Rāllapaḷḷi Ananthakrishṇa Śarma and the late Chennakēśaviah, the term Pallavi does not figure as such in anyone of our ancient music treatises.

According to Prof. Sandyāvandhaṁ Sreenivasa Rao the roots of Pallavi exposition lie in the Jātis of Bharata, its flowering in Śāraṅgadēva's Rūpaka ālāpti and its fruiting in the Nādarasa of the Trinity. According to him the following short passage in the Prakīrṇaka Adhyāyā of Saṅgīta Ratnākara represents the quintessence of the Pallavi of our times : 'Roopakasthēna rāgēṇa tālēnacha vidheeyate yaprāktā roopakālāpti so punar dvividha bhavēth prathigrahanīkaikanyā bhanjanthyubidheeyate'.

Prof. Sambamorthy however, dismisses this allusion to Pallavi exposition in the Saṅgīta Ratnākara as very vague. Coming to the other meaning of the term Pallavi, there is a comencing portion in each of Jayadēva's Ashṭapadis called Dhruva which also serves to connect up with the end of each charaṇam. Basavaṇṇa refers to this Dhruva as Pallava in respect of his vachanas. Annamācharya too has composed his songs in different sections starting with Pallava. It is significant that the term Pallavi to denote the initial part of a musical compositions seems to have emerged round about the time of the Trinity as also Pallavi exposition as we know it today which too is believed to be just 200 years old as evidenced by the fact that the earliest reference to this aspect in the history of Carnatic music is the Pallavi contest between Śyāma Sāstri and Bobbili Kēśavayya.

The credit of being the pioneer in introducing Saṅgatis into musical compositions goes beyond doubt to Saint Tyāgarāja and the Pallavis in particular of his compositions are veritable storehouses of beautiful and highly delectable Saṅgatis. It is quite in the realm of probability that musicians who were Tyāgarāja's contemporaries, stirred by the excellence of the Pallavi moiety of his compositions replete with Saṅgatis, started elaborating them with Neraval and Svaraprasthāra and this aspect became the major segment of their concerts. This would appear to be the genesis of the tradition of Pallavi exposition in Carnatic music. The fact that the sāhitya of many ancient Pallavis consisted of the initial words of Tyāgarāja's compositions lends supports to this view as for example 'Nannupālimpa naṭachitivo', 'Māmava raghurāma', 'Rāmaṁ bhajēhaṁ', 'Bhajare raghuvīram', 'Sreerāma jayarāma', etc. Later on the commencing portion of the songs of other eminent composers also came to be used for pallavi exposition like 'Dēvi brōva samayamidhē' (Śyāma Śāstri), 'Nīrajākshi Kāmākshi' (Muthuswāmi Dīkshitar), 'Gānalōla karunālavāla' (Chinnaswāmi Dīkshitar), 'Mahimateliya taramā' (Ānai Ayyā) and 'Koniyaḍe taramā' (Garbhapuri).

Pallavi consists of three sections. They are Eḍuppu or the beginning, the Aṛudi or Padagarbha and the Muktāyi. The Eḍuppu can be of 4 types--Anāgatam, Samaṁ, Atītam or Vishamaṁ. The end of the first moeity of the Pallavi is Aṛudi or Padagarbha. In a pallavi the Aṛudi plays an important role in maintaining the balance between the Prathamānga and the Dvitīyānga and it should be sufficiently long, covering at least 4 aksharakālas of the tāḷa. Joining the end with the Eḍuppu is Muktāyi. The Eḍuppu swara and the Muktāyi swara should be coined appropriately in such a manner that invariably the Muktāyi swara is the succeeding one to the Eḍuppu swara. The Sāhitya can be developed according to one's manōdharma during Neraval but the punctuation must always be constant without altering the placement of sāhitya or words throughout and care should be taken to see that the syllables of the sāhitya fall at the identical places in the āvarta as in the fundamental scheme.

Pallavi itself is construed as made up of the initial syllables of the following three terms—padam (meaning words), layam (meaning time measure or rhythm) and vinyāsaṁ (meaning variations). The sāhitya of the pallavi is confined to one of the south Indian languages and may be sacred or secular-amorous or based on Shringāra rasā (e.g. Kamalākshi viraha mōrvane samamugara dhīsalubrōve), humourous (e.g. Kutthālattu kuraṅgē maratthaiviṭṭiraṅgē) or satirical (e.g. Ninyākō ninna hanyākō). An example of the sahitya of a vichitra pallavi is Upparaikkāśu, Puḷiyaraikkāśu, Miḷakaraikkāśu, Kaḍukaraikkāśu nalarai reṇḍukāśu.

From the point of view of musical construction, pallavis may be classified into Chaukkakāla pallavi, Madhyamakāla pallavi,

Duritakāla pallavi, Shaṭkāla pallavi, Naḍai pallavi, Dvitāḷa pallavi, etc. An example of Rāgamālikā pallavi is Śaṅkarābharaṇanai aihaztthōdi vāḍi kalyāṇi darbārukku and of Rāgamudra Pallavi, Bhairavi mahā Tripurasundari. Reṭṭai pallavis or double pallavis are an interesting variety and are unique by themselves; the entire pallavi in this case consists of two independent pallavis comprising separate Padagarbhas with the first pallavi suggesting the theme of the second and leading on to it (e.g. Chakkaga nī bhajana Jēsēvāriki thakkuva galada Ō rāma Anudinamu). As the names imply, the svarasthāna pallavi is replete with svarāksharas (e.g. Sariga paga Dichchēne sadhā paga Dichchēra) and the Konnakkōl pallavi, with śolkaṭṭus (e.g. Dhittaḷāṅgu mani veḍalina śrī Gaṇapati). In Yati pallavi treatment of Yati pattern is to be found in the sāhitya (e.g. Gōpuchcha yati Śrōtovahayati Samayati, etc.).

Anulōma and Pratilōma

In anulōma while keeping the tempo of reckoning the tāḷa constant the sāhitya is rendered at double and quadruple speed; as a consequence the sāhitya will be heard twice and four times respectively within the time span of the original duration. Vilōma is said to consist in retracing the steps backwards in the reverse direction in an identical manner and ending just as the pallavi is commenced. According to one version, Pratilōma consists in keeping the tempo of reckoning the tāḷa constant and rendering the sāhitya at half and quarter speeds; as a consequence the full sāhitya will be heard sucessively in twice and four times the time span of the original duration. According to another version, in Pratilōma the sāhitya as well as the tāḷa reckoning is started in duritakāla and while keeping the speed of reckoning the tāḷa constant, the sāhitya is sung sucessively in Madhyama kāla and Vilaṁba kāla. But, in fact this is no different from Vilōma. Actually Pratilōma consists in commencing both the sāhitya and tāḷa of the pallavi in its appropriate chosen kālapramāṇa and while keeping the speed of singing the sāhitya constant, the tāḷa is reckoned with the hand successively at double and quadruple tempo with the result that the tāḷa is heard twice and four times respectively within the same time span.

Anulōma and Pratilōma are more appropriate in the case of

Chaukka kāla pallavis of 2 or 4 kaḷais. No doubt a high degree of laya gñānam is an essential pre-requisite for their accurate and correct rendering. But even so they only serve to confirm that the debutant has carried out painstaking homework. They are merely optional whereas the indispensable aspects of pallavi exposition are beyond doubt variegated neraval or vinyāsaṁ and exquisite swaraprastāraṁ. Only these would reveal the singer's depth of scholarship and bear testimony to his or her level of manōdharma improvisation.

Conclusion

In order to nurture and upgrade the pallavi traditions, it is incumbent on the part of music institutions, music sabhās, Government and private music colleges etc., to arrange for frequent participation by students, music lovers as well as aspiring amateur musicians in advanced pallavi classes and pallavi demonstrations by distinguished and worthy exponents as well as periodical pallavi competetions.This is the surest method of resurrecting the tradition of pallavi singing and preserving it for posterity, bringing about a renaissance in the field, paving the way for the emergence of a generation of budding musicians well-versed in this dying art and thereby restoring Carnatic music to the glorious traditions of the bygone days.

TAMIL PADĀS AND THEIR VĀGGĒYAKĀRĀS

The principal aim of all art is to provide aesthetic pleasure and music does this far more effectively and extensively than any other art. It has a spiritual appeal too. It elevates the soul through its bhāva and provides eternal bliss.

In the words of Alan Danielou, the famous French musician and musicologist, "Most of the music of the West and the Far East today is either mental or sensual. It does not change the heart; it does not uplift the soul. This is just what Indian music can do and whenever musicians in far away parts of the world have had an opportunity of hearing some of the best music of India, of learning something of its theory, it has opened up further new vistas and horizons, new fields which they are eager to explore".

Music should be devotional in character and wedded to bhakti; for such music alone would be conducive to spiritual salvation. Over the years, a large number of musical forms have evolved in South Indian music for the expression of its manifold beauties with the result that at present it can boast of a rich variety of compositional types. In order to obtain a clear and thorough knowledge of our ragas, different types of compositions like Varṇa, Kṛiti, Padaṁ etc., have to be studied and mastered. The quintessence of each raga is delineated in a beautiful and vivid manner in the Padams. A detailed picturisation of the rāga in the Padam is rendered possible through its slow tempo and the characteristic use of subtle gamakas for the music.

In a very literal sense, the term 'Padam' indicates just a word or saying. In 'Saṅgīta Ratnākara', Śārṅgadēva makes mention of the Prabandha with six aṅgas--Svara, Biruda, Pāṭa, Tēnaka Pada and Tāḷa. Here pada means merely an expression in words. The term 'Pallavi' is made up of the first syllables of the three words, Pada, Laya and Vinyāsa. Here, too Pada has the same meaning. According to Venkaṭamakhi, Pada, which is one of the aṅgās of prabandha, is the line of sāhitya which describes the heroic qualities and achievements of the hero. Till the beginning of the 17th century, the term Padam used to denote a sahitya portraying any rasabhāva.

It was only during the early part of the 17th century that it came to be definitely identified with Śringāra rasa in particular. It was the Nāyak king of Tanjore, Vijayarāghava Nāyak (son of Raghunātha Nāyak) who, in his yakshagāna 'Raghunāthābhyudayam' referred to Padam as a musical piece depicting love or śringāra rasa. In present day musical parlance, the term Padam is confined to a composition which belongs to the realm of dance music and treats of diverse aspects of madhura bhakti.

The earliest known songs in our music belonging to this compositional category were Annamāchārya's 'Śringāra sankīrtanālu' based on the Nāyaka-Nāyika bhāva. These were patently the model for Kshētragña in composing his unique and inimitable Padams. Kshētragña, the greatest and most celebrated of the Padam composers, gave fresh impetus to this musical form and in his hands it reached the pinnacle of perfection with the sections like Pallavi, Anupallavi and Charaṇam couched in a grand musical setting.

Till Kshētragña's time, Padams too, like most other musical compositions, were just doxologies - in other words, the themes of the Padams were restricted to the praises and glorification of various deities. But subsequently, the subject matter of most Padams degenerated into adulation of mortals and many Padam composers sprang up who substituted the deities by the reigning monarchs or zamindars who were their patrons. Scores of Padams have been composed by different court poets on the various Marāṭha rulers of Tanjore. The Padams of Ghanam Krishṇa Iyer, one of the foremost composers of Tamil Padams, are in praise of not only different deities, particularly Śri Soundararāja, the presiding deity of his native village, but also some of his patrons like King Amarasimha of Tiruviḍamarudūr and Kachchiranga, Zamindar of Uḍayarpāḷayam.

As already pointed out, Padam is a 'tridhātu prabandham' with pallavi, anupallavi, and charaṇam. It is interesting to trace the evolution of the Tamil padams from the medieval prabandhas. Prabandhas have been classified into 3 types - Sūḍa, Alikrama and Viprakirna Compositional varieties known as Ēla, Karaṇa, Ḍhenki, Vartani, Jhēmpaḍa, Lambhaka, Rasa and Ēkatāli belong to the Sūḍa type of prabandhas. Matanga, the author of 'Brihaddēśi' makes mention of Nādavati, a variety of Gāna - Ēla prabandha specially suited for the exposition of Śringāra rasa. Venkaṭamakhi, in the Prabandha chapter of his work 'Chaturdaṇḍi Prakāśika', defines Ēla-prabandhas (ślōka, 318). Subsequent ślōkas contain a description of the four varieties of Ēla-prabandhas-Gāna, Mathra, Varṇa and Dēśa ēlas. The Dēśa-ēlas are the earlier counterpart of Padams. These Dēśa-ēla prabandhas were composed in the five regional languages - Karṇāṭa, Lata, Gauḍa, Āndhra and Drāviḍa. The Ēla-prabandhas in Drāviḍa, which are presumably the fore-runners of the Tamil Padams, are reported to be pregnant with bhāva and rasa but devoid of prāsa. It is, however, worthy of note that this alleged absence of prasa is not borne out by the sāhityas of the Tamil Padams of modern composers as can be seen later.

Padams being essentially dance forms, their musical potentialities are realised in full only when heard in dance performances. The dancer is rightly the best interpreter of the meaning and music of Padams. The music of the Padams is majestic and learned and is meant for the elite and musicaly initiated rather than the lay public. Owing to their technical excellence, Padams earned popularity, also as art musical forms and came to be practised by musicians. When Padams are rendered in musical concerts, the introduction of sangatis is out of place in view of the slow and highly emotive music.

Composers of Tamil Padams

The most well known composers of Tamil Padams are Ghanam Krishṇa Iyer, Subbarāma Iyer, Muthu Thāaṇḍavar, Kavi Kuñjara Bhārathi, Pāpavināśa mudaliār, Mookku Pulavar, Eṭṭyāpuram Nārāyaṇaswāmi Iyer, Vēdanāyakaṁ Piḷai, Mārimuthā Piḷḷai, Rāmaliṅga Swāmigaḷ, Madhura Kavi, etc. Coloquial words also figure in the Padams of some of these composers. Their signatures (mudras) may occur in the Pallavi, Anupallavi or Charaṇam.

Tāḷas in Tamiḷ Padams

The rhythm of the Padams is not very rigid due to the preponderance of melody. It flows in a slow and natural manner. Pata or thythmic sylables are absent in Padams - a fact which ascribes this compositional type to the sphere of nṛitya or expressive dance.

The tāḷas Ādi, Rūpaka and Miśra chāpu are most commonly met with in the vast majority of Tamil Padams. Tripuṭa and Aṭa tāla are also used in some Padams. During medieval times, Ādi tāḷa was referred to as Jhampaṭa tāḷa. Names of tāḷas like Aṭṭa chāpu, Ēka, Jhampa and Maṭhya are found in the Padams of manuscripts in Dr. U.V. Swāminātha Iyer's library at Adyar (A descriptive catalogue of Tamil Mss. Vol. IV, Madras - 1967). As regards the Grahās of the tāḷas, one can find 'Sama' or Anāgada eḍuppus in the Tamil padams.

Vilambita and Madya laya are usually used in Tamil Padams. A few of these Padams are in Madhyama Kāla couched in simple diction. Besides the usual anupallavi and charaṇa, some of these Padams also have madhyama kāla sāhitya called 'Pin Muḍukugaḷ' (known as 'Kaṭka' in Sanskrit).

Rāgas in Tamil Padams

The idea of conceiving God as the Nāyaka and the human soul as the Nāyika - the Paramāthma - is quite ancient. Spiritual literature centred on divine eroticism of the Vaishṇava cult is found in the Bhāgavata and in the Ashṭapadis of Jayadēva. It also finds expression in the works of Tamil Saivite and Vaishnavite saints like Māṇikkavāchagar (Tiruvāchagam), Āṇḍāḷ (Tiruppavai), etc. Thisconcept of Nāyaka-Nāyika bhāva, with the dual significance of spiritual and mundane love in all their ramifications, provided the requisite background for the evolution and development of the musical form Padam.

The chief basis for Padam compositions is the Madhura bhakti approach to God. Among the themes of different compositional types, those of the Padams are most ideally suited for the depiction of diverse types of rasas. Śringāra rasa and its various uparasas are the main rasas of Padams. The composers of Tamil Padams have reached unsurpassable heights in portraying erotic mysticism or Śringāra rasa coupled with bhakti and these Padams have developed to a very high degree of perfection at their hands. Most of the Tamil Padam compositions deal with one or other phase of love in a state of amorous separation or union with ample scope for varied exposition. The mood of a particular context in a Padam is usually complex and is the outcome of various circumstances and situations of an involved and emotional nature. The sāhitya of the Padam by itself may not be adequate to unravel the mood of the context adequately. But the inarticulate language of rāga possesses the unique power to portray more by suggestion the deepest and subtles of the feelings which the articulate words fail to convey. It is therefore possible to forcefully express the import and content of the sāhitya through the use of appropriate music as the vehicle for this purpose.

In the case of the Tamil Padams, the emphasis is found to be equal on both the music and the sāhitya; and the music and emotional content of the sāhitya seem to be inseparable in each case. The Dhātu and Mātu present a harmonious whole, the latter expressing the meaning in words. The composers of Tamil Padams have exercised great care in their selection of apt rāgas ideally suited to their themes and the sentiments and atmosphere of the sāhityas calculated to bring out the rasas in a forceful manner. The rāgas have been so chosen as to bring forth their delicate shades and emotional aspects quite vividly. All the Tamil Padams are invariably set in rakthi rāgas for portraying the rasas of the sāhityas faithfully. Kāmbōdhi, Bhairavi, Tōḍi, Kalyāṇi, Śankarābharaṇam, Pantuvarāḷi, Śahāna, Kēdāragowḷa, Śāma, Aṭhāna, Khamās, Bilahari, Suruṭi, Nādanāmakriya, Sāvēri and Āhiri are the rāgas most frequently handled by the composers of Tamil padams. Kāmbōdhi in particular accounts for the maximum number of Tamil padams. It is a point of interest that Kshētragña, too, has composed the maximum number of Padams - as many as 37 - in this rāga.

Examples

"Yār pōyiśolluvār" of Ghanam Krishṇa Iyer in Tōḍi raga is fully expressive of the Nāyaki's love-sick state of mind.

"Manamurugudhu vizhi puṇal pooṇudhu" of Muttutāṇḍavar is in Nādanāmakṛiya rāga. This rāga portrays sadness combined with viraha tāpa in this padam.

'Manamurugudhu vizhi puṇal pūṇudu
maiyal perugudu madianal mūḷudu
varumuruvili śaramennai tīṇḍudu'

"Sarasadurai" of Mookkupulavar is in Sāma rāga. The mood of this rāga is śāntha and this rasa eminently fits the sāhitya.

"Niddhirayil soppanathil" of Ghanam Krishṇa Iyer is in Pantuvarāḷi rāga. Here this rāga is picturised as the joyful rāga.

"Nāyakar pakshamaḍi" of Vēdanāyakam Piḷḷai is in Bilahari rāga which is ideally suited to depict Vīra rasa is portrayed in this piece. The sāhitya "Pāyōr piḍithavan enna seyvānē pānai piḍitthavan bāggiyanthānē" in the charaṇa is a well known proverb of Tamilnadu.

"Anjugamē" of Subbarāma Iyer is in Kēdāragowḷa, an ancient and auspicious rāga. The sāhitya of this Padam aptly fits the mood of this rāga which evokes both Karuṇa and Bhakti rasas. This is an example of a Padam wherein the eḍuppu influences the emotion produced by the rāga.

"Inienna pēchchu" of Subbarāma Iyer is in Śahāna. This rāga evokes Karuṇa rasa and the mood of the sāhitya is angercoupled with this Padam is from Mandra sthāyi Dha to Tārastāyi Madhyama.

"Manadariyāmalē" by Muttutāṇḍavar is in Kāmbōdhi, a highly rakti rāga which is ideally suited for descriptive purposes and diverse moods. It beins with Madhyastāyi Madhyama and extends to Thārastāyi Shaḍja and from there to Tārastāyi Madhyama. From there it descends to Madhyastāyi Madhyama and comes to a stop at this svara; there is no sañchāra below Madhyastāyi Madhyama. One can find beautiful swarākshara eḍuppus in the commencement of Pallavi, anupallavi and charaṇa.

"Summā summā varumā sugam" by Ghanam Krishṇa Iyer has the same melodic structure as the well-known kṛiti of Tyāgarāja 'Ēpāpamu' in Aṭhāṇa rāga. It is said that Krishṇa Iyer was inspired into composing this Padam after listening to some of Tyāgaraja's disciples singing this masterpiece of the saint.

Likewise Ghanam Krishṇa Iyer's Kāmbōdhi padam "Engaḷ Jānakiyai" was composed on the model of Tyagaraja's famous kṛiti 'Mā jānaki' in the same rāga.

There are a number of Padams in the Telugu and Tamil

languages with sahityas conveying identical meanings and it is noteworthy that many of these similar Padams are in the same raga. Instances of such pairs are Kshētragña's Padam 'Mōsamāye' and the Tamil Padam 'Mōsamānēne' both in Āhiri and Sārangapāṇi's Telugu Padam 'Magudochchi pilachidē' and the Tamil Padam 'Kaṇavan vandazhaikkirān' both in Śahāna. There are however, exceptions where Padams in these two languages portraying the same moods and contexts have been composed in different rāgas. The pair of Padams 'Thelisēnurā' in Sāvēri and 'Arivēnayya' in Aṭhāṇa in Telugu and Tamil respectively is a case in point.

Prosodical beauties

The Tamil Padams are replete with diverse prosodical beauties like Dvitīyākshara prāsa, Antya prāsa, Anu prāsa, Svarāksharas and Svarasthāna padas.

Dvitīyākshara prāsa

The rhyming of the second syllables of pairs of lines in the sahitya or a pada is known as Dvitīyākshara prāsa or Eḍukai in Tamil. The following lines taken from Ghanam Krishṇa Iyer's Padam in Aṭhāṇa and Mārimuthā Piḷḷai's Padam in Tōḍi exemplify this prosodical beauty.

Aṭhāṇa : Andi nēranthannil mundikkel
pengaḷ kaṇṇil sandikkāmale nī
vandu vandu nindrāl manda
mārutam anda vēḷai nēram enda
nanda kumaranai nayandu

Tōḍi : Ennēramum
Ponnādar
Nannādar

Antya prāsa

Antya prasas refers to the rhyme inherent in the ending syllables of the lines of a pada. The following lines taken from Subbarāma Iyer's Padam 'Araikkaṇṇuḍaiy yānenḍru' and Muthutāndavar's Padam 'Teruvilvarānō'.

"Ettāy muppurathēyum seydāy nakaitthu
Iruvarumoru vagaiyoyen paḍaittu
Patthi sey subbarāman paṇiyum senchaḍaiyanai
paṛikkum vazhiyillāda parutta venviḍaiyanai
Teruvil vārāno Tirumbi pārānō
Vāsal mun nilāno Vāchakam sōllānō
nēsamay pullāno rājanai vellānō"

Anuprāsa

Anuprāsa denotes the repetition of similar letters, syllables and words in the sāhitya. The Pallavi of Ghanaṁ Krishṇa Iyer's Padam in Khamāṣ and charaṇam of his Padaṁ in Aṭhāṇa which are reproduced below, provide good example.

Khamās

"tān tān tānāyirukka sakalamuṁ
tānāyirukka sachidānanda gahaṇamē

Aṭhāṇa

pārthu kangaḷ-pārthatu pōl-pārtha vidamellāṁ"

Svarākshara

We come across profuse examples of svarākshara beauties in the Padam 'Padari varugudu' in Subbarāma Iyer in Kāṁbōdhi.

Svaras

'Padari varugudu paḍaikkudu pāḍuvār kāṁbōdhi māyappōḍi'

Svarasthāna padas

Poets like Kaḍigai Mūkku Pulavar and Nārāyanaswāmi Iyer who flourished in the court of Veṅkaṭēśwara Eṭṭappa Mahāraja of Eṭṭayapuram were adepts in composing Svarasthāna padas.

According to Prof. Sambamoorthy, svarasthāna pada is a composition wherein at the commencement of each āvarta, the svarakshara beauty is met with. But some of the svarasthāna padas of the Eṭṭayāpuram composers are at variance with this definition as can be seen from the examples given below.

For instance, in the svarasthāna pada 'Ādi ārambakkalavyilē' of Mūkku Pulavar in Tōḍi, svarākshara is not present at the begining of all the āvartas, but svaras play the role of the sāhitya in the latter part of the Anupallavi as well as the entire Charaṇam. Another noteworthy feature of this Padam is that the Muktāyi swarā has been set in the Anulōma Vilōma krama.

On the other hand, svaras entirely play the role of sāhitya throughout the svarasthāna pada (including Pallavi, Anupallavi and Charaṇam) 'Pārikkanni' of Nārāyaṇaswāmi Iyer in Kalyāṇi rāga.

Mudras in Tamil Padams

Different varieties of Mudras or signatures are met with in Tamil padams. The Padams of Subbarāma Iyer abound in 'Rāga Mudras'. The words 'Kalyāṇi rāgam pāḍi' in his Kalyāṇi Padam 'Thaiyyale unnai ninaindu' and 'Pāḍuvār Kāmbōdhi' in his Kāmbōdhi Podam 'Padari varugudu' are nice examples.

One can find the svanāma mudra of the composer in the Charaṇam of Subbarāma Iyer's Śahāna Padam 'Ini enna pēchchu'.

In Ghaṇam Krishna Iyer's Padam 'Vēlavare'in Bhairavi, paryāya mudra can be seen in the use of different synonyms from the very beginning of the sāhitya to refer to Vēlan or Muruga.

The Padams 'Niddirayil' of Ghanam Krishṇa Iyer in Pantuvarāḷi and 'Sarasadurai' of Mūkku Pulavar inŚāma contain Rāja mudra or Pōshaka mudra.

Pantuvarali : "muthan amarasimhen drabhūpan kīrti śollum...

Sama : thāyaippōle samāna māna kumāra eṭṭēndira..."

In Kavi Kuñjara Bhārati's Padams we find the prabandha mudra in the words 'señchol padam pāḍi, kavikunar padam pāḍi' etc.

Nāyaka Mudras are found exclusively in Padams whose themes treat the deity as the Nayaka in the context of the Nāyaka-Nāyika relationship. Examples are the words 'Tiruvoṭṭriyūr Tyāgarājan' in Ghanam Krishṇa Iyer's Padam in Aṭhāṇa beginning with the same words and the words 'Karigirivaradan' in Subbarāma Iyer's Padam 'Añjukamē' in Kēdāragauḷa.

One can find Kshētrą mudra also in the above Padam 'Añjukamē' in the words 'Kanchi nagaril vāzhuṁ'. Another example of Kshētra mudra is the words 'Arooril vāsare' in the Paḍam 'Mukhattai kāṭṭiye' of Pāpavināśa Mudaliār in Bhairavi.

The words 'Viṭhanka Tyāgarājare' in the Charaṇam of the last mentioned Padam by Pāpavināśa Mudaliar exemplifies the Dēvatā Mudra.

Mythological Anecdotes in Tamil Padams

Composers like Muthu Tandavar and Mārimuthā Piḷḷai have composed a number of 'Ēsal padams' and 'Nindā stuti padams' in Tamil. Many Tamil Padams make profuse mention of incidents from ancient Puranic stories. To cite just one example, the Padam 'Ennēramum' by Mārimuthā Pilai in Tōḍi is replete with references to mythological anecdotes like those dealing with Dhaksha yagnam. Mārkkaṇḍēya charitram, Oordhva tāṇḍavam, churning the milk ocean, Thāṇḍava darśana for Patañjali and Vyāgkrapātar, gift of Paśupatha arrow to Arjuna etc.

It can thus be seen that the Tamil Padams are not only full of rāga bhāva and rasā bhāva but are also compositions of unsurpassed literary excellence. The composers of these Padams occupy an honoured place among the great Vāggēyakāras. They have made an invaluable contribution to the enrichment and refinement of Carnatic music and at the same time to Tamil culture.

KUCHIPUḌI DANCE DRAMA

Since ancient times, dance has been the most effective form of the expression of joy. In India, the art of dancing has originated and developed since ancient times. Indian dance is mainly of two types - religious and secular. The temple was the centre of religious types of dance which was performed by Devadasis as a form of worship, whereas, secular dance (as also dances of classical and religious themes) were practised by professional artistes outside the temple.

Andhra Dance

In the realm of Indian dance, the dances of Andhra Pradesh have always had their own distinctive character and appeal. Andhra's classical dance can also be divided into two types, viz., 'Nāṭyamāla' and 'Naṭṭuvamēla'. The former consists of dance-dramas, whereas the latter comprises of pure dance forms. The well-known Kuchipuḍi dance-drama is popular in every nook and corner of Andhra Pradesh and its reputation even in adjacent States is a measure of its significant and remarkable contribution to Indian culture. For several centuries it has been an essential feature of the programmes in public functions, in temples and in the courts of Kings. The organisations responsible for preserving the purity of the Kuchipuḍi art were known as Bhāgavatamēḷas or Brāhmaṇamēḷas. Their noteworthy feature was that all the members were Brāhmins who led a pure and religious life. No women artistes were allowed to take part in the Kuchipuḍi dance-dramas. They dedicated their whole life to the propagation of this art form. They were known as Kuchipuḍi Bhāgavatars and the art itself was known as Bhāgavatam as it was related mainly to themes based on stories of Lord Kṛishṇa from the classic Bhāgavata Purāṇa.

Long before Kuchipuḍi artistes adopted dancing as their profession, there existed dance-dramas in folklore. The main achievement of the Kuchipuḍi dance directors lay in lifting the dance-drama from folklore status to classical level.

Kuchipuḍi

Kuchipuḍi is a village in Divi taluk of Krishṇa district in Andhra Pradesh about 15 miles from Masulipaṭaṇam and 3 miles from Muvva, the birth-place of Kshētragña, the Carnatic pada composer. This tract of land has been famous for cultural and fine arts right from the 3rd century B.C. One of the rulers of the area, Sultan Abdul Hassan Tanesha, was a greater lover of fine arts with a secular outlook. During one of his tours, he happened to stay for sometime in Kuchipuḍi. This provided an opportunity for the Kuchipuḍi dancers to exhibit their art and talents before Sultan Tanesha. The latter admired the dance-dramas so much that he became a keen patron of the art and in appreciation of their attainments, he gifted away the entire village extending over 600 acres as a charitable endowment for the Kuchipuḍi artistes with hereditary rights.

Melas

The Kuchipuḍi Bhāgavatamēḷas were itinerant troupes who entertained the people by enacting popular purāṇic stories and thereby kept up the religious and devotional fervour in the country. The traditional worship through this art began from the time of Kākatīya Kings (12-13 century) who were ardent patrons of this art. From the local records of the Mackenzie Mss., we learn that the Kuchipuḍi artistes staged a kēḷika in the court of Vīra Narasiṁhadēva, the then King of Vijayanagar. This establishes the fact that this art had flourished as early as 1500 A.D. Later Achyuthappa Nāyak, the ruler of Tanjore granted a whole colony known as Achyutharāyapuram, later called Melaṭṭūr, to the Bhāgavatars and since then Melaṭṭūr Bhāgavatamēḷas came into prominence. Even today, a number of dramas written by the Telugu composer, Venkaṭarāma Sastri, a senior contemporary of Tyāgarāja, are enacted in Melaṭṭūr during the annual Bhāgavatamēla festival.

Abhinaya

The next stage in the development of Kuchipudi began with the introduction of Kshētragña Padas into this art as a means for depicting abhinaya. These padas deal with the Nāyaka-nāyaki bhavas comprehensively in all their manifold varieties and stand out as masterpieces of erotic themes. The performance given by modern Kuchipuḍi Bhāgavatars generally fall into two types, viz., Veedhināṭakas or Yakshagānas such as the Prahlāda Charitram, Ushā Pariṇayam, etc., and Kalāpas such as the Bhāmā Kalāpa, Gollakalāpā, etc. In all these dramas, the padas of Kshetragña are prominently included as a special feature for Rasābhinaya.

The Bhāgavatars of Kuchipuḍi are exponents of not only Kshetragña Padas, but also of the Taraṅgas of Nārāyaṇa Tīrtha. They have adopted certain forms from Bharaṭanāṭyam as well as Yakshagānas based on the Bhāgavata Purāṇas, the Mahābhārata and the Rāmāyaṇa. Girijākalyāṇa, Kīchakavadha, Hariśchandra nāṭaka, Kirātārjunīya, Kāḷīyamardhana, Śaśirēkhapariṇaya, Rukmāṅgada charitra, Rāmanāṭaka and Gajōpākhyāna are examples of some of them.

Tradition

According to tradition, Siddēndra Yōgi is the originator of the Kuchipuḍi shcool of dance. While it is believed that he belonged to the 14th century, it is a point of debate whether he was originaly a native of Kuchipuḍi village or not. To begin with, he was an illiterate and after seeking initiation at Banaras and later at Śringēri, he became an eminent scholar and Yōgi and taught Nāṭya in Kuchipuḍi. He is the author of the famous Kuchipuḍi dance and drama - Bhāmākalāpam, mainly a dialogue between Satyabhāmā, Śri Krishṇa's consort and her maid Mādhavi. He also composed the Pārijātapaharaṇa in the form of a unique type of dance-drama and taught the play to the Kuchipuḍi artistes and since then, it has been the best item in the repertoire of the Kuchipuḍi school. He persuaded the artiste families of Kuchipuḍi village to take a vow by which every male member of the family pledged to practise the art and play the part of Satyabhāmā at least once in his life time. He was also responsible for the issue of a tāmra śāsana, copper plate order of grant to the residents of Kuchipuḍi village by the Nawab of Golconda.

Training

The members of the Kuchipuḍi troupes are given intensive training in Sanskrit and Telugu languages and are taught in detail treatises like Nāṭyaśāstra, Abhinayadarpaṇa, Rasamañjari and Tāṇḍavalakshaṇa. They also undergo rigorous training in Nṛitta, Nṛitya and Abhinaya. Among the plays Bhāmākalāpaṁ tops the list. It is a Śriṅgāra Kāvya with more than 80 darus each ending with an intricate Tirmānaṁ with beautiful footwork. Among the forms that are found in the Kuchipuḍi dance are Taraṅga Nṛitya, Padābhinaya, Śabda, Muktāyi, Timmānam, Jakkini Daru, Śabda Pallavi, Maṇḍūka śabda, Kandaram, etc.

Enactments

The Kuchipuḍi dance-dramas were usually enacted on a simple open-air stage. The spectators sat on three sides. On the fourth side, a white decorated curtain was held by two persons as there were no curtain arrangements fixed on the stage in those days. After prayer, the herald would announce the arrival of the principal actor and the actor would enter the stage, stand behind the curtain and announce his name and title of the dance-drama by way of an introductory song called Praveśa Daru. Immediately the curtain would be raised and the drama would commence. The stage-director, sūtradhāra would stand behind the actors and conduct the drama. He would repeat loudly for the benefit of the entire audience what the characters spoke and sometimes he would himself act in minor roles.

The orchestra consisted of the mṛidaṅga, flute, violin, taṁbura or harmonium and two or more background singers. The actors would wear beautifully designed crowns and ornaments according to their status in the drama. The ornaments were of diverse sizes and shapes exquisitely carved out of light teniki wood.

The intricate rhythmic patterns set to tala are the noteworthy feature of Kuchipuḍi dances. The Bhāgavatars master the technique, interweaving rhythm with beautiful tune appropriate for abhinaya.

Chinta Veṅkaṭarāmayya, the founder of the Veṅkaṭarāma Nāṭya Maṇḍali, was one of the foremost exponents of Kuchipuḍi dance. He had a number of disciples and among them Vēdāntam Lakshmīnārāyaṇa Śāstri and his son Vēdāntaṁ Satyanārāyana are widely known for their extraordinary skill in this art. Indeed the latter emerged as the most gifted portrayer of Satyabhāma, consort of Lord Krishṇa!

RASA AND BHĀVA IN DANCE COMPOSITIONS

Bharatha's Nāṭyaśāstra is the source book for comprehensive information on the status of diverse contemporary arts like dance, drama and music in ancient India. In the sloka starting with the words 'Muninā Bharathēna' in his work Vikramōrvaśīya, Kāḷidāsa refers to sage Bharatha not merely as an authority on Sanskrit drama but the procreater of a particular play in which was incorporated the delineation of eight rasas. Bharatha's work remains the earliest and richest reference treatise on dance and matters pertaining thereto. The dances described in ancient Tamil classics like Śilappadikāram also closely resemble those mentioned by Bharatha. However the term Nṛithya, which stands for the present day Indian dance with predominance of Abhinaya, does not figure in the Nāṭyaśāstra. Kōhala (4th century A.D.) is reported to have codified and regularised Nṛithya which may be regarded a hybrid art involving the fusion of Abhinaya with pure Nṛitta. The fact that it finds mention by Amarasiṁha, the earliest Sanskrit lexicographer of the 5th century A.D., bears testimony to the fact that by his time Nṛithya was sufficiently developed to find a place in his lexicon. That it was already a full-fledged art during Kāḷidāsa's period is revealed by the fact that in his play Māḷavikagnimitra, the heroine Māḷavika is said to interpret a verse set to music with Abhinaya. Nṛithya was a highly developed and popular performing art during the Gupta period and its brightest era were the days when Indian culture left its strong impress even beyond the shores of India - particularly in many regions of South East Asia - first through Buddhism and later through Hinduism.

The term Bharatanāṭyam itself came into vogue only during the early decades of this century though it occurs in Purandaradāsa' Dēvarnāma 'Ādidheno raṅga'. Earlier it was known as Sadir, Chinnamēḷaṁ, etc. In Telugu the term Chadura was used which is actually featured in one of Kshetragña's Padams. It is this word that came down to us as Sadir and its claim to be called Bharatanāṭyam appears quite legitimate in view of the retention therein of many of the dance patterns described in the Nāṭyaśāstra.

The term Abhinaya is derived from the Sanskrit root 'abhi'

indicating to or towards along with the root 'ni' meaning to lead. It connotes the dancer's act of sending forth impulses to the consciousness of the spectators or the dancer's process of communication with the audience. Abhinaya stands for the representation or exposition of a certain theme or exhibition of the import of that which is depicted. Abhinaya is done by the use of meaningful hand gestures called Hasthas as well as facial expressions to bring out varying shades of inner emotions. Their functions, usages and significance are comprehensively explained in the dance treatises. Abhinaya has an unlimited range of interpretation through employing the technique of sañchāris. A dancer can render abhinaya even while seated without any body movement except for the hand and face. She is in a sense a lyrical narrator employing them to communicate in the language of Abhinaya. No dance in any other part of the world has given so much thought to bodily gestures in depicting expression as Indian Nṛithya. Spiritually, psychologically, aestheticaly and visually every gesture is devised in detail and the dancer is made aware of the dual function of the art in elevating the physical to the sublime level. Bharatanāṭyam lives only in Abhinaya and not in the scrupulously gained accuracy of the laya. Abhinaya alone can win laurels for an artiste for having transformed an audience from mere gazers into participating Sahṛidayās. Abhinaya is not easy to master nor can it be taught in its finer aspects and the knack has to be inborn. Knowledge of the language, a correct understanding of the import, a grounding in Nāyaka-Nāyika bhāva and a precise comprehension of the motifs of the characters portrayed are all indispensable for mastering Abhinaya.

Everyone is familiar with the emotional experiences one goes through on witnessing the diverse situations in a dance or drama. This is the basis of rasa as understod in the field of Indian art and the onlooker becomes a Rasika. Rasa means essence or flavour. The rasa theory is the creation of the Indian genius. Bharata has classified Rasas into eight main types - Śringāra, Hāsya, Karuṇa, Raudra, Vīra, Bhayānaka, Bhībatsa and Adbhutha. This same list is also mentioned in ancient Tamil classics like Tolkāppiyam. To this list a ninth rasa - Śānta rasa - was added later and these are the generally accepted Navarasas. The meaning of rasa is roughly conveyed by sentiment or motif but artistic experience or aesthetic experience would perhaps be the nearest English equivalent. Rasa is outstanding in variety and depth and provides animation to dance. Śringāra is the king of rasas in the context of dance. The Vedic hymns as well as our epics like the Rāmāyaṇa and the Mahābhārata are replete with rasas. When the term is used as a factor in arts, it refers to the much needed criterion of the beautiful as against the merely agreeable and pleasant. The temporary identification of the dancer with the character and the portrayal of the theme as well as the temporary involvement of the spectator with the atmosphere and the theme - even though everyone is aware all the time that it is all just an illusory depiction- are the direct results of the atmosphere created by rasa. Thus through the evocation of rasa the aesthetic experience of dance is greatly enhanced and better rapport is established with the audience. This certainly is the ultimate glory of Indian dance.

This leads us to the concept of bhāva in dance. Beauty of form, grace in movement and response to rhythm are comparatively direct in appeal - often eye-filling. But there in classical dance something that transcends the eye and the ear - something that reaches for the mind and the cultural consciousness of the viewer. According to Bharata, bhāvas or states are so called because, through words, gestures and representations of temperament, the Bhāgavanthas infuse the meaning of the play in the spectators. The term bhāva is derived from the root bhavaya meaning to pervade. The bhāvas or states cause the rasa to pervade the mind of the spectator. The tendency of bhāva is to pass into action - bhavathi ithi bhava. Bhāva does not mean to be but to become. The finer sense of the term would imply affecting the viewer to become what the artist intends. This aesthetic transmission is what Abhinavagupta would seem to imply when he cites the analogy of the musk and clothes where the communication - in this case fragrance - occurs even without contact through the medium of air. The different cross-currents of emotions can be portrayed by bringing into play the various anubhavas and vyabhichāri bhāvas. Gestures and expressions can be employed to elucidate with telling effect diverse sañchāri bhāvas such as weakness, exhaustion, weariness, agitation, recollection, dreaming, depression, discouragement, despair, distraction, etc. While depicting the main emotion which in most cases is Vipralamba śringāra, several transient feelings like anxiety, impatience, yearning, indignation, etc., can be brought on to enhance the main mood of the dance. This technique of sañchāri bhāvas must be revealed through creative faculties of expressing the various emotions in a subtle suggestive way calculated to evoke the rasa in the minds of the audience. The dancer must possess the knack to lift herself to awaken to an existence where feelings and refined emotions could easily engage the rasikas in rapport with their own rasānubhava. Rasānubhava is inculcated through the communication of the rasa in the composition through the dancer's abhinaya. In this manner Bharatanāṭya transports the audience to the acme of divine bliss.

Rasānubhava connotes aesthetic delight and its enjoyment. The source may be visual or aural or mental. one of our Alaṅkāras has defined it as a ripple on the surface of a tranquil mind. This ripple is caused by a situation read or heard or seen. What is read or heard is couched in language because there can be no thoughts without words and there can be no feeling without thought. As such sāhitya is as essential as music for the evocation of rasānubhava. Sāhitya is the real fountainhead of rasa. While the rāga abides in the svaras, rasa abides in the bhāvas. Sāhitya generates the rasa while saṅgīta enhances and elevates it.

The quintessance of rasānubhava is poetry set to music because the poet and the musician are aesthetitians par excellence in the Indian tradition. The linkage between poetry and dance as a fundamental tenet dates back to the Nāṭya śāstra wherein Bharata declares that to reflect the inner sense of what the poet has in mind is bhāva in dance. It is the dramatic style of such poetry that lends itself readily to representation on the stage; the skill and sensitivity of the dancer lies in exploring every nuance of the sentiment by probing into the meaning of each phrase - may even a word. That produces rasānubhava. It takes its origin in lyrics and poetry but emotion is its sap. In the choice of music it is good to recognise that rasas and Nāyikas are central.

The theme of most dance compositions is invariably the protestation of love by a love-lorn maiden pinning for union with her lord who may be a deity or king or chieftain. The superiority of śriṅgāra in commanding the contribution of a multitude of sañchāri bhāvas towards establishing itself as a dominant rasa is undoubtedly due to its own versatality in presenting the dual possibilities of Vipralamba śringāra and Sambhōga śringāra. Further it is only Vipralamba śringāra which gives immense scope for a variety of fleeting emotions. The mixture of several changing moods and responses kindles creation unfathomable depths of expression when Vipralamba śringāra is portrayed. The other rasas such as Vīra or heroism (attributed to the Lord) or Bhayānaka or fear (attributed to his victories) come out of auxiliary or sañchāri bhāvas with śringāra forming the base. The erotic content or format can vary within limits. While the pangs of separation may form the starting point, the rest of the song can be a plea for union or taunt for his collousness or for flirting with the other woman while part of the song may detail the glories of the Lord, his heroism, victories, his beauty and great compassion. Śringāra rasa has certainly played its part in the spiritual adventure of the human soul down the ages. Bhāgavatha, which is the very foundation of devotion, abounds in the Madhura bhakti rasa of the Rāsa Kṛeeḍas staged on the green meadows of Brindāvan amidst sylvan surroundings. The Vaishnavite Bhakti poets - the Āḻwārs of Tamilnadu - viewed themselves as forlorn beloveds of Lord Krishṇa and they have poured out all their devotion in Vipralamba śringāra in their Pāśurams replete with Nāyaka-Nāyika bhāva. True love is divine, whatever its context. Among the Navarasas we speak of śringāra as the only one which can take in all the others as a part of its diverse situations and moods. That is the reason why many types of love lyrics and varieties of śringāra literature have become the largest segment of our dance repertoire.

Passing on the subject of music vis-a-vis dance, the main function of music in this context is to accentuate rasānubhava. There is a world of difference between music in a music concert and that in a dance concert. The former is marked chiefly by the singer's virtuosity with the main attention being paid to improvisation in the form of rāga ālāpana, neraval, svaraprasthāra, pallavi exposition etc., and bhāva mostly takes a back seat. In a dance concert music functions only as an aid to Nṛitta and Nṛitya - particularly the latter. Dance music calls for perfect blending between sāhitya and rāga and the rāga bhāva must be brought out clearly.

Different rāgas are deemed to be conducive to evoke diverse rasas. Let us in the first instance consider the relationship between the saptasvaras and rasas.

Shaḍja	evokes	Adbhutha and Vīra
Ṛishabha	,,	Raudra
Gāndhāra	,,	Śānta
Madhyama	,,	Hāsya
Pañchama	,,	Śriṅgāra
Dhaivata	,,	Bībatsa
Nishda	,,	Karuṇa

As for the twelve svarasthānas, Shaḍja (as already mentioned) evokes Adbhutha and Vīra. Śuddhaṛishabha evokes laziness and sorrow; Chatuśruti ṛishabha evokes consciousness with laziness and so on.

There are some rāgas which portray a single rasa like Punnāgavarāḷi and Nādanānakṛiya as well as rāgas capable of delineating multiple rasas such as Śaṅkarābaraṇam and Kalyāṇi. But it is generally accepted that certain rāgas possess the powerful effect of evoking particular rasas like :

Aṭhāṇa	evokes	Vīra rasa
Gauḷipantu	,,	Karuṇa rasa
Sāma	,,	Śānta rasa
Sāraṅga	,,	Adbhutha rasa
Kantaḷavarāḷi	,,	Hāsya rasa
Khamās	,,	Śriṅgāra rasa
Śubhapantu-varāḷi	,,	Bībhatsa rasa
Bilahari	,,	Raudra rasa

Passing over to the subject of rhythm in the context of dance, generally viḷamba or slow tempo is best suited for subjects of grave and sober nature like śānta, karuṇa and śriṅgāra rasas. For sport, merriment, etc., madhyamakāla suits best. Durita kāla goes well with vīra and raudra rasas. Ārabhi, Nāṭa and Suraṭi are examples of rāgas which shrine in medium tempo. Sāvēri, Ānandabhairavi, Nīlāmbari, Sahāna and Yadukulakāmbōji are suited to slow tempo. Aṭhāṇa, Darbār and Behāg go well with fast tempo.

In a Bharatanāṭyam concert the first portion, right upto Śabdam, is taken up predominantly by Nṛitta. It is only thereafter that Nṛitya comes into play. The main items giving scope for elaborate Abhinaya are Varṇam, Padam and Jāvaḷi. Among others, Ashṭapadis of Jayadēva are delectable dance compositions. The medium through which Jayadēva depicts divine love has rendered it śriṅgāra swarūpa. It is well known that Gītagōvinda is supremely suited for Abhinaya and that Jayadēva's wife Padmāvathi herself used to render the Ashṭapadis in dance. Many Dāsa sāhityas as well as masterpieces of Tamil composers like Aruṇāchalakavi, Gōpālakṛishṇa Bhārati, Muthu Tāṇḍavar etc., are also ideal dance pieces in the same class of Padams and Jāvaḷis. Some kritis of the Trinity of Carnatic music also fall in this class. Among the modern composers, the Anthapura Geethe of the late D.V. Guṇḍappa are ideally suited for dance. Many slokas are also nice dance pieces. The use of all such composition would help expand one's dance repertoire and pave the way for diversifying and upgrading the range and level of dance concerts.

(This paper was presented at the Annual Seminar of NUPURA at Bangalore, 1986.)

DEVELOPMENT OF INDIAN AND WESTERN MUSICAL SCALES

The unique feature which distinguishes Indian music from the music of other nations is the system of Raga or melody types. This supreme innovation enables Indian musicians to display their powers of improvisation on the spot (or Manōdharma) to an unlimited extent in their concerts. The basis of the Rāga system is the groupings of scales with different varieties of notes. An attempt is made in this article to present a study of Indian scales in comparison with those of other nations. First the Heptatonic or seven note scales, then the Pentatonic or five note scales or Oudava, then the Hexatonic or six note scales or Shāḍava and finaly the Modern scales will be dealt with. Since the tonal basis of the scales are the notes, we shall begin with the evolution of the seven notes in Indian as well as Western music.

Our music tradition in the North as well as the South remembers and cherishes its origin in the Sāmavēda. Sāmavēda is just the musical version of the Rigvēda. Seventyfive verses of the Rigveda were recited in the Sāmavēda in the form of liturgical melodies. This vedic music possessed three definite pitches called Udatta, Anudatta and Svarita. The Saman scale was recited in a downward movement, at first to the notes of D C B and later in the form of a tetrachord E D C B. As time passed on, the number of notes in the Sāman scale was gradually increased to seven.

The influence of Greek music on Western music is considerable. In ancient Greece, the lyre had only three strings to start with. Later one more string was added and it was tuned to a tetrachord, in the order of a semitone and two tones starting with B C D E. Terpander, an eminent musicologist of the 7th century B.C., increased the number of strings from four to seven. He added another tetrachord E F G A above B C D E to form the heptachord B C D E F G A. Later one more tetrachord A B C D was added to E F G A making altogether three tetrachords i.e., B C D E, E F G A, A B C D. This system was called Conjunct because in this arrangement the last note becomes the starting note of the succeeding tetrachord. Here, in the third tetrachord, a new note B flat occurs. In this progression another new note E flat is arrived at in the fourth tetrachord D E F G.

Sometimes later, experiments were carried out in the hexachordal system in three ways - one starting with F, another with C and the last with F i.e., F G A B^b CD, CDEFGA and GABCDE. In the hexachord the third and fourth notes are always separated by a semitone, all other notes being separated from each other by whole tones. In the above arrangement the last two notes of each hexachord form the first two notes of the suceeding hexachord. In the above mentioned hexachords we can notice two types of B : B^b B^+.

During the 6th century B.C. Pythagores introduced the octave scale by adding an eight string to the lyre. He invented the Monochord and with the help of the movable fret,he could arrive at the intervals of the octave, fifth and fourth, which are the most important consonances. The interval between the perfect 4th and 5th known as Tone, became the basis of Western music. It is a point of interest that Ārabhi rāga of South Indian music takes the frequencies of the Pythagorean scale for its notes. In the scale of Pythagores, we get the Pythagorean E i.e., 81/64, slightly higher than the true Major 3rd, 5/4. The difference between these two E's is 81/80 (Pythagorean Comma) and it is worthy of note that this is equal to the Pramāṇa Śruti of Bharata.[1]

A few centuries after Pythagores, Bharata experimented with his two Veeṇas and assigned twentytwo śruti values to seven notes. Through this experiment he discovered the prime interval of 81/80, i.e. Pythagorean Comma. The important śruti values 4, 3, 2 given by Bharata correspond to the Major tone. Minor tone and Semitone of Western music. In Bharata's days there were seven placed or pure notes and two displaced or impure notes known as Antara and Kākali. It may be recalled that in the Greek tetrachordal system also the displaced notes E and B occur.

The three hexachords beginning with F, C and G about whicn mention has already been made, paved the way for the respective Clefs i.e., F clef, C clef and G clef in Western musical notation. A striking similarity to this can be seen in our own Grāma system inasmuch as the Madhyama Grāma, Shaḍja Grāma and Gāndhāra Grāma also begin with the respective svaras. In his Grāma-Mūrchchana system, Bharata has mentioned the Shaḍja and Madhyama Grāmas with fourteen mūrchchanas. Out of these only seven mūrchchanas, considered to be more important, were retained with the names of their starting notes.

The counterpart of Mūrchchanas in Western music are the Modes and the Greek music was based upon a system of eight modes. By varying the arrangement of tones and semitones in a total ofsix notes, the different modes were obtained. Among these eight modes the 1st, 3rd, 5th and 7th were called the Authentic modes introduced by St. Ambrose and the 2nd, 4th, 6th and 8th modes were called Plagal modes introduced by St. Gregory, a little later. The plagal modes were the same as the Authentic mode but with a different range. In both the pairs of Authentic and Plagal, the tonic is the same but in a different position. The tonic in the Authentic is the commencing note, while in the Plagal it lies near the middle of the octave, having three notes below and four notes above.

Round about the 16th century A.D. the Swiss monk St. Glarenus introduced two more Authentic modes with their Plagal modes. The Greek modes of ancient times were in the descending order whereas the medieval church modes were in the ascending order. The modes of the medieval times were Dorian, Phrygian, Lydian, Mixolydian, Aeolian and Ionian. Their plagal modes were Hypodorian, Hypophrygian, Hypolydian, Hypomixolydian, Hypoaeolian and Hypoionian.

In Western music we have the option of commencing a mode from any key. If we take C as the tonic note in these modes we arrive at the corresponding Melas of South Indian music.

Dorian	-	Kharaharapṛiya
Phrygian	-	Hanumathōḍi
Lydian	-	Kalyāṇi
Mixolydian	-	Harikāmbōdhi
Aeolian	-	Naṭabhairavi
Ionian	-	Śaṅkarābharaṇaṁ

The Plagal modes resemble Madhyama śruti rāgas of South Indian music like Kuruñji, Saindhavi, Navarōj, etc.

Authorities on Indian music are of the opinion that the Saman notes were sung to a fixed scale in the Shadja grama, but controversy exists with regard to the original scale. By shifting the tonic from Prathama to Dvitīya and so on till Mandra, one gets Thōḍi, Śaṅkarābharaṇa, Naṭabhairavi etc. Therefore the view that all the Gānas of the Samaveda should be sung in the same scale is untenable and the scholars who say that the basic scale is Kharaharapriya are as much in the right as others who call it any one of the other scales mentioned above.

If we consider the Sāman scale, we notice the occurrence of most of these Mēḷas in the above church modes. The peculiarity is that all these modes take only white keys. Since all these modes were considered pure, they were adopted for the sacred or church music. The reason for Sāmagāna as well as Church music gradually fading away is their restricted use for religious purpose confined to certain classes of Brāhmins and priests.

At present in Western music, only the Major scale and the Minor scale (Ionian and Aeolianmodes respectively) have been retained. The reason for this is that by the use of the Chromatic notes B^b (the first chromatic note to be experimented with) F^+ E^b and, G^+ on the Lydian, Mixolydian, Dorian and Phrygian modes respectively these four modes merged into the popular Major and Minor scales.

In the music of Shaḍja grāma of Kuḍimiyāmalai inscription of the 7th century A.D., all the notes of an octave occur consisting of the four varieties of D, E, A and B. King Mahēndravarman combined one scale with another and ushered in a new chromatic scale particularly through the use of two E's in conjunction. This paved the way for the formation of the seventy-two Mēḷas of Veṅkaṭamakhi on the basis of only seven placed and five displaced notes.

It is a point of interest that Western Music is also based upon the same system of seven placed and five displaced notes, the five chromatic notes being B^b, E^b, F^+, C^+, G^+. Chromaticism was first introduced into Western music by Adrian Willeart in the 16th century A.D.

The 17th century saw the dawn of the era of Harmony. With a

view to favouring the development of Harmony, Western music came to be based on the cycle of fifths and fourths rather than the division of the strings and its octave unit, as in Melody. For the purpose of Harmony, the pianoforte with the range of 7¼ octaves was constructed and the Equal temperament system with twelve equally divided semitones in an octave was adopted.

At this stage modulation became almost indispensable. Modulation may be defined as a take off into a new key from the original key for a short period, keeping the intervals in the same sequence using sharps and flats. Modulation (<u>Śrutibhēda</u>) is practised in South Indian music also, in a different way since the sharps and flats are not admissible as in Western music.

It is interesting to note that some of the scales resulting from modulation in Western music correspond to some of the scales of the seventytwo Mēḷas scheme propounded by Venkaṭamakhi.

G	Major scale	- G A B C D E F	- Kalyāṇi
F	Major scale	- F G A B^b C D E	- Harikāmbōdhi
B^b	Major scale	- B^b C D E^b F G A	- Kharaharapriya
A^b	Najor scale	- A^b B^b C D^b E^b F G	- Tōḍi
A	Minor scale	- A B C D E F G	- Naṭabhairavi
A	Harmonic minor	- A B C D E F G+	- Kīravāṇi
E	Harmonic minor	- E F+ G A B C D+	- Hēmavati
C+	Harmonic minor	- C+ D+ E F+ G+ A B+	- Kōsalaṁ
D^b	Harmonic minor	- D^b E F G A B C+	- Vakulābharaṇa

The Melodic minor scale as well as those obtained by its modulation resemble some of the scales in the new scheme of 5184 melas formulated by late Prof. P. Sambamoorthi.

A	Melodic minor scale	- Gowrimanōhari	- Naṭabhairavi
E	Melodic minor scale	- Vāchaspati	- Kharaharapriya
B	Melodic minor scale	- Śaṅkarābharaṇa	- Harikāmbōdhi
D	Melodic minor scale	- Chārukēśi	- Thōḍi

The seven note scales are to be found in the music of Arabia, Turkey, Egypt, Iran, China, Spain, England, Scotland, France, Poland, Hungary, Bulgaria, Czechoslovakia and Brazil.

<u>Arabia</u> : In present day Arab Music, a seven note scale with

seventeen śrutis is used, the śruti values being in the order of 3, 3, 1, 3, 3, 1, 3 taking C as the first śruti. The important fixed intervals in Arab music are C, F and G and with two pairs of variable notes D, E and A, B different scales are formed resembling Veṅkaṭamakhi's Mēḷa scheme. The Arabs do not make any distinction between consonances and dissonances but know only the increasing and decreasing degrees of them like Vādi, Saṁvādi and Vivādi of South Indian music. The counterpart of the Indian Mēla scales in Arabian music are the Maqams and Arabs possess twelve Maqams. Among them four Magams, namely, Iraq (which has the notes : C, E^{bb}, F^{b}, F, A^{bb}, B^{bb}, B^{b}, D^{bb}), Mezmoum, Edziel and Djorka correspond respectively to Harikāmbōdhi, Kalyāṇi, Thōḍi and Naṭabhairavi rāgas.

Turkey : Turkish music is based on a fundamental scale containing twentyfour microtones to the octave. The scale of the mode Tchariguiah (pronounced as charr-e-gu-ah) corresponds to the Pythagorean scale while another mode called Raste is the same with the difference that E and B have the ratios of 5/4 and 15/8.

Egypt : Egyptians also use a scale containing twentyfour microtones to the octave based on the Turko-Arabian system with seven Diatonic intervals. It corresponds to the Harikāmbōdhi of South Indian music.

Iran : According to Sina, the famous musicologist, Iranian or Persian music is based on twelve primary modes. Four of these are of Arabian origin while the others are indigenous. One of the modes of the former group known as the Nava mode takes the notes C D E F^{+} G A B. The use of slightly sharpened F along with natural F in this scale is analogous to the sharpened F in the Bēgaḍa rāga of South Indian music. Some of the modes of the later group correspond to the Indian melas if C is taken as the tonic note :

Mahur	:	C D E F G A B C	- Śaṅkarābharaṇa
Humayan	:	G A(-B) C D D E^{b} F G	- Chārukēśi
Baya-i-Ispahan	:	C D E^{b} F G A (-B)(-C)	- Gowrīmanōhari
Shur	:	G A (-B^{b}) C D (-E^{b}) F G	- Naṭabhairavi

During the Mohammedan period of Indian history, Persian tunes came to be added to Indian music. In the 13th century, Amīr

Khusrau, the reputed musicologist, introduced some of the Persian scales into the Indian classical stock.

China : In ancient China, a twelve note scale was used, correlated with the 12 months, 12 hours and 12 signs of the Zodiac. This has a parallel in India in Saṅgīta Makaranda's description of singing rāgas according to time, day, hour, etc. During the 6th century, Buddhist monks introduced the Indian gamakas and quarter tones into Chinese music. Using quarter tones, the Chinese formed scales of 53 to 60 notes. One can notice the interval of the Pramāṇaśruti 81/80 in the excess of the 12th fifth from their tonic note F (E^+). The Chinese-seven note scale starting from F corresponds to the Śaṅkarābharaṇa rāga with the perfect 4th. Another seven note scale of the 12th century has an augmented 4th with Diatonic intervals equivalent to the Kalyāṇi rāga of South Indian music.

Spain : The Arabs remained in Spain for a considerable period and so the influence of Arabian music on Spanish music is discernible. Spanish popular melody is based upon a series of intervals taking the notes of Harikāṁbōdhi of South Indian music.

England : Nearly half of the English tunes are derived from the Diatonic scale or Śaṅkarābharaṇam of South Indian music and the rest of the tunes from Harikāṁbōdhi and Kharaharapriya. In most of the tunes, the 6th degree seems to be absent leading to the doubt as to whether they are of Aeolian or Dorian origin.

France & Poland : French and Polish music use extensively the seven note scales of Naṭabhairavi, Kharaharapriya, Tōḍi, Harikāṁbōdhi and Kalyāṇi of South Indian music.

Scotland : The Panmure Vocal manuscript of the 16th century describes the Scottish melodies similar to Kharaharapriya, Kalyāṇi and Harikāṁbōdhi of South Indian music. The preeminent position of melodies corresponding to Śaṅkarābharaṇa and Naṭabhairavi of South Indian music is also noticeable.

Hungary : In Hungarian music two varieties of the so-called Gypsy scale starting from C (i) C D^b E F G A^b B and (ii) C D E^b F^+ G A^b B correspond respectively to Māyāmāḷavagauḷa and Siṁhēndramadhyama rāgas with two Augmented seconds.

Bulgaria : Bulgarian music is based on Diatonic scale and Chromaticism usually appears by way of altered diatonic notes with addition of foreign chromatic note to that scale. This corresponds to the prevalence of Bhāshāṅga rāgas in South Indian music. While the majority of the scales are in the range of Naṭabhairavi, in some regions one can hear Kharaharapriya and Tōḍi and occasionally Kalyāṇi. Two Bulgarian modes starting with (i) G A^b B C D E^b F^+ and (ii) G A^b B C D E F correspond to the Māyāmāḷavagauḷa and Chakravāka rāgas of South Indian music.

Brazil : In Brazilian music, most of the composers have drawn freely from the rich and colourful folk music of both Portugese and Red Indian origin. The scales of three of their modes correspond to Vāchaspati, Kalyāṇi and Harikāmbōdhi of South Indian music.

Next to the Heptatonic, the Pentatonic scale having five notes to an octave is most widespread in the music of the different nations. This is of two types. The first type is called the Tonal Pentatonic in which no semitones or tritones can be found. In Western music we find such tonal pentatonic scales starting from F and its varieties. These scales correspond to Śuddhasāvēri, Mōhanam, Śuddadhanyāsi, Hindōḷam and Madhyamāvati of South Indian music. One can hear the same varieties of Tonal Pentatonic in Chinese and Polish music also.

The second type is known as the Semitonal pentatonic or Ditonic with semitones and ditones. They are to be found mostly in the music of the Eastern countries.

Japan : Buddhist monks spread Chinese, Indian and Korean music to Japan. The principal pentatonic modes of Japanese music are (i) Hirajoshi (ii) Kumoi and (iii) Iwato. The absolute pitch is F^+. The Hirajoshi mode has two types of tunings - C D E^b G A and C D E G A^b and they correspond respectively to Śaṅkrandanapriya and Vāsanti[2] rāgas.

Two new scales formed out of these modes correspond to Revati scale (C D^b F G B^b) and Karṇāṭaka Śuddhasāvēri scale (C D^b F G A^b). The scale called Zokugakusempu formed out of these two scales is frequently used in Japanese music. This scale resembles the

Melodic scales of Western music. Considering the notes of Karṇāṭaka-Śuddhasāvēri which falls in the Bhairavā scale of North-Indian music or Māyāmālavagauḷa scale of South Indian music, we get clear evidence of the influence of Indian music on Japanese music.

Java : The Pentatonic scale of Javanese music is peculiar in having the notes C D F G A consisting of five equal intervals of a whole tone plus a quarter tone in an octave.

Bulgaria : In Bulgarian the distinctive feature is that all the pentatonic scales start with G. We find both the varities of tonal and semitonal pentatonics in Bulgarian music. Taking C as the tonic we get the following scale :

Śuddhadhanyasi	from the scale	G B^{b} C D G
Nāgasvarāvaḷi	,,	G B C D E
Śuddhasāvēri	,,	G A C D E
Mōhanaṁ	,,	G A B D E

Hexatonic scales are found chiefly in Russian and French music.

Russia : It is noteworthy that Russians have a six note scale introduced by Alexander Scriabin (19th century). This scale takes the notes C D E F^{+} A B^{b} correspondig to a rare rāga in Carnatic music 'Paramēshṭi' - a janya rāga of Vāchaspati.

France : In French music, Claude Debussy introduced a six note scale associated with his name - Debussy whole tone scale. This contains six degrees of equally divided whole tones in an octave and corresponds to Indian scale 'Gōpriya' - a janya raga of Ṛishabhapṛiya. This scale has the notes C D E F^{+} A^{b} B^{b}.

Coming to modern scales, two examples are given below. Tcherepnin of France has formulated a nine note scale in the order of a Semitone, Tone and a Semitone. The scale has following notes : C C^{+} D^{+} E F G G^{+} A B. Another scale called 'Blues Scale' consisting of all the tones of Major scale and the additional note E and B of the Minor scale. They are C D E^{b} E F G A B^{b} B C.

It can be seen that the musical scales in vogue in the different nations of the world are enormous. All of them have equally served the purpose of allowing man to express his emotions. The depth of the scales of some Indian ragas like Todi, Śaṅkarābharaṇam, Kalyāṇi, Karaharapriya etc., can be seen from the fact that they pervade the music of most nations. Modern composers often experiment with new scales of their own contrivance like Dīpāvaḷi (C D E F F+ A B)[3], Haricharaṇ (C C+ E F F+ A B)[4], Hēmāṅgi (C C+ D F G+ A)[5], Śubhaśri (C C+ D F F+ G+ A)[6] etc. While some of these may perhaps be too artificial, others have their own beauty and individuality. We should not also fight shy of borrowing some of the popular melodies from the music of other nations. This is the surest way of enriching our music and avoiding stagnation.

NOTES

1. The calculation of intervals, particularly of the more complicated ones, can be simplified by disregarding the octave or in other words, the factor 2. For convenience one can take the prime numbers instead of fractions for easy calculation. Starting from G, in the cycle of 5ths, i.e., C D E F G, G A B C D, D E F G A one gets higher G in the 12th place beyond two octaves. Therefore, by reducing it to one octave, G becomes 3/2 x 2/1 = 3. Major 3rd (E) is 5/4. To get a higher E, one will have to repeat eight times i.e., C D E, E F G, G A B, B C D, D E F, F G A, A B C and C D E, beyond two cotaves. Adopting the same process as in the case of G, E becomes 5/4 x 8/2 = 5. So 3rd (E) is 5 and 5th (G) is 3. Pythagorean E is 5th raised to the power of 4, i.e. 3^4. Natural 3rd is 5 x 8 x 2. The difference between the two E's is therefore : 3 •

$$3^4 \div \text{3rd i.e. } \frac{3 \times 3 \times 3 \times 3}{5 \times 8 \times 2} = 81/80$$

2. Cf. R. Raṅgarāmānuja Iyengar's 'History of South Indian (Carnatic) Music', Bombay, 1972. Apendix III, p. Lxiv the rāga numbered as 701.

3. Dīpāvaḷi or Śaṅkarābharaṇam without pañchama and with two Madhyamas.

(b) sign indicates Flats and (+) sign indicates Sharps.

4. Harichharaṇ or Sūryakāntam without pañchama and with two Madhyamas.

5. Hēmāṅgi or Kanakāṅgi without pañchama.

6. Śubhaśri or Kanakāṅgi without pañchama and with two madhyamas.

(This paper was presented at the Annual Conference of the Music Academy, Madras in 1979.)

ROYAL PATRONAGE AND CONTRIBUTION TO INDIAN MUSIC

Indian music, in its classical forms, is one of the most ancient types still surviving. It has, of course, inevitably altered over the years; nevertheless its basic elements would appear to be much as they were over two thousand years ago.

The enlightened kings of India have nurtured our music with tender care and have been its willing captives. In fact, musical training formed an indispensible item of royal education. Many were the rulers of India who were profound scholars in the theory and practice of this art. Several of them have perpetuated their names by bequeathing an imperishable legacy of scholarly musical treatises to posterity. Also, nowhere else in the world has royal patronage and encouragement to music probably been as continuous and rich as in India.

Around 2000 B.C. the Aryans came to the subcontient and with their arrival, India entered the Vedic period of her history. The sacred scriptures consisted of the four Vēdas viz, Ṛig, Yajuṛ, Sāma and Atharva. These, together with the two epics, the Rāmāyaṇa and the Mahābhārata and various Purāṇas, had a close connection with music for the verses were chanted in set musical patterns. The Rāmāyaṇa throws considerable light on the musical culture of the age and abounds in references to music and dancing. The Mahābhārata too contains references to students of music, teachers of music, professional musicians, instrumentalists, etc.

Authentic chronicled history of India begins with the rule of the Mauryan dynasty in the north and of the Cēras, Pāṇḍyas and Cōḷas in the south. There is no denying the fact that royal interest in literature and the fine arts including music was evident even at the time of the Mauryas (325-188 B.C.) and continued during the reign of the Suṅga dynasty (188-76 B.C.) and the Kaṇva dynasty (76-31 B.C.). However, sustained encouragement and patronage to music can be said to have commenced only with the rulers of Gupta dynasty. Chandragupta I (320-330 A.D.) and Chandragupta II(375-413 A.D.) deserve particular mention in this context. The latter was better known as Vikramāditya and it was in his court that renowned poets like Kāḷidāsa and Aśvaghōsha flourished.

The Pallava rulers of Kāñchi, Mahēndravarman I and Narasimha-varman (7th century) were also great patrons of music and other fine arts. The first Royal patron to have himself made a significant contribution to the science of music is Mahēndravarman I, the engraver of Kuḍimiyāmālai and Tirumayyam inscriptions (near Pudukkōṭṭai) which enshrined many new ideas for the later musicians and musicologists. Mahēndravarman, in fact, laid the foundation for the development of notation in Indian music with different varieties of notes and rāga formulations.

In the far north, a little later, Dāmōdara Gupta wrote Kuṭṭaṇimata under the patronage of the Karkōṭaka King Jayapīḍa Vinayāditya of Kashmir. This treatise reveals that by the 8th century vocal music had attained a status comparable with instrumental music.

Many Cōḷa kings whose reign extended over the 11th and 12th centuries encouraged and nurtured musicians and other artists in diverse ways including munificent gift of lands (in some cases even whole villages) as evident from numerous inscriptions and edicts ascribed to this period. Special mention needs to be made in this context of Rājarāja I, (985-1018 A.D.), Rājēndra I(1012-1044 A.D.), Rājādhi Rāja (1044-1054 A.D.), Rājēndra II (1052-1064 A.D.), Rājēndra III (1070-1122 A.D.) and Rājarāja III (1146-1173 A.D.).

Contemporaneous with the later Cōḷas were a number of royal scholars in different parts of India who distinguished themselves in diverse fields of music. The Chālukyan king Sōmēśvara II wrote the encyclopaedia work <u>Mānasōllāsa</u> of Abilashitārthachintāmaṇi (1100 A.D.) which deals in detail with all the subjects known in his time; its section on music highlights for the first time the importance of ragas and their classification. <u>Sarasvati Hṛidayālankāra</u> (1100 A.D.) of Nāyadēva, the ruler of Mithila lists 160 rāgas including some dēsi rāgas while <u>Saṅgīta Sudhākara</u> (1170 A.D.) of the Gujarathi king Haripāla Dēva, abounds in reference to tāla, gīta and gīta-prabhandas. Other noteworthy kings of this period who enriched our musical heritage with their monumental treatises are Nānyadēva's illustrious brother Kīrtirāja of Kāśi (Commentary on Nāṭya-Śāstra, 1100 A.D.); Pratāpa Chakravarti Jagadēkamalla II (Saṅgīta Chūḍāmaṇi

1140 A.D.) and Gouraṇārya (Saṅgīta Lakshaṇadīpika). Lōchana Kavi, the author of the well known work Rāgataraṅgiṇi (1160 A.D.) was the court poet ofthe Rāshṭrakūṭa monarch Kīrtirāja of Kāśi. The most noteworthy poet of this period who enjoyed royal patronage was Jayadēva, the author of the famous Gītagōvinda, who flourished in the court of king Lakshmaṇasēna of Bengal. The Gītagōvinda heralded the introduction of Sanskrit verses in music. In fact it is the first known musical opera or dance drama written in Sanskrit. It also set the pattern for the treatment of themes like erotic love and mundane and profane love in Indian musical texts and songs. The fact that more than 150 poets have attempted at various periods to imitate this epic in different languages throughout the length and breadth of the country bears testimony to its greatness and popularity.

During the 13th century, Sōmarājadēva, the feudatory under Ajayapāla (Saṅgīta Ratnāvali, 1200 A.D.) the Kākatīya King Gaṇapati Dēva (Gītaratnāvaḷi, 1220 A.D.) and king Sēnāpati (Nṛityaratnāvali) contributed in no small measure towards enriching our musical repretory. In the north, king Hammīra of Mēwār (a forefather of Rāṇa Kumbha) wrote the treatise entitled Saṅgīta Śriṅgārahara (1283 A.D.) which enumerated more than 50 alaṅkāras and varieties in music beginning from Sāmavēda. While Siṅgabhūpāla (Lāsyarañjana, 1220 A.D.) flourished in Vīra Ballāla II's court, Niśaṅka Śāraṅgadēva wrote his magnum opus Saṅgīta Ratnākara (1230 A.D.) under the patronage of the Yādava king Siṅghana. This veritable ocean of music is the pioneering work to discuss almost all aspects of Indian music including the lakshaṇas of various contemporary prabhandhas and gītas. The fact that Saṅgīta Ratnākara is the one musical treatise on which the largest number of commentaries have been written by illustrious scholars over several centuries is a measure of its greatness. The closing years of the 13th century saw the beginnings of Muslim influence on Indian Music. The pioneer among the royal Muslim patrons of India was Allaudin Khilji (1296-1316 A.D.). The renowned musicologist Amīr Khusru flourished during his reign while Gōpāla Nāyaka was his court musician.

Passing on to the 14th century, Ballāla III (Bharatasāra Saṅgraha, 1310 A.D.), Sudhākalaśa (Saṅgītōpanishadasārōddhara, 1320 A.D.), Bhuvanānanda (Saṅgītalōka 1350 A.D.) and Kumāragiri Reḍḍi

(Vasantharājīyam, 1350 A.D.) were some of the royal scholar poets who made valuable contributions to our musical culture and heritage. The great Vidyāraṇya, who inspired the Vijayanagar Empire into being, is reported to have written a work on music known as Saṅgītasāra (1340 A.D.) for which no authentic manuscript is yet available. One has to gather the contents of this work from references and quotations available from other musical treatises like Saṅgīta Sudhā of Ragunātha Nāyaka, Bharatasārasaṅgraha of Chikkabhūpāla, etc. Vidyāraṇya seems to have described in this work more than 15 mēḷas and 50 rāgas prevalent during his time. Siṁhabhūpāla king of Mithila wrote Saṅgītasudhākara, a critical commentary on Śāraṅgadēva's Saṅgīta Ratnākara. Siṁhabhūpāla's genealogy begins with Harisiṁhadēva, the patron of Jyōtiriśvara whose work, Varṇaratnākara, contains references to various types of musical forms existing in Mithila during his time. Palkurukti Sōmanātha (Basavapurāṇa and Paṇḍithārādhya Charita, 1300 A.D.) received royal encouragement from the Reḍḍi kings of Andhra Pradesh.

During the 15th century, Pedda Kōmaṭi Reḍḍi (commentary on Vasantharājīyam, 1400 A.D.), Vēmbhūpāla (Saṅgīta Chintāmaṇi, 1402 A.D.), the ruler of Kaḍa who was the feudatory under Hussain Shah Sharqi (Saṅgīta Śirōmaṇi, 1499 A.D.) and Sikandar Lōdi (1488-1506 A.D.), the author of the first work on Indian music in the Persian language (Labjat-e-Sikandar Shahi) were the royal stalwarts who distinguished themselves as the harbingers of our musical renaissance. Rāṇa Kuṁbha of Mēwār (1433-1468 A.D.) has more than 10 musical works to his credit including the monumental treatises Saṅgītarāja and Rasikapriya. While the latter is a commentary on the Gītagōvinda of Jayadēva, the former abounds in descriptions of various rāgas, their lakshaṇas, dhyānas, Sūḍa Prabhandas, etc. In Orissa Purushōttamadēva composed the dance drama Abhinava Gīta-gōvinda (1470 A.D.) on the model of Jayadēva's Gītagōvinda using 54 rāgas instead of only 16 rāgas used in the parent work. Ibrahim Shah of Jaunpur (1411-1440 A.D.) was himself an accomplished musician. Husain Shah Sharqui of Jaunpur (1458-1528 A.D.) invented Khyāl while Raja Man Singh of Gwalior (1486-1518 A.D.) was responsible for evolving the Dhrupad style of singing. He has to his credit numerous Dhrupads in rare rāgas as well as many new rāgas and tunes named after his queen. A host of Rāja Mān Singh's court musicians compiled a treatise entitled Man Kutūhal embodying the latest theories in music and dedicated this work to their patron. Among the musicologists who enjoyed royal support during this era, mention may be made of Maṇḍaṇa, the Prime Minister under Hoshang Gori (1405-32 A.D.) who wrote the Saṅgīta Maṇḍaṇa; Kallinātha, the author of Kalānidhi(1450 A.D.) the famous commentary on the Saṅgīta Ratnākara, who flourished in the court of Immaḍi Dēvarāya; and Dēvaṇṇa Bhaṭṭa (Saṅgīta Muktāvali, 1450 A.D.) who was patronised by Prauḍha Dēvarāya.

Adverting to the 16th century, Nijaguṇa Śiva Yōgi, the chieftain of the Śambhuliṅga hill near Mysore (Vivēkachintāmaṇi and Kaivalya Paddhati, 1500 A.D.), Harināyaka (Saṅgītasār, 1502 A.D.), Mēshakarṇa (Rāgamāla, 1509 A.D.) and Achyutarāya (Tāḷakālavāridhi, 1530 A.D.) were the prominent royal scholars in music. Lakshmīnārāyaṇa alias Lakshmaṇa (Saṅgīta Sūryōdaya, 1520 A.D.) and Sōmabhaṭṭa (Commentary on the Tāḷakālavāridhi) were inspired in writing these works by Krishṇadēvarāya (1509-30 A.D.), Rāmāmātya, author of the well known Svaramēḷakalānidhi (1550 A.D.) flourished in thecourt of Rāmarāya (1536-58 A.D.). The versatile Puṇḍarīka Viṭṭhala (1510-65 A.D.) wrote a number of musical treatises like Shaḍrāgachandrōdaya Rāgamañjari, Rāgamāla and Nartananirṇaya under the patronage of Burhan Khan of Farqy dynasty, Mādhavasiṁha and Akbar.

Beginning with the closing years of the 15th century and throughout the 16th and 17th centuries Indian music was fostered and nurtured by the Mughal rulers starting with Babur (1483-1530 A.D.) followed by Humayūṇ (1530-56 A.D.), Akbar (1556-1605 A.D.), Jehāṅgir (1605-27 A.D.), Shāh Jahān (1628-58 A.D.) and Auraṅgazeb (1658-1707 A.D.). Under their patronage flourished musicologists like Ahōbala (Saṅgīta Darpaṇa, 1653 A.D.) and Faqirullah (Rāgdarpan, the translation of Man Kutūhal, 1663 A.D.); composers like Jagannāth Kavirāj; and musicians like Tānsen and Bāz Bahādur. The later Mughals such as Bahādur Shah I (1707-11 A.D.), Bahādur Shah II (1711-12 A.D.) and Muhammad Shah Raṅgila (1719-48 A.D.) devoted the greater part of their time to the pursuit of music and other artistic endeavours as a sort of spiritual and emotional compensation for the gradual decline and fall of their empire.

During the 17th century musical treatises were written by a number of scholars such as Subhaṅkara Ṭhākura, the ruler of Mithila

(Saṅgīta Dāmōdara, 1610 A.D.), Jagajyōtirmalla (Saṅgīta Sārasaṅgraha, 1620 A.D.), Ibrāhim Ādil Shāh II (Kitab-e-Naweas, 1623 A.D.), Mummaḍi, Chikkabhūpāla (Abhinavabharata-Sārasaṅgraha, 1630 A.D.) and Hṛidaya Nārāyaṇa (Hridaya Kantaka, Hridaya-Prakāśa - 1677 A.D.). King Anup Siṅha co-authored Bhāvabhaṭṭa to write Anūpa Saṅgītaratnākara, Anupāṅkuśa and Anūpa Saṅgīta Vilāsa. The dawn of the 17th century saw the emergence of Tanjore as the centre of intense musical activity first during the rule of the Nāyaks and later under the Marāṭṭas. Raghunātha Nāyak was the most illustrious among the Tanjore line of Nāyaks as well as the main prop of their fame and glory. The origin of the dance drama form, Yakshagāna, is attributed to him. Raghunātha Nāyak is best known as the author of Saṅgīta Sudhā (1620 A.D.) which he wrote jointly with his minister Gōvinda Dīkshita. This work explains for the first time the ṭechnique of fixing frets on the Vīṇa as at present. Gōvinda Dīkshita's son Veṅkaṭamakhi wrote his magnum opus Chaturdaṇḍi Prakāśika under the patronage of Raghunātha Nāyak's successor, Vijayarāghava Nāyak. Veṅkaṭamakhi's greatest contribution is the codification of the system of 72 Mēḷakarthas or Janaka Rāgas. Among the Marāṭha rulers of Tanjore who succeeded the Nāyaks, King Shāhji (1690-1710 A.D.) was a prolific composer as well as a musicologist of repute. He has to his credit more than 25 musical works inclusive of dance dramas, musical operas, Yakshagānas, Kuravañji Nāṭakas, etc. With the help of his court musicians, he determined the lakshaṇas of all the rāgas in vogue during his time, which remained in 10 manuscripts in the Sarasvathi Mahal Library at Tanjore. King Shāhaji's younger brother, Tulājaji is the author of Saṅgīta Sārāmṛita, an authoritative work on contemporary music. In fact, the Marāṭṭa rulers of Tanjore laid the foundation for the present day system of Carnatic music and it was no mere coincidence that the Marāṭṭa kingdom was blessed soon after with the Trinity of Carnatic Music viz., Tyāgarāja, Muthuswāmy Dīkshitar and Śyāma Śāstri, all of whom were born near Tanjore at Tiruvārūr, the abode of Tyāgeśa, the family deity of the Marāṭṭa rulers.

The 18th century witnessed the beginning of a remarkable musical renaissance, particularly in South India. The crucial figure in this efflorescence were the Trinity of Carnatic Music. However, among them only Muthuswāmi Dīkshitar can be deemed to have enjoyed some measure of royal patronage and that too only during the closing years of his life at the court of the Mahārāja of Eṭṭayāpuram. The royal scholars of this period included Chikkarāja Woḍeyār (Gītagōpāla, 1701 A.D.), Nārāyaṇadēva, the Gajapati king of Orissa (Saṅgīta Nārāyaṇa, 1766 A.D.) and Bālarāmavarma Mahārāja of Travancore (Bālarāmabharataṁ, 1760 A.D.). On the lines of Sōmēśvara's Mānasōllāsa, Basappa Nāyaka wrote the encyclopaedic work Śivatattuvaratnākara (1720 A.D.), wherein musical aspects were dealt with in Taraṅgas. Raṅganātha of Śrīraṅgapaṭna wrote the work Saṅgīta Śāstra Dugdhābhi under the patronage of Krishṇarāja Woḍēyar II (1714-31 A.D.).

During the beginning of the 19th century, at the initiative of the Mahārāja of Jaipur, a large number of musicians and musicologists met for the first time and the results of their discussions were made known to the public. Mohammad Reza wrote his Mamat-e-Aspahi in 1813 A.D. The dawn of this century also saw the emergence of Svāti Tirunāḷ Mahārāja of Travancore as a prolific composer as well. as patron of musicians. Svāti Tirunāḷ's contribution to music can be classified into literary and musico-literary works. While the former comprises works like Bhakthimañjari, Padmanābha Śatakam, etc., the latter includes musical operas as well as diverse types of compositions of all forms like Svarajati, Varṇam, Kṛithis, Padas, Jāvaḷis, Rāgamālikas, Tillānas, etc. The musicians who enjoyed patronage in his court numbered more than a hundred including such stalwarts as Paramēśwara Bhāgavathar, Irayimman Tampi, Shaṭkāla Gōvinda Mārār, Mēruswāmi, the Tanjore Quartette, etc. Other distinguished royal composers of this century were King Serfoji of Tanjore (Kāvyacha Sāhityacha Jannas or Dance compositions in Marathi) and Vijayaraghunātha Toṇḍaimān of Pudukkoṭṭai. Among the Sētupatis of Rāmnāḍ, Muthurāmaliṅga Sētupati was a great composer with more than 100 compositions to his credit in rare as well as popular rāgas. Krishṇarāja Woḍeyār III of Mysore (1799-1868 A.D.) wrote Svarachintmaṇi and Śrītattvanidhi while Kaḷale Nañjarāja, the author of Saṅgīta Gaṅgādhara (1850 A.D.) flourished in his court. Subbarāma Dīkshitar, the author of the monumental work, Saṅgīta Saṁpradāya Pradarśini, enjoyed the patronage of both Veṅkaṭēśvara Eḍḍappa III of Eṭṭayapuram as well as Bhāskar Sētupati of Rāmnāḍ.

During the early decades of the 20th century, a number of music conferences were held largely as a result of royal effort. The 1st All India Music Conference was convened by the Mahārāja of Baroda at Delhi (1910 A.D.), the 2nd and 4th conferences by the Maharaja of Rāmpur at Delhi (1918 A.D.) and Lucknow (1925 A.D.), respectively and the 3rd conference by the Mahārāja of Benaras (1919 A.D.). These conferences greatly stimulated the advancement of music by providing an opportunity of the front-rank musicologists and musicians to know one another which helped to crystalise their views on different aspects of music for mutual benefit. The first half of this century also witnessed a great spurt in musical activity in the Royal courts at Travancore and Mysore. Dr. Muthiāh Bhāgavatar wrote his work Saṅgīta Kalpadruma (1933 A.D.) under the patronage of Chittira Tirunāḷ Mahārāja of Travancore. The encouragement given to musicians by Krishṇarāja Woḍeyar IV of Mysore (1897-1943 A.D.) during his reign is a bright page in our cultural history. His court was adorned by musicians like Vīṇa Śēshaṇṇa, Vīṇa Subbaṇṇa, Bidāram Krishṇappa, Vāsudēvāchar, etc. Because of his special interest in Vina Mysore was able to establish a tradition of Vaiṇikas with a distinct bāṇi or style of Vīṇa playing. The last among the Wōḍeyar rulers of Mysore, the late Jayachāmarāja Woḍeyar (1943-75), was a prolific composer with nearly 100 compositions to his credit.

Great indeed are the mighty kings of India who have laboured unceasingly in all the fields of our music and kept alive our vast musical heritage. Not only did they sow the seeds of a musical system which reigned supreme continuously for several centuries and propped it up with permanence both in principle and practice, but they invigorated it by absorbing and assimilating many an alien musical influence which dared to rival it. The deep-probing enquiry, the composition of theoretical treatises as well as richly varied and musico-literary patterns and the expansion of musical practice achieved during the prosperous reigns of these kings are, in magnitude and excellence, unparalleled. Most of the important compositional patterns current both in the South as well as the North viz., Kṛiti, Varṇa, Tillāna, Jāvaḷi, Pada, Khyāl, Dhrupad, Tappa, Gazal, Bhajans, etc., are largely traceable to both royal endeavour and patronage. Indian Music would not have risen to the present status of excellence but for the liberal patronage and contribution made by our Royal stalwarts. In fact we owe a debt of gratitude to these scholar-patrons for the efforts they have made in preserving and propagating the different systems of our music from the dawn of history down the present day.

(This paper was presented at the Annual Conference of the Music Academy, Madras in 1980.)

MUSICOLOGY IN TAMILNADU : A SHORT SURVEY

Throughout India it has been our stalwart kings who over the ages nurtured our music with tender care. In fact, musicial training formed an indispensable and vital item of royal education. Many were the rulers of India who were profound scholars in the theory and practice of this art. Several of them have perpetuated their names by bequeathing an imperishable legacy of scholarly musical treatises to posterity. Also nowhere else in the world has royal patronage and encouragement to music probably been as continuous and rich as in India. And Tamilnadu has been no exception to this general trend in the development of Indian music.

So far as Tamilnadu is concerned the development of musicology can be said to have flourished mainly during the epochs of three dynasties which held sway over the Tamil country during different periods. These were : (1) the Pallava rulers of Kāñchi (7th century); (ii) the Nāyak kings of Tanjore (17th century) and (iii) the Marāṭha kings of Tanjore (17th and 18th centuries). It is only in modern times (19th and 20th centuries) that individuals who did not belong to royal clans have contributed to musicology in good measure.

I. PALLAVA RULERS OF KANCHI

Indeed no country in the world has ever risen to the acme ofpre-eminence which had not art as the prime force prompting its growth and civilisation. And in the list of illustrious Tamil monarchs whose deeds have illumined the pages of India's history, there are few that have better earned a niche in the temple of fame and a place in the hearts of their countrymen through their contribution and patronage of art than Mahendravarman I, the accomplished Pallava artiste and musicologist. Like his contemporary, King Harshavardhana of Kanauj, Mahēndravarman was a man of considerable talents and rare gifts. The Kuḍumiyāmalai inscription, near Pudukkōṭṭai, stands as a fitting monument to Mahēndravarman's attainments in the field of musicology wherein he has portrayed, in a characteristic innovative manner, the notation of music as was either current in his time or was invented by him. Scholars have little hesitation in ascribing the authorship of the inscription to this Pallava king in view of the fact that the characters and formation of letters closely resemble those in other inscriptions in Tamil Nadu which are known definitely to belong to the Pallava period and contain unequivocal references to the same ruler. The Kuḍumiyāmalai inscription itself contains a colophon at the extreme right end of the bottom, which reads : '<u>Rudrāchaara sishyēṇa parama mahēśvarēṇa rajña sishyahitārthaṁ kṛitah svarāgamāḥ</u>' i.e., <u>svarāgamaḥ</u> made for the benefit of the king - a Mahēśvara and a disciplie of Rudrāchārya.

The inscription occupying a space of about 13 ft. by 14 ft. is engraved on the slope of a rock facing east behind the Sikhanāthasvāmi temple on the right side of the cave temple known as Mēlakkōvil and lies between two rock-cut Gaṇēśas (one a Valaṁpuri and the other an Idampuri). Commencing with a salutation to Lord Śiva, the inscription is arranged in 7 sections. Each section has several subsections and each subsection throughout comprises 15 sets of four svaras each. The combination of four svaras in each of the seven sections are arranged under specific headings mentioned in order as :'Madhyama grāma chatusprahāraḥ svarāgamaham, Sādhārite chatusprahāraḥ svarāgamāḥ...and so on'. It is believed by some that the seven sections in the inscription correspond to the seven classical rāgas of the time. On the other hand, there is no reference to rāga as such in the inscription. It appears more plausible that the seven sections represent not the permutations and combinations of svaras of rāgas but rather of grāmas and jātis which are some of the fundamental facets of music.

One ofthe striking features of the Kuḍumiyamalai inscription is the vowel endings of svaras - a, i, e and u. These have been construed to stand for the Ēka, Dvi, Tri and Chatus sruti of a particular śvara. Thus, for instance, Sa represents the Eka-sruti Shadja; Si, the Dvi sruti Shadja; Se, the Tristruti Shadja; Su, the Chatusruti Shadja and so on. The various sections of the inscription portray permutations and combinations of svaras of various srutis involving consequently <u>śruitibhēda</u> or modulation. Again, one can also [illegible] ts on top of some of the notes and these probably represent '<u>Aṁśa</u>', - one of the ten criteria determining the jatis.

Below the colophon of the inscription already referred to, there is the following postscript in Tamil : 'Eṭṭiṛukkuṁ ēḻiṛukkuṁ ivai uriya'. This probably refers to the fact that after trying his notes on the seven stringed Vīṇa, Mahēndravarman discovered the possibility of playing the same successfuly on the eighth string too.

From the inscription one can also infer that Mahēndravarman possessed the title Saṅkīrṇajāti. According to the late Gopinatha Rao, this might refer to the Pallava ruler being born of mixed caste. But the interesting point is that Saṅkīrṇajati is also the name of one of the five Tāḷas or time scales, now in vogue in Carnatic music, the other four being Chaturaśra, Tiśra, Miśra and Khaṇḍa. Significantly enough only the last four jātis are mentioned in the Tāḷalakshaṇa of Nandikēśvara but not Saṅkīrnajāti. It appears highly probable that being an accomplished musicologist, the Pallava ruler was also a master of laya and was responsible for inventing the new time scale, Saṅkīrṇajāti. That is the likely genesis of the epithet Saṅkīrṇajāti associated with Mahēndravarman in the Kuḍumiyāmalai inscription.

The chief contribution of Mahēndravarman in the realm of musicology is his innovation in musical notation, making it possible to depict svaras with different srutis through appropriate vowel endings. He was also the originator of the idea of śrutibhēda or modulation in Indian music as portrayed by the combination of svaras with different srutis in his Kuḍumiyāmalai inscription. Here all the notes of the octave occur consisting of the four varieties of Ri, Ga, Dha and Ni. Mahēndravarman combined one scale with another and ushered in a new chromatic scale particularly through the use of two Madhyama in conjunction. Based on the system of seven placed and five displaced notes, this paved the way for the formation of the seventytwo Mēḷas of Veṅkaṭamakhi, - another musicologist who was born and flourished in the Tamil country nearly ten centuries later.

II. NAYAK KINGS OF TANJORE

For almost ten centuries after Mahēndravarman, there was a comparative lull in the development of musicology in Tamil Nadu. However, magnum opuses in musicology like Saṅgīta Ratnākara (by Śārṅgadēva), Swaramēḷakalānidhi (by Rāmāmātya) and Bṛihaddēśi (by

Matanga) appeared in other parts of India during this period. They contained numerous references to the rāgas and _paṇṇs_ existing in the realm of Tamil music and contributed, albeit indirectly, to the development of music in the region. The revival of activity in the field of musicology in Tamil Nadu took place only at the beginning of the 17th century with the establishment of Nāyak rule at Tanjore.

The Nāyak rulers of Tanjore originally came from Andhra Pradesh and they brought with them a large number of Telugu speaking people to Tamil Nadu who were well versed in various forms of art. They evolved a colloquial form of Telugu with a large admixture of Tamil words. In spite of being 'foreigners', they made the Tamil country their home and spared no pains to develop fine arts like music, dance and drama.

Raghunātha Nāyak was the most illustrious and accomplished among the Tanjore line of Nāyak kings as well as the main prop of their fame and glory. His rule was one of tranquility and peace and witnessed the revival and development of the many sided cultural activities for which Tanjore has been justly famous through the ages. Literature and art flourished side by side and Tanjore became under him the greatest seat of learning and culture of the time in South India as well as the home of Carnatic music. It is no exaggeration that but for Raghunātha Nāyak, the history of the Tanjore Nāyaks would have remained obscure and insignificant. He richly deserved the title of Abhinava Bhōja in view of both his attainments and patronage of art.

Yakshagāna, an important form of dance-drama, had its origin during Raghunātha Nāyak's time. Raghunāth Nāyaka himself composed not less than 225 Telugu dramas and _Yakshagānas_. They formed the nucleus of the famous Tanjore palace library which was considerably improved and expanded later by the Marāṭha rulers. There was also a royal theatre which presented these dramas and _Yakshagānas_.

Among the great scholars who adorned Raghunātha Nāyak's court, special mention may be made of Gōvinda Dīkshita, his minister, and his two sons, Yagñanārāyaṇa and Veṅkaṭamakhi. A versatile minister who had also served under Raghunātha's father (Chēvappa Nāyaka) and grandfater (Achyutappa Nāyak), Gōvinda Dīkshita was mainly responsible for the peace, prosperity and cultural progress of Tanjore. He was hailed as Ayyan and this name has become immortal since many memorials such as Ayyanpēṭṭai, Ayyankuḷam, Ayyan bazar, Ayyan choultry, Ayyan street, etc., were named after him. It is said that in reality Gōvinda Dīkshitar wrote the magnum opus Saṅgīta Ṣudhā and passed on the authorship to Raghunātha Nāyak, - a view corroborated by the former's son Veṅkaṭamakhi. The more widely accepted belief, however, is that Raghunātha Nāyaka co-authored his minister, Gōvinda Dīkshita, in writing this monumental work on contemporary musicology.

The whole treatise consists of 6 chapters. In the first chapter, the origin ofsounds, śrutis, the seven svaras, 12 different svarasthānas, their family and origin, chandas, different kinds of metre, different modulations, prastāras, 63 alaṅkāras, jātis, lakshaṇas, etc., are dealt with in detail. The second chapter, Rāga Vivēka, is concerned with the gamut of Rāgas, Uparāgas, Bhāshā, Vibhāsha, Antarbhāsha, etc. In the third chapter, Prakīrṇa Adhyāya, gāyaka-guṇa-dōshas, śārīra, its good and bad qualities, gamaka, sthāyi, etc., are elaborated Thirty verses are devoted to depict a clear picture of a singer pointing out that a cultivated voice in perfect trail, with instant charm of appeal, facile execution of gamaka, and intimate knowledge of Rāgāṅga, Bhāshāṅga, Kṛiyāṅga, Upāṅga and other rāgas and connected details are the essential qualities of an ideal <u>gāyaka</u>. The fourth chapter deals with Udgraha, Mēlāpaka, Dhruva, Ābhōga, the six divisions of tāḷas, different kinds of Prabandhas, etc. The fifth and sixth chapters are concerned with tāḷas, their varieties, layas, measure of tāḷas, names of 120 tāḷas, different kinds of musical instruments, etc.

Saṅgīta Sudhā refers to Mataṅga as the pioneer in the treatment of Rāgas and mentions his thirteen elements of rāgas viz., graha, aṁśa, etc. However, in the treatment of rāgas, the authors have preferred to adopt Śāraṅgadēva's six steps for rāga-ālāpti, viz., Ākshiptika, Rāgavardhani, Vidāri, Stāyi, Vartani and Nyāsa. In fact, in writing Saṅgīta Sudhā, Raghunātha Nāyaka and Gōvinda Dīkshita seem to have derived inspiration mainly from Śārṅgadēva as is borne out by the fact that it has been planned largely on the model of Saṅgīta Ratnākara, the main difference being in the metre adopted. The other authorities whom the authors have consulted are Yashtika, Hanumān, Umāpati, Nandīśa and Vidyāraṇya.

Saṅgīta Sudhā deals with the following fifty ragas : Nāṭa, Gujjari, Saurāshṭram, Mēchabhauḷi, Chāyagauḷa, Guṇḍakṛiya, Sālaṅganāṭika, Śuddhavasanta; Nādarāmakṛiya, Gauḷa, Bhauḷi, Karṇāṭakabaṅgāḷa, Lalita, Malahari, Pāḍi, Sāvēri, Rēvagupti, Varāḷi, Śrīrāga, Sālagabhairavi, Ghanṭa, Vēlāvali, Dēvagāndhāri, Rītigauḷa, Malavasri, Madhyamavati, Dhanyasi, Bhairavi, Jayantasena, Bhinnashaḍja, Hindōḷavasanta, Hindōḷabhūpāla, Śaṅkarābharaṇa, Ārabhi, Pūrvagauḷa, Nārāyaṇi, Nārāyaṇagauḷa, Āhari, Ābhēri, Vasantabhairavi, Sāmanta, Kannaḍagauḷa, Kāmbōdhi, Mukhāri, Suddharāmakṛiya, Kēdāgarauḷa, Nārāyaṇagauḷa, Hejjuji and Dēśākshi. Among them the rāga Jayantasēna seems to be Raghunātha Nāyak's invention and a new tāḷa, Rāmānanda tāḷa was also invented by him.

Another noteworthy feature of Saṅgīta Sudhā is that it refers, for the first time, to the fretting of the Vina as is current today. Raghunātha Nāyaka is credited with the construction of a vīṇa named after him : the Raghunātha Mēḷa Vīṇa. It was undoubtedly the innovation of a master mind. Till his time the frets had been tied to the Vīṇa daṇḍi with guts.. It was Raghunātha Nāyak who for the first time hit upon the idea of fixing the frets on wax. Placed in position, they could be shifted with ease when necessary.

Thus Saṅgīta Sudhā brought classical musical traditions to a cleạrer focus with rare originality in the treatment of the subject. Its main value lies in the fact that it gives an authoritative account of the developments in contemporary music.

Veṅkaṭamakhi

Gōvinda Dīkshita's son Veṅkaṭamakhi, became minister in the court of Vijạyarāghava Nāyak who succeeded Raghunātha Nāyak to the Tanjore throne. The outstanding achievement of Veṅkaṭamakhi in the field of musicology lies in the fact that for the first time he propounded a scientific classification of the Mēḷas on the basis of their svạras. At the behest of his royal patron, Veṅkaṭamakhi wrote his magnum opus, Chathurdaṇḍi Prakāśika, which means the exposition of the 4 pillars (chathurdaṇḍi) or the four channels, through which the rāga manifests itself. Out of the 10 chapters of the treatise, the last and part of the ninth chapter have not been traced. Only 1200 couplets in Anushṭup metre have survived. The different chapters deal in detail with such topics as Vīṇa, Śruti, Svara,

Mēḷa, Rāga, Ālāpa, Ṭhāya, Gīta, Prabandha and Tāḷa. The most important portion of the treatise, however, is the one relating to the 72 Mēḷakarta schemes for deriving which Veṅkaṭamakhi is indebted to Sōmanātha, the author of Rāgavibōdha. The 72 Mēḷakarta scheme is based on the universally recognised twelve notes of the gamut. The work explains the scheme of 72 mēḷas without assigning any nomenclature for them. It was the author's grandson Muddu Veṅkaṭamakhi who assigned the nomenclature of Kanakāmbari, Phēnadyuti, etc., which came to be known as the Asampūrṇa Mēḷapaddhati. In his Saṅgrahachūḍāmaṇ, Gōvindāchārya later changed the names to Kanakāṅgi, Ratnāṅgi, etc., and this came to be known as Sampūrṇa Mēḷa Paddhati. Veṅkaṭamakhi called the 19 Mēḷakartas in vogue during his time as Kalpita Mēḷakartas. These were Mukhāri, Sāmavarāḷi, Bhūpāḷa, Hejuji, Vasanta bhairavi, Gauḷa, Bhairavi, Āhari, Śrīrāga, Kāmbōji, Śaṅkarābharaṇa, Nāṭa, Dēśākshi, Sāmanta, Suddhavarāḷi, Pantuvarāḷi, Śuddharāmakri, Siṁhārava and Kalyāṇi. They correspond respectively to the 1st, 3rd, 8th, 13th, 14th, 15th, 20th, 21st, 22nd, 28th, 29th, 30th, 35th, 36th, 39th, 45th, 51st, 58th and 65th melas in the 72 Mēḷakarta scheme. Veṅkaṭamakhi called the other 53 Mēḷas (not current in his time) as the Kalpyamāṇa and Kalpayishyamāna varieties (immediate and remote possibilities, respectively).

According to Veṅkaṭamakhi, a Mēḷa was defined as a scale of Sa Ri Ga Ma Pa Dha Ni, each note being chosen from its own category of two in the case of Ma, and three in the case of Ri, Ga, Dha and Ni. The 72 Mēḷas were arranged systematically. Half of them took Śuddha madhyama and the other half Prati madhyama. The first section was known as Pūrva mēḷas and the second as Uttara mēḷas. These two sections were divided into six equal groups of six and each group was known as chakra. The chakras are : Indu, Nētra, Agni, Vēda, Bāṇa, Ritu, Vasu, Brhma, Diśi, Rudra and Āditya. The 72 mēḷas, later named Asampūrṇa and Sampūrṇa mēḷas on the lines of the formulae enunciated by Veṅkaṭamakhi, are as follows :

PURVA-MELA WITH CHAKRA SUDDHAMADHYAMA

1	Kanakāmbari	Kanakāngi
2	Phēnadyuti	Ratnāngi
3	Gānasāmavarāli	Ganamūrti
4	Bhānumati	Vanaspati
5	Manōrañjani	Mānavati
6	Tanukīrti	Tānarūpi
7	Sinagraṇi	Sēnāvati
8	Janatōdi	Hanumatōḍi
9	Dhunibhinna shaḍja	Dhēnuka
10	Naṭābharaṇam	Nāṭakapriya
11	Kōkilārava	Kōkilapriya
12	Rūpavati	Rūpavati
13	Gēyahejjuji	Gāyakapriya
14	Vāṭīvasantabhairavi	Vakuḷābharaṇa
15	Māyāmāḷavagauḷ	Māyāmāḷavagauḷa
16	Tōyavēgavāhini	Chakravāka
17	Chhāyāvati	Sūryakāntam
18	Jayaśuddhamālini	Hāṭakāmbari
19	Jhaṅkārabhṛamari	Jhaṅkāradhvai
20	Rītigauḷa	Naṭabhairavi
21	Kiraṇāvali	Kīravāṇi
22	Śrī	Kharaharapriya
23	Gaurīvēḷāvali	Gaurīmaṇohari
24	Vīravasantha	Varuṇapriya
25	Śarāvati	Mārarañjani
26	Taraṅgini	Chārukēśi
27	Sauraśēna	Sarasāngi
28	Harikēdāragauḷ	Harikāmbōdhi
29	Dhīraśankarābharaṇa	Dhīraśankarābharaṇa
30	Nāgābharaṇa	Nāgānandini
31	Kalāvati	Yāgapriya
32	Rāgachūḍamaṇi	Rāgavardhani
33	Gaṅgātaraṅgiṇi	Gāngeyabhūshaṇi
34	Bhōgachyānāṭa	Vagadhīsvari
35	Śailadēśakshi	Śūlini
36	Chalanāṭa	Chalanāta

UTTARA-MELA WITH CHAKRA PRATIMADHYAMA

37	Saugadhini	Sālaga
38	Jaganmōhana	Jalārṇava
39	Dhāḷivarāḷi	Jhālavarāḷi
40	Nabhōmaṇi	Navanītam
41	Kumbhiṇi	Pāvani
42	Ravikṛiya	Raghupṛiya
43	Gīrvāṇi	Gavāmbōdhi
44	Śravaṇi	Bhavapṛiya
45	Śivapantuvarāḷi	Śubhapantuvarāḷi
46	Sthvarāja	Shaḍvidhamārgiṇi
47	Sauvīram	Suvarnaṅgi
48	Jīvantika	Divyamaṇi
49	Dhavalāṅgi	Dhavaḷāmbari
50	Nāmadēśi	Nāmanārāyaṇi
51	Kāśirāmakriya	Kāmavardhani
52	Ramāmanōhari	Rāmapriya
53	Gamakakṛiya	Gamanaśrama
54	Vamśavati	Viśvambari
55	Śyāmala	Śyāmalāṅgi
56	Chāmaram	Shaṇmukhapriya
57	Sumadyuti	Simhēndramadhyama
58	Dēśisimhāravam	Hēmavati
59	Dhāmavati	Dharmavati
60	Nishāda	Nītimati
61	Kuntaḷam	Kāntāmaṇi
62	Ratipṛiya	Rishabhapriya
63	Gītapriya	Latāṅgi
64	Bhūshāvati	Vāshaspati
65	Śāntakalyāṇi	Mēchakalyani
66	Chaturaṅgini	Chitrāmbari
67	Santānamañjari	Sucharitri
68	Jyōti	Jyōtisvarūpiṇi
69	Dhautapañchama	Dhātuvardhani
70	Nāsāmaṇi	Nāsikābhūshaṇi
71	Kusumākara	Kōsalam
72	Rasamañjari	Rasikapṛiya

The beauty of the names assigned the Mēlas according to the

Sampūrṇa paddhati lies in the fact that its serial number in the 72 Mēḷakartha scheme can be arrived at therefrom by applying the Kaṭapayādi system. Taking Dhīraśankarābharaṇam as example, dhi indicates the number 9 and ra, 2. By reversing these numbers, we get the figure 29, denoting that Dhīraśankarābharaṇa is the 29th Mela.

Tamil Nadu can justly be proud that one of her eminent musicologists gave to the world of music the ingeneous and unparallelled 72 mēḷakarta scheme which forms the scientific basis for the classification of rāgas. He maybe called the Paṇini of modern Carnatic Music. It is noteworthy that both Tyāgarāja and Muthuswāmi Dīkshitar adopted and followed Venkaṭamakhi's scheme in their compositions, the Sampūrṇa mēḷapaddhati and Asampūrṇa Mēḷapaddhati, respectively. To Subbarāma Dīkshitar, the most prominent modern musicologist of Tamil Nadu, goes the credit of having preserved the only original manuscript of Chaturdaṇḍi Prakāśika of Venkaṭamakhi.

III. MARĀṬHA RULERS OF TANJORE

The Maratha kings of Tanjore, who succeeded the Nāyak rulers in 1674, were no less enthusiastic and liberal patrons of art and music. The rulers of this dynasty, who contributed to the development of musicology were Shahaji, Tulajaji Ikand Serfoji II.

King Shāhaji

King Shāhaji succeeded his father Ēkōji in 1685. One can get a detailed account of his life in the Bhōsalavamśāvali of Gangādhara Vājpeyin. Shāhaji was a great patron of learning and fine arts and most of the grants of Ināms to the families of scholars in Tanjore district were his charity. He has been eulogised in scores of kāvyas and hundreds of songs which are now preserved in the Tanjore Sarasvati Mahal Library. His reign was the golden age of art, literature and philosophy in the Cauvery delta. The titles of Dakshiṇa Bhōja and Abhinava Bhōja are well-merited tributes to his extensive patronage of artistes and scholars.

In addition to being a great patron of art and learning, King Shāhaji was also a versatile man of letters and composer of

Prabandhas and Nāṭakas. In spite of the fact that his own mother tongue was Marāṭhi and that of the majority of his subjects was Tamil and most of his court poets were Sanskrit scholars, Shāhaji had a distinct preference for compositing in Telugu. However, a few of his plays are in Marāṭhiand Sanskrit and there is a lone work in Hindustani also.

Coming to Shāhaji's contribution to musicology, he has to his credit a number of both lakshya and lakshaṇa manuscripts on music which have been preserved in the Sarasvati Mahal library. With the help of his court musicians, Shāhaji collected most of the Gītas, traditional alapas etc., of almost all the rāgas current in his time and one can find these in about 20 manuscripts. In the ālāpa section, rules are laid down for the elaboration of the following 40 rāgas :

Ābhēri, Ārdradēśi, Bhauḷi, Bhinnapañchama, Chāyāgauḷa, Dīpaka, Gurjari, Gāndhārapañchama, Guṇḍakriya, Hindōḷavasantha, Hejjuji, Kannaḍabaṅgāḷa, Kannaḍagauḷa, Māḷavaśrī, Maṅgaḷakaiśika, Mēgharañjani, Māruva, Mallamāruva, Mēchabhauḷi Malla, Sālaṅganāṭa Nāgadhvani, Nārāyaṇi, Mādhavamanōhari Malla, Mādhyamāvati, Nārāyaṇagauḷa, Pūrṇapañchama, Pūrvagauḷa, Pāḍi, Rāmakriya, Rēgupti, Sāmanta, Sālaṅganāṭa, Sālagagauḷa, Sālagabhairavi, Śuddhadēśi, Suddhavasantha, Surasindhu, Ṭakka, Vēlāvali, Vasanthabhairavi.

In addition to this collection of lakshya, King Shāhaji also determined with the help of his court musicians the lakshanas of all the ragas in vogue at his time. These lakshaṇas are to be found in 10 manuscripts. In one of these lakshaṇa manuscripts, Shāhaji has assigned the Mēḷa status to 20 rāgas and he has grouped all the then current rāgas (amounting to about hundred in number) under these twenty Mēḷa rāgas. A uniformly striking feature of his lakshaṇa manuscripts is that the lakshya quotations therein are invariably made form Ālāpa, Ṭhāyaṣ, Gītas, Sūlādis and other Prabandhas.

The number of svaras mentioned in these lakshaṇa manuscripts are greater in number than those propounded by Venkaṭamakhi. Shāhaji and his musicians added four more svaras to the sixteen already in vogue, making it twenty in all. There are four Rishabhas, four Dhaivatas, four Gāndhāras, four Nishādas, two Madhymas, one Shadja and one Pañchama as shown below :

Śuddha, Chatuśruti, Pañchaśruti and Shatśruti for Rishabha and Dhaivata	4 x 2 = 8
Śuddha Shādhāraṇa, Antara and Chyutamadhyama Gāndhāra	4 x 1 = 4
Śuddha, Kaiśiki Kākali and Chyuta Shadja Nishāda	4 x 1 = 4
Shadja and Pañchama (1 each)	2 x 1 = 2
Chyuta Pañchama and Śuddha for Madhyama	2 x 1 = 2

Tulājāji I (1728-36 A.D.)

King Tulajāji I was the younger brother of King Shāhaji and King Serfōji I and succeeded the latter to the Tanjore throne. His versatality is evident from the fact that he has to his credit works on such varied subjects as medicine, astrology, mantra sastra, dharma śāstra, rāja dharma etc. not to speak of musicology. He was also a composer of padas and operas. The rāgas used in his Yakshagāna 'Śivakāmasundari Pariṇaya' are : Mallār, Saurāshṭra, Kalyāṇi, Gauri, Asāvēri, Kāpi, Brindāvani, Pahaḍi, Gummakāmbōdhi, Yerukalakāmbōdhi, Husēni, Punnāgavarāḷi, Bhairavi and Madhyamāvati.

His work on musicology 'Sangīta Sārāmṛita' consists of the following 14 chapters. The 1st chapter, Śrutiprakaraṇa, contains the genealogy of the Bōnsle family and deals with Nāda, its varieties, different sthāyis and the 22 śrutis with various quotations from Śārṅgadēva, Matanga, Viśvavasu, Tumburu, Kōhala, etc. The 2nd Chapter, Śuddhasvara prakaraṇa, is concerned with Śuddhasvara, 12 different svaras, the genesis of 22 srutis from 7 svaras, jātis and their varieties etc. The 3rd chapter, Vikṛatasvara prakaraṇa, deals with the 7 śuddha svarās in their threefold aspects of sthānas, 12 vikrita svaras, vādi, vivādi, anuvādi and samvādi and lastly the kula, jāti, varṇa, rasa, deities, metres and rasas of the seven svaras. The 4th chapter, Grāmamūrchana prakaraṇa, describes the different grāmas, their mūrchchanas and 2 kinds of Tānas. In the 5th chapter, Sādhāraṇa prakaraṇa, most of the material is taken from Sārṅgadēva but differentiation is shown for jāti and svara sādhāraṇa. The 6th chapter, Varṇālankāra prakaraṇa, defines Varṇa as Gānakṛiya; 4 kinds of varṇas and alaṅkāras with illustrations are given. The 7th chapter, jāti prakaraṇa, deals with 7 śuddha jātis and 11 vikṛita jātis; 13 characteristics elements of jātis are explained. The 8th chapter, Gītiprakaraṇa, speaks of Kapāla and kambāla gītis. The 9th chapter, Mēḷaprakaraṇa, discusses the definition, origin and development of rāgas, their classification into rāgāṅga, bhāshāṅga, kriyāṅga, etc., and the 10 lakshaṇas of a rāga. The 10th chapter, Rāgaprakaraṇa, which deals with the diverse aspects of Rāgas, is the most important and noteworthy chapter in this work. Tulajāji begins the rāga chapter with a brief description of the nature of the rāga on the authority of Bharata and Mataṅga. After ascertaining that the scales which give rise to rāgas are based only in Shaḍja grāma, he mentions the svara varieties for various rāgas. According to him the 72 mēḷas of Veṅkaṭamakhi were formulated as a matter of Prastāra and that in fact only 19 mēḷas, existed. In his opinion, among these 19 mēḷas, Śrīrāga is the foremost. The glory of sanctity associated with this rāga is traceable to its antiquity, being the offspring of Shaḍja grāma which was itself the scale of Sāmagāna. The other mēḷas are : Śudhanāṭi, Māḷavagauḷa, Vēlāvali, Varāḷi, Śuddharāmakriya, Śaṅkarābharaṇa, Kāmbhōji, Bhairavi, Mukhāri, Vēgavāhini, Sidhurāmakṛitya, Hejjuji, Sāmavarāḷi, Vasantabhairavi, Bhinnashaḍja, Dēśākshi, Chāyānāṭa, Sāraṅga. The 11th chapter, Vādyaprakaraṇa, deals with Vādyas which are classified under 4 groups viz., Taṭa, Shushira, Avanadhdha and Ghana. Details regarding varieties of Vīṇa including Śuddhamēḷa Vīṇa, its technique of play, posture etc., are given. The 12th chapter, Gītaprakaraṇa, describes Gītas and its varieties, six limbs of composition, Sūlādi gītas, Prabandhas, etc. The noteworthy feature of this chapter is that the compositions of Puṇḍarīka Viṭṭhala, Veṅkaṭamakhi and Nyāsāchārya are used as examples. A couple of gītas from Purandaradāsa are also cited including a Sūlādi. The 13th chapter, Tāḷaprakaraṇa, deals with Tāḷa, Mārga and Dēśi and its varieties, constituent aṅgas etc. About 125 Dēśi tāḷas are enumerated and defined. The 14th and last chapter, Prakīrṇaka adhyāya, discusses in detail 4 kinds of voice, Gāyaka Guṇa dōshas, classification of singers, groups of singers, etc. The following rāgas have been mentioned in the above work.

Ānandabhairavi
Āndhāḷi
Ābhēri
Ārabhi
Ārdradēśi
Āhari
Indughanṭārava
Īśamanōhari
Udayaravichandrika
Kannaḍa
Kannaḍagauḷa
Kalyāṇi
Kāphi
Kāmbōdhi
Kurañji
Kēdāra
Kēdāragauḷa
Gāndhārapañchama
Guṇḍakṛiya
Gurjari
Gauḍamallāra
Garumanōhari
Gauḷa
Gauḷipantu
Ghaṇṭārava
Ghāyāgauḷa
Rītigauḷa
Rēvagupta
Lalitapañchama
Lalita
Varāḷi
Vasanta
Vasantabhairavi
Vēgavāhini
Vēlāvaḷi
Śaṅkarābharaṇa
Śuddhadēśi
Śuddhadhanayāsi
Chāyātaraṅgiṇi
Chāyānāṭa
Jayantasēna
Julavu
Ṭakka
Tōḍi
Dīpaka
Dēvakṛiya
Dēvagāndhāra
Dēvmanōhari
Dēśākhsi
Dhanyāsi
Naṭanārāyani
Naṭagāndhāri
Nāgadhvani
Nāṭa
Nāṭakuruñji
Nādarāmakṛiya
Nārāyaṇagauḷa
Nārāyaṇadēśākshi
Nārāyaṇi
Pantuvarāḷi
Pāḍi
Pūrṇachandrika
Pūrṇapañchama
Pūrvi
Śuddhanāṭi
Śuddhasādhārita
Śuddhasāvēri
Śrīrañjani
Śrīrāga
Sarasvatīmanōhari
Sāma
Sāmanta
Sāmavarāḷi
Sāraṅga
Sāraṅganāṭi
Sālagabhairavi
Pūrvagauḷa
Phalamañjari
Balahaṁsa
Bhauḷi
Bibhāsu
Bilahari
Bhinnapañchama
Bhinnashaḍja
Bhūpāla
Bhairavi
Maṇiraṅgu
Madhyamagrāma rāga
Madhyamāvati
Malahari
Magadhi
Mādhavamanōhari
Māruva
Māḷavaśrī
Māḷavi
Mēgharañji
Mēchabhauḷi
Mukhāri
Mōhana
Mōhanakalyāṇi
Yerukulakāmbōdhi
Rāmakṛiya
Sāvēri
Sindhurāmakṛiya
Surasindhu
Saindhavi
Saurāshṭra
Hindōla
Hindōḷavasanta
Husēni
Hejjuji

The names of authors and works quoted in Saṅgīta Sārāmṛita
are ás follows :

Kallinātha, Mataṅga, Kīrtidhara, Yajnavalkya, Kóhala,
Viṭṭhala, Garbhōpanishad, Vidyāraṇya, Gōpālanāyaka,
Viśvavasu, Granthantara, Vēna, Chaturdaṇḍiprakāśika and its
author, Vyasapācharya, Tāṇappa, Sáraṅgadēva, Tamburu Sīta-
samhita, Tulajā (as composer of song), Sutasamhitavyākhyāna,
Dhanañjaya, Sōmēśvaramata, Nandin, Saubhāgyalakshmīkalpa,
Nārada, Svaramēlakalānidhi, Purandaradāsa, Svāti, Bharata.

In his Saṅgīta Sārāmṛita, King Tulajāji has spared no pains
to incorporate the lakshaṇas of all the rāgas as they prevailed at
his time along with sancharis and appropriate Thāya, Gīta, Prabandha
and Sūlādi as supporting evidence. The chief value of Shāhaji's
lakshaṇa and lakshya manuscripts together with the Saṅgītasārāmṛita
of Tulajāji lies in the fact that they help us in obtaining a clear
picture of the state of Carnatic music in Tamil Nadu during the era
immediately preceeding that of the Trinity (Tyāgarāja, Muthuswāmi
Dīkshitar and Śyāma Sāstri) and judging how far, if at all, any
departure was made by the Trinity and their contemporaries from the
tradition as handed down from this period.

King Serfōji II

King Serfōji II succeeded Tulajāji II to the Tanjore throne
in 1798. His reign coincided with the golden age of Carnatic music
in .Tamilnadu as he was the contemporary of the Trinity. Besides
being a great patron of musicians, Serfoji was also a composer. His
'Kāvyache sāhityache Jinna' is a vast collection of dance pieces in
Marathi. He has also written a book in Marathi on Rāgas and
Rāgiṇis.

Serfōji is to be remembered chiefly as the architect of the
Tanjore band. He was a multilinguist and contemporary records show
that he was a scholar in English, French and German in addition to
various Indian languages. He is also credited with the ability to
compose tunes based on Western music. Indian rāgas and tunes set to
European Staff notation are to be found in many of his music books.
He trained a band with instruments brought from Europe and his

orchestra consisted of several native and western instruments richly ornamented with pearls and diamonds. This combined orchestra became popular and famous as the Tanjore Band.

Serfōji's minister Varahappier, who was also the main Vīna player in the Tanjore Band, became deeply interested in the violin when he took his Band to Madras to play before the Governor. With the Governor's help, he learnt the technique of violin play from competent English violinists and adopted it to playing Indian melodies. To Varahappier, along with Bālusvāmi Dīkshitar, the younger brother of Muthuswāmi Dīkshitar, goes the credit of introducing the violin into the realm of Indian music.

To Serfōji also goes the credit of building up the Tanjore Sarasvati Mahal Library. While returning from a pilgrimage to North India, he brought with him quite a large number of rare and valuable old manuscripts on music and had fair copies made of them by a host of Pandits. Serfōji was thus responsible for adding the single largest collection of manuscripts to the library for proper care and preservation. As a fitting tribute to this great patron and scholar, the library has been named after Serfoji.

IV. MODERN MUSICOLOGISTS OF TAMILNADU

To the modern musicologists of Tamil Nadu we owe a deep debt of gratitude, for, but for their labours of love, the continuity in our musical tradition would have been seriously impaired and the renaissance in our art would have suffered both in quality and substance.

These modern musicologists can be considered in two groups : those whose contributions covered the 19th century and the first decade of this century and others who belonged to the 20th century. To the former group belong Subbarāma Dīkshitar, Chinnaswāmi Mudaliār and Abrahām Paṇḍitar. Among the musicologists of more recent times, mention may be made of Gāyakaśikhāmaṇi Muthiāh Bhāgavatar and Prof. P. Sambamoorthi.

Subbarāma Dīkshitar

Subbarāma Dīkshitar was the most accomplished among the modern musicologists of Tamilnadu. He belonged to the lineage of

Muthuswāmi Dīkshitar who was his maternal grandfather. Subbarāma Dīkshitar was born in 1839 at Tiruvārūr. He was a person of considerable energy and varied talents. On the purely literary side stands to his credit his translation into Tamil of the Telugu Mahābhārata. He has also composed several songs in Sanskrit and Telugu.

It was at the insistance and constant prompting of his close friend. A.M. Chinnaswāmi Mudaliār, Superintendent at the Madras Secretariat, that Subbrāma Dīkshitar wrote his magnum opus in musicology, entitled Saṅgīta Sampradāya Pradarshini. Chinnaswāmi Mudaliār was also instrumental in successfully persuading Jagadvīra Rāma Veṅkaṭēśvara Eḍḍappa, the Raja of Ettayāpuram, to meet the cost of printing the work.

Saṅgīta Sampradāya Pradarśini appeared in 1904 in two parts running to 1700 pages. It comprises 76 biographies of personages famous in the history of Carnatic music beginning with Śārṅgadēva. Two sections are devoted to the science of music. The work contains an exhaustive tabular statement of Rāgas, Rāgāṅgas, Bhāshāṅgas, and Upāṅgas with their mūrchchanas. There is also a detailed descriptive guide in Tamil and Telugu to the Gamaka and Tāḷa signs employed in the book. The main text of the work gives 72 Mēḷas and all their Janyas together with their Rāga lakshaṇas, relevant lakshana gītas and illustrative pieces selected mainly from the composition of Muthuswāmi Dīkshitar, Tyāgarāja, Śyāma Śāstri, etc.

The detailed explanation of the distinguishing characteristics of each raga and the delineation of the special notes of phrases together with elaborate sancharis under each raga bear eloquent testimony to Subbarāma Dīkshitar's erudition and all round knowledge of music and musicology. The chief value of Saṅgīta Sampradāya Pradarśini lies in preserving in an authentic and systematic manner the vast knowledge in the field, accumulated during the golden age of Carnatic music. It is an encyclopeadic storehouse of musical lore and has become a valuable reference book for the present day musicians and musicologists.

Chinnaswāmi Mudaliār

Reference has already been made to the role of A.M.

Chinnaswāmi Mudaliār in the publication of Saṅgīta Sampradāya Pradarsini. Mudaliār's greatest contribution to musicology, however, was the introduction of western musical notation into the realm of Carnatic music. He was the pioneer in showing the possibility of writing Carnatic music compositions in Western musical notation. Mudaliar obtained the authentic vernamettus of a large number of songs from the disciples of Tyāgarāja and other composers, had them written in staff notation and checked the scripts with the aid of violinists trained in Western music who were asked to play them by sight. These songs in Western notation were first published serially in 10 issues of the Journal, 'Oriental Music', which had a wide circulation among readers interested in Music. In 1895, these were published together in the form of a book containing 800 compositions of the Trinity as well as various other composers such as Mārgadarsi Sēshayyaṅgār, Swāti Tirunāḷ Mahārāja, Mysore Sadāsiva Rao, Paṭnam Subramaṇya Iyer, Vīṇa Kuppayyar etc., in staff notation. In addition to clear cut instructions regarding the use of the signs and symbols of Western music as applied to Carnatic music, the book also contains an 'elaborate account of the fundamental aspects of Western music. Chinnaswāmy Mudaliār was the architect of the gigantic project of presenting oriental or Carnatic music in European staff notation. The importance of his work lies in the fact that it has helped to spread Carnatic music in the west.

Abraham Panditar

Abrahām Paṇḍitar was an authority on Tamil music. His book 'Karṇāmṛuta Sāgaram', which was first published in 1912, deals with various facets of Tamil music. This book in two volumes dealing respectively with the theoretical and practical aspects. Abrahām Paṇḍitar was also the chief organiser of the First All India Music Conference held at Baroda in 1912. The deliberations of this Conference have been reported in detail in the Karṇāmṛuta Sāgaram.

Dr. Muthiāh Bhāgavatar

Gāyakaśikhāmaṇi Dr. Muthiāh Bhāgavatar was a musician, Harikathā performer, musicologist and music composer, rolled into one. His dominent role in the discussions on the science of music at the Annual Conferences of the Madras Music Academy bear eloquent testimony to his deep erudition in musicology. He has also written a book on musicology entitled 'Saṅgīta Kalpadrumam'. As a composer, his greatest contribution is the large number of songs in new rāgas. He was steeped in the rules relating to harmony and consonant notes (Vādi and Saṁvādi) and had a genius for inventing new melodies. Rāgas like Haṁsānandi, Mōhanakalyāṇi, Valaji, Gauḍamallār, Vijayanāgari etc., which have become popular on the concert stage, are largely the result of his endeavours.

Prof. P. Sambamoorthy

Prof. P. Sambamorthy, the first Head of the Department of Music of the Madras University, was the pioneer in musical pedagogy. He was chiefly instrumental for the introduction of music in the curricula of schools and colleges in Tamil Nadu. Prof. Sambamorthy has written text books on music of varying standards to suit students from the elementary classes to the Post-graduate level. Among his numerous publications, his Dictionary of Music deserves special mention. This encyclopeadic work gives the meanings of different terms used in the field.

Thus, from the earliest times down to the present day, the contributions of the musicologists of Tamilnadu have been considerable. The Kuḍumiyāmalai inscription stands as a monument in stone to Mahēndravarman's musicological genius. It was again another son of Tamil Nadu, Veṅkaṭamakhi, who gave to the world of music the scientific system of rāga classification based on 72 Mēlas in his Chaturdaṇḍi Prakāsika. Tamil Nadu can also boast of other magnum opuses in the field of musicology like Saṅgīta Sudhā, Saṅgīta Sārāmrita, Saṅgīta Sampradāya Pradarsini and Karnāmruta Sāgaram. We owe to the musicologists of Tamil Nadu certain innovations like playing on the Vīṇa with a fixed fret, introduction of the Western instrument, violin, which has currently become the foremost accompaniment on the concert stage and use of the western Staff notation in thefield of Carnatic music which has helped to popularise oriental musical forms in the West. In short, the achievement of Tamil Nadu in musicology compares most favourably with that of other states - Andhra Pradesh, Karnataka and Kerala - where also Carnatic music flourishes but the language is different.

This paper was presented at the International Conference of Institute of Tamil Studies, Madras, 1980.

ORIGIN AND DEVELOPMENT OF TŌḌI RĀGA

Kalita vipan̄chi vipinē
lalita hariṇā ruṇāmbara hariṇi
dhavalāṅga rāga rachanā
mṛidu vachanā bhūshita tōḍi

This is Sōmanātha's Dhyāna śloka for Tōḍi Rāga, according to which Tōḍi Rāga dēvatha is to be contemplated in the form of a young lovely damsel of green colour bewitchingly decorated with the most attractive ornaments. Wearing golden yellow dress, She is surrounded by deers. As the rāga is to be performed usually at midday, the Rāgini picture shows a nymph standing in an open landscape in the brilliant sun clothed in a snow white saree perfumed with camphor. In her hands she holds a Viṇa. As the musician sings or plays Tōḍi, he is required to conjure up before the audience the scene of this picture.

Tōḍi rāga presumably derives its name from the tune originally belonging to the Tōḍa people who are of non-Aryan origin and still survive in some parts of Chōṭṭa Nāgpur and the Nīlgiris. Its name changed to Tōḍika during the period preceeding the Mohammedan invasion of India, but became Tōḍi again under the Muslim rule. Amīr Khusru the court musician of Alaudin Khilji (13th cent.) made a very interesting innovation in introducing a number of melodies by crossing Indian rāgas with Persian airs and one such was Turushka Tōḍi.

There is no doubt that Tōḍi rāga is of very ancient origin. It corresponds to the Phrygian mode of Greek music. It finds mention in the musical texts ascribed to Brahma, Bharata and Hanumān - all prior to the dawn of the Christian era. In different musical treatises, Tōḍi rāga is referred to under diverse names such as Tōḍi, Turushka Tōḍi, Tōḍika, Chāyā Tōḍi, etc. Shaḍja Grāma roughly corresponds to modern Kharaharapriya which in mūrchchana represents Tōḍi. In Bharata's Nāṭyaśāstra, Tōḍi is considered as a Śuddha Rāga. However there is no mention at all of this rāga in Mataṅga's Brihaddēśi or Tulajā's Saṅgīta Sārāmṛita. In most early works Tōḍi is invariably given the status of a janya rāga, being regarded variously as a derivative of Pañchama, Kannaḍagaula, Dipika, Vasantha, etc. According to Saṅgīta Makaranda by Nārada it was called Troti under the Mēḷa Pañchama. Rāmāmātya's Svaramēḷakalānidhi refers to this rāga as Turushka Tōḍi and puts it under the Mēḷa Kannaḍagauḷa. According to Rāgamāla by Mēshakarṇa Tōḍi is a Sthree rāga (feminine) and a janya under the Mēḷa Dīpaka. Puṇḍarīka Viṭṭhala also regards Tōḍi as a Sthree rāga but under the Mēḷa Hindōḷa. Nārada's Pañcha Saṁhita puts Tōḍi under the Mēḷa Vasantha and so does Dāmōdara Miśra. Pārśvadēva, the author of Saṅgīta Samaya Sāra, was the first to refer to Tōḍi as a Sampūrṇa rāga in his scheme of 20 Rāgāngas. He also mentions about the great popularity of Tōḍi during his time as a rāga capable of evoking the emotion of joy. Tōḍi finds mention as a Mēḷa rāga for the first time in Lōchana's Rāga Taraṅgiṇi forming the 2nd Mēḷa in his scheme. Bhāvabhaṭṭa too assigns to Tōḍi the Mēḷa status and this view is shared by Sōmanātha in his Rāgavibōdha. In fact the description of this Rāga as found in Rāgavibōdha closely corresponds to the lakshaṇa and lakshya of the present day Tōḍi rāga. The Tōḍi kritis of the Musical Trinity are based on the characteristic of this raga as expounded in Rāga Vibōdha and Saṅgrahachūḍāmaṇi. Although the idea underlying the present system of 72 Mēḷakartas was suggested by Venkaṭamakhi according to his Asampūrṇa Mēḷapaddhati, he propounded only 19 Mēḷas in the first instance among which Tōḍi does not find a place. When his grandson Muddu Veṅkaṭamakhi enlarged and perfected this system, it was included as the 8th Mēḷa under the name Janatōḍi. In the Sampurna Mēḷapaddhati formulated by Gōvindāchārya, too, Tōḍi forms the 8th Mēḷa but under the title Hanumatōḍi. In Tamil music, Tōḍi corresponds to Vilarippālai.

A very interesting anecdote concerned with Tōḍi raga relates to a musician at King Serfoji's court in Tanjore known as Tōḍi Sītārāmayya so called because of his incomparable exposition of this Rāga. When the musician ran into financial difficulties, he could obtain a loan from the money lender only by pledging his favourite rāga on condition that until the debt was discharged, he should not sing Tōḍi before anyone. When the King came to know of this, he was amused by the cuteness of the money lender and he not only paid up the loan on Sitarāmayya's behalf, but also rewarded the money lender for his sense of musical values.

Thus we can see that Tōḍi has undergone many vicissitudes from the earliest times to the present day. It does not seem to have been handled by Jayadēva (12th century) and the Taḷḷapākkam Composers (15th century), Kshētragña (16th century) has used it rather sparingly compared to many other rāgas. Tōḍi attained its maximum popularity at the time of the Trinity, i.e. Saint Tyāgarāja, Muthuswāmi Dīkshitar and Śyāma Sāstri (18th century). Tyāgarāja has composed 31 songs in this rāga - which is more than his songs in any other rāga. One of Tyāgarāja's song in Tōḍi, 'Kōṭinadulu' is interesting from the standpoint if the aptness of the use of this rāga for the kṛiti. In his Ārabhi song 'Nādasudhā' there ocurs the phrase 'Vararāgamu Kōdaṇḍamu' by which Tyāgarāja compares the system of superior rāgas or rakti rāgas to Rāma's bow. Though Tyāgarāja accepts the scheme of 72 mēḷas, he speaks of only vara rāgas, as forming the Kodaṇḍa. The first or earliest rāga in that system or the lowest in the arrangement with all Kōmaḷa swaras should be Tōḍi. When Rāma struck the earth with his bow, the end of the bow must be the lower end. Tōḍi is therefore the significant or appropriate rāga for referring to Dhanushkōṭi or the bow's end.

An important feature of Tyāgarāja's songs in Tōḍi is that each gives a picture of different facets of the rāga with Eḍuppu in different swaras. Thus

'Āragimpavē'	Rūpakam	Starts in	Madhya	Stāyi	Shaḍja
'Vāridhi nīku'	M. Chāpu	,,	,,	,,	Rishabha
'Karuṇa jūda'	Ādi	,,	,,	,,	Gāndhāra
'Kaddanuvāriki'	Ādi	,,	,,	,,	Madhyama
'Jēsinadalla'	Ādi	,,	,,	,,	Pañchama
'Dāchukōvalena'	M. Jhampa	,	,,	,,	Dhaivata
'Koluvamara-gada'	Ādi	,,	,,	,,	Nishāda
'Tappi pṛadiki'	Rūpaka	,,	Tāra	,,	Shaḍja

Like Tyāgarāja, Muthuswāmi Dīkshitar too has composed a number of kṛitis in Tōḍi rāga, though not so extensively. In the case of Dīkshitar's songs also, each has a different Eḍuppu in different swaras. Thus :

'Vēdaraṇyēśvara'	Ādi	starts in	Tāra	Stāyi	Shaḍja
'Śrī Subrahmaṇyō'	Ādi	,,	Madhya	,,	Gāndhāra

'Mahāgaṇapatim'	Rūpaka	starts in	Madhya Sthāyi	Madhyama
'Pālayamām'	Rūpaka	,,	,, ,,	Pañchama
'Dākshāyaṇi'	Rūpaka	,,	Mandra ,,	Dhaivata
'Rāmachandrāya'	M.Chāpu	,,	Madhya ,,	Dhaivata
'Kamalāmbike'	Tiśra Ēka	,,	,, ,,	Nishāda

Śyāma Śāstri has composed only two songs in Tōḍi rāga.

'Ninnē Nammi nānu'	M.Chāpu	starts in	Madhya Sthāyi	Pañchama
'Karuṇā nidhi'	Ādi	,,	,, ,,	Shadja

Swāti Tirunāḷ has composed 7 songs in Tōḍi. Three of these viz., 'Bhārati Māmava' (Navarātri kṛiti), 'Mandharadhara' and 'Sāmōdam' start in Tāra Sthāyi Shaḍja while the rest viz., 'Dēva Dēva mām', 'Pankajāksha' 'Sarasijanābha' and 'Śrī Rāmachandra' start in Madhya Sthāyi Shaḍja.

At present Todi takes the notes of :

Shaḍja	Śuddha Ṛishabha	Sādhāraṇa Gāndhāra	Śuddha Madhyama	Pañchama	Śuddha Dhaivata
256*	273*	303*	341*	384*	409*

Kaiśiki Nishāda
455*

(* vibrational values)

These vibrations have been derived by observations on the Sonometer. This rāga takes except for Shaḍja and Pañchama, which are immutable notes on the scale which are all flat.

Through the process of Śruti Bhēda, Tōḍi gives rise to the following rāgas if all the 6 notes are taken for Graha Bhēda.

Ṛishabha	-	Kalyāṇi mēḷa
Gāndhāra	-	Harikāmbōdhi
Madhyama	-	Naṭabhairavi
Pañchama	-	Śuddha bhavāni with both Madhyama
Dhaivata	-	Śankarābharaṇa
Nishāda	-	Kharaharapriya

Thus Tōḍi rāga can be rightly called a Sarva Svara Mūrchchanākāraka Mēla rāga.

If only 5 notes (leaving Shaḍja and Pañchama) are taken for śruti bhēda, we get the following ragas :

Ri-Ga-Ma-Da-Ni-Ri	Mōhana
Ga-Ma-Da-Ni-Ri-Ga	Madhyamāvati
Ma-Da-Ni-Ri-Ga-Ma	Hindōḷam
Da-Ni-Ri-Ga-Ma-Da	Śuddhasāvēri
Ni-Ri-Ga-Ma-Da-Ni	Suddha dhanyāsi

Tōḍi is one of the Ghana rāgas which gives unlimited scope not only for extensive rāga ālāpana and Tāna, butalso for niraval and as such it is one of the favourite rāgas for the exposition of Pallavi. The following are highly apt passages for niraval in different compositions.

(A) Tyāgarāja's Compositions

"Tambūrā chēkoni guṇamula cheluvandha pāḍuchu" in Koluvamaragada.

"Sāramaina Divyānnamu shaḍrasayuta bhakshaṇamulu" in Āragimpavē.

"Āśa kannēṭri nannēla inchuṭakamunu" in Jēsinadalla

"Nēmamuna paricharya nērpuṇa pogaḍuvela" in Dāchukovalēna

(B) Muthuswāmi Dīkshitar's Compositions

"Śaṅka chakra gadā padma vana mālam" in Śrī Krishṇam Bhaja

"Bālachandra sēkhari bālā paramēśvarī" in Pālayamām

"Dīksha santhushṭa manase dhīravana hasta sarasē" in Dākshāyaṇi.

(C) Śyāma Sāstri's Compositions

"Kāmākshi kañchadaḷāyatākshi" in Ninnē namminānu

"Dēvi kōmaḷa mṛidu bhāshiṇi" in Karuṇānidhi.

Tōḍi is a highly versatile rāga all pervading in its scope

and as such we meet with almost all types of compositions in this rāga. The following are examples :

1. Ādi tāla varṇa : 'Ēṟā nāpai' by Paṭnam Subramaṇya Iyer
2. Aṭa tāla varṇa : 'Nā mīdha dayayuñchi' by Poinniāh Piḷḷai
3. Pada varṇa : 'Dānike tagunā' by Ponniah Pilai
4. Jatiswara : by Swāti Tirunāl
5. Swarajati : 'Rāvé Himagirikumāri' by Ṣýāma Sástri
6. Dēvarnama : 'Ēnu danyuḍō' by Purandaradāsa
7. Tarañgam : 'Jāne Bhuvana srushṭi' by Nārāyaṇa Tīrtha
8. Padam : 'Kanna nīvu' by Kshetragña
9. Jāvaḷi : 'Balumiyāla bālāmaṇi' by Paṭṭābhi-rāmayya
10. Tillāna : by Rāmanāthapuram Śrīnivāsa Iyengār

Thus Tōḍi rāga has been one of the earliest rāgas to be found in practice and also mentioned in treatise written on Music. That Tyāgarāja alone has composed more than thirty compositions in this rāga shows the popularity Tōḍi rāga had attained in those times. At present there are more than 300 compositions in this rāga.

A NEW THEORY OF KUḌUMIYĀMALAI INSCRIPTION IN MUSIC

Among the musical inscriptions the two most important are the Arichalūr and the Kuḍumiyāmalai Inscriptions. The former one is in the village of Arichchalūr near Erōḍe in Tamilnadu, which has tāḷa mnemonics in Brāhmi script set to archaic Tamiḷ language belonging to 3rd century A.D. The latter has gained considerable importance and popularity.

Kuḍumiyāmalai, literally means the hill of the Lord who has the tuft. It is the site of Śikhānāthaswāmi temple near Mēlaikkōvil in the Pudukōṭṭai state in Tamilnadu. This inscription engraved on the rock slope of the hill behind the Śikhānāthaswāmi temple was discovered by archaeologists in 1904. The earlier impression that the Kuḍumiyāmalai inscription belonged to the Pallava period and the author was Mahēndravarman is doubtful now. Here we have tried to evolve a new theory as to its period, date, authorship, technique of approach, format etc. Since the characters of the Brāhmi and Grantha script in the inscription agree with those of the period of Pāṇḍyas also, the inscription is presumably a later one belonging to the late Pallava or early Pāṇḍya period.

The characteristic short label read in 'Parivādini' is found in more than one cave temple besides Kuḍimiyāmalai i.e. at Tirumayyaṁ, Malaikkōvil, Satyagīrīśwara temple and the Gōkarṇēśvara temple at Tirugōkarṇaṁ. The Tirumayyam temple which also once consisted of a series of music records like that of the Kuḍimiyāmalai but they have now been oboliterated and replaced with another irrelevant record. But still there are stray inscribings showing words like Ṛishabha, Gāndhāra etc. It is probable that the Malaikkōvil and Tirugōkarṇam cave temples too had similar sets of musical records of the same format which were lost in the blasting away of the rock. This opinion is put forward by many archaeologists including Sri K.R. Srinivasan.

The Tamil colophon at the end of the Kuḍimiyāmalai inscription is read as 'eṭṭiṛkkum ēḻiṛukkuṁ ivai iriya' by many scholars. But in fact it should be 'Pāṭṭiṛkkuṁ Yāzhiṛukkum ivai uriya'. It would also appear that the Tirumayyam record though meant to be practiced on the Parivādini would lend itself to the two branches of music, i.e. vocal and instrumental. In the light of this, it would certainly appear that the colophon should be read as above and not as 'eṭṭiṛukkum ezhiṛukkum ivai uriya' meaning common for 8th and 7th notes. While the label Parivādini connects all the above temples, they reveal differences in their architectural mode. In this they show characteristics of non-Pallava tending to Pāṇḍyan affinities. The cave cell type and particularly the Kuḍumiyāmalai facade pillars are not found in any other cave temples of the Mahēndravarman period or Pallava style.

Besides the sculpture pointing to a style other than the Pallava, it is known that the Pallava authority of rule did not extend to the Kāvēri till the time of Nandivarman II i.e., a century later. Hence the inscription under reference belongs to the late Pallavas and early Pāṇḍyas.

As scholars have pointed out, the iconographic contents would indicate a later date than Mahēndravarman, for example, the liṅga and the liṅga pīṭha. Another noteworthy feature would be the prescence of Gaṇēśa sculpture in the maṇḍapa as in Tirugōkarṇa and in the Kuḍimiyāmalai cave temple, the presence of Gaṇēśa being a regular feature in many other cave temples of undoubted Pāṇḍya origin and apparently the Kuḍumiyamālai inscription antedates Pallavas. Nowhere a Gaṇēśa is found in the works of any Pallava structure or temple.

The eastern cave temple in Malaikkōvil with the musical label and the lines mentioning Guṇasēna is found in an Pāṇḍyan inscriptions of 1220 A.D. (vide Pudukkōṭṭai inscriptions No. 246 of 50th year of Jātavarman Kulaśēkhara I) as the temple of Śrīvara indicates more affiliation to the Pāṇḍyas. All these facts taken together wouldindicate that these five cave temples including the Kuḍumiyamālai would be of Pāṇḍyan affiliation excavated between 710 to 800 A.D.

There are other external evidences like the sculpture of Saptasvaramūrthi belonging to the same period (early 8th century). This sculpture is at present exhibited at the Prince of Wales Museum at Bombay. Here Lord Śiva is depicted as the lord of the seven notes or modes with Gaṇēśa accompanying Him with the Yazh and the Parivādini. Since the Kuḍumiyāmalai inscription has seven sections for 7 different modes or rāgas, these seven mūrtis also correspond to represent these seven modes. The label Parivādini in the inscription is also represented in this piece or work, wherein a Gaṇa plays on the Parivādini instrument. Since Parivādni is the main communicative instrument, the sculpture under reference also indicates Lord Śiva singing the seven sections of the Kuḍumiyāmalai inscription to the accompaniment of Parivādini.

This inscription does indicate the possibilities of a compositional format. This is so because no author before or after this particular inscriptional work has attempted to use all the varieties of the seven notes of the 22 śrutis in the same composition. Scholars' opinions that this text was meant to teach students of music in Vīṇa or the text has short phrases of many rāgas combined in different phrases of the same section have little value now under the present circumstances because any one string instrument cannot produce four kinds of Shaḍja and Pañchama simultaneously in the same string.

Grāmas in Kuḍumiyāmalai Inscription

Just as Madhyamagrāma is obtained in a particular mūrchchana of Shaḍja grāma can be obtained in that Mūrchchana of Madhyama grāma where Dhaivata is lowered by two Śrutis and is given the place of Gāndhāra. Thus Grāma and mūrchchana are interchangeable terms in the sense that one grāma is nothing else but a particular mūrchchana of the other. This is the main theme of the Kuḍumiyāmalai inscription.

The tradition of tuning the main string of the Vīṇa in madhyama svara has been handed down to us from early times. Thus the svara Shaḍja is obtained on the 7th fret when madhyama is located on the main string. This shaḍja is the madhyama of Shaḍja grāma which has been described by Bharata also. When this madhyama of Shaḍja grāma is taken as the starting note - in other words, when the mūrchchana of Shaḍja grāma is constructed - the Harikāmbōdhi scale is obtained. Thus in developing this inscription into a compositional format, this principle is followed.

In Śilappadikāram, and its commentaries, we find description of Tamil musical scales. The main scale when calculated to Śruti intervals is the Sempālai which is the equivalent of the modern Harikāmbōdhi or madhyama grāma. The Sempālai was the fundamental scale and other scales were derived by the model shift of tonic as stated earlier. Taking the Pañchama of the Sempālai as Shaḍja, the scale Arumpālai is produced which is the Kharaharapriya or Shaḍja grāma. It is also reasonable to suppose that along with the Shaḍja grāma, the seven letters, SA, Ri, Ga, Ma, Pa, Dha and Ni were also adopted in the music of the South. The usage of these syllables is followed for the first time in the Kuḍumiyāmalai inscription. These points have been corroborated by Dr. S. Rāmanāthan through his several writings.

Regarding the rāgas in Kuḍumiyāmalai, as Bharata points out, earlier the terms Gāna and Jāti denote rāgas. Mataṅga later interprets these Gāna and Jāti as Rāgagītis meaning seven rāgas. Among them one variety is Bhinna out of which the five mūrchchanas or rāgas in the Kuḍumiyāmalai are denoted. These five rāgas or rāga-gītis differ in their form and value due to the different setting of tones and microtones. The Kuḍumiyāmalai inscription represents two Grāma rāgas and five rāga-gītis, in other words, two Mēḷakartas and five janya rāgas.

Technique of Kuḍumiyāmalai Inscription

It is worthy to mention that the two Grāmas or the first two sections are assigned the names Madhyama Grāma and Shaḍja Grāma consisting of seven notes. The next five sections have different names like Shāḍavē, Shādhārite, Pañchame, Kaiśika madhyamē and Kaiśikē. They all have less than seven notes and they are janya rāgas or rāga-gītis. But, it is noteworthy that all these five janya rāgas have the Antara and Kākali varieties of Gāndhāra and Nishāda notes. These mēḷa ragas and janya rāgas correspond as follows :

1. Madhyama Grāma - Harikāmbōdhi Mēla - m p d n s r g m
   m g r s n d p m

2. Shaḍja Grāma - Kharaharapriya Mēla - s r g m p d n s
   s n d p m g r s

(Pañchama Mūrchchana of madhyama grāma, Pa being the next note in the ascending scale).

3. Shāḍave - Madhūlika rāga - s r m p d n s

s n d p m r s

(Ṛishabha mūrchchana will be Naṭabhairavi and Shāḍava is a janya rāga of this mēḷa).

4. Kaiśki Madhyama - s r m p d s

s d p m r s

(Dhaivata mūrchchana will be Tōḍi and this is a janya of Tōḍi mēḷa with prati madhyama).

5. Pañchamē - Padmini rāga - s r m p d n s

s n d p m r s

(Shaḍja mūrchana will be Harikāmbōdhi and Pañchama is a janya rāga of this mēḷa).

6. Kaiśiki - Karṇāṭaka Suddhasāvēri - S r m p d s

S d p m r s

(Gāndhāra mūrchchana will be a janya of tōdi raga with the first use of two madhyamas simultaneously)

7. Sādhārita - Vandanadhāriṇi - S r m p d s

S d p m r s

(Nishāda mūrchchana will be Kalyāṇi and is a janya rāga of of this mēḷa).

The presence of Antara and Kākali i.e. Antara Gāndhāra and Kākāli nishāda can be noted only in Janya rāgas and not in mēḷa rāga. This definitely means that the usage of Antara and Kākali occuring in only jānya ragas are foreign or Bhāshānga swaras to them. The Antara and Kākali varieties have only three vowels and the conspicuous absence of 'I' for antara and 'ki' for Kākali is noticeable. If we again notice the text of the Kuḍumiyāmalai inscription, use of these foreign notes is rare and not frequent. This has also evolved the possibility of Bhāshānga rāgas.

Another noteworthy feature in the inscription is that each ākshiptika in each section end with the same notes and different ākshiptika with different notes. For example in the Shaḍja grāma section the first ākshiptika ends with the note Sa and the seven ākshiptikas end with the notes Sa Ri Ga Pa Dha Ni and Ma respectively. The main thrust of the inscription is on its vowels and dots. Certainly the vowels are not different varieties of the same swara, but indicate the different tāḷa or rhythmic measures, because it is totally impossible to render the four varieties of Shaḍja, Ṛishabha, etc, in the same grāma or rāgas especially the Shaḍja Pañchama. Here we have assigned the following time measures or tāḷa aksharas to the four vowels.

the vowel Ā indicates 1 aksharakala
the vowel Ī indicates 2 aksharakala
the vowel Ū indicates 3 aksharakala
the vowel Ē indicates 4 aksharakala.

Another reason for assigning different aksharakālas to the four varieties of seven notes are because no musicologist would deliberately compose all the varieties of the same note in the same phrase - that too in the same ākshiptika. There are totally 2378 notes in the inscription out of which 729 are dotted ones. It is a rule that the octave should be indicated both at the top and bottom of the swara. Here the dots are represented by only on the top of the svaras and not below them.

The dots above each note indicate the presence or occurance of sāhitya or text for the inscription. But it is unfortunate that the text has not yet been identified and traced so far. It is for the scholar musicians and for the scholar musicians and musicologists to arrive at a definite conclusion on the basis of the aforesaid interpretations.

This paper was presented at the Annual Conference of the Music Academy, Madras in 1983.

INSCRIPTIONS ON MUSIC IN TAMILNADU

Authentic chronicled history of India begins with the rule of Mauryan dynasty in the north and of the Chēras, Pāṇdyas and Chōḷas in the South. There is no gainsaying the fact that royal interest in literature and the fine arts including music was evident even at the time of the Mauryas (325-188 B.C.) and continued during the reign of the Suṅga dynasty (188-76 B.C.) and the Kaṇva dynasty (76-31 B.C.). However, sustained encouragement and patronage to music can be said to have commenced only with the rulers of the Guptā dynasty. Chandragupta I (320-330 A.D.) and Chandragupta II (375-413 A.D.) deserve particular mention in this context. The latter was better known as Vikramāditya and it was in his court that renowned poets like Kāḷidāsa and Aśvagōsha flourished.

The Pallava rulers of Kāñchi, Mahēndravarman I and Narasiṁhavarman (7th century), were also great patrons of music and dance. The former's name is associated with the famous Kuḍumiyāmalai Inscription (600-625 A.D.) concerned with the evolution of musical notation. In the list of ilustrious Tamiḷ monarchs whose deeds have illuminated the pages of India's musical history, there are few that have better earned a niche in the temple of fame and a place in the hearts of their country men through their contribution to art than Mahēndravarman I, the accomplished musician and musicologist. His inscription stands as a fitting monument to his attainments in the field of musicology wherein he has portrayed, in a characteristic manner, the notation of music as was neither current in his time or was invented by him. Since many scholars have delved deep into the significance of this inscription we may refrain from any further discussion of this subject.

To reveal the art history of music further, art forms like inscription, painting, sculptures, frescos etc., are being consulted during the last few decades. In this paper we shall attempt to bring to light some of the inscriptions found in Tamil nadu and a few in the adjoining states, with themes relating to music and musicians.

Many Chōḷa kings whose reign extended over the 11th and 12th centuries encouraged and nourished musicians and other artistes in diverse ways including munificent gifts of lands (in some cases even whole villages) as evident from numerous inscriptions and edicts ascribed to this period. Special mention needs to be made in this context of Rājarāja I, Rājēndra I, Rājādhirāja I, Rājēndra II, Rājēndra III and Rājarāja III.

Before we discuss the inscription, it would not be out of place to consider the general conditions in the Chōḷa empire so far as music was concerned. That this art was highly developed becomes clear from contemporary accounts of the technique of music, musical instruments and dance. Musicians were greatly encouraged and music itself was given a very important place in the life of the people, especially in the field of devotional music. The rulers were themselves knowledgable patrons and were able to enjoy and appreciate good music. The music of those days was, however, different from the music as we know it today. Though they were not conversant with the Raga system, music has evolved continously from the Saṅgam age down to the present and this progressive evolution was definitely encouraged by the Chōḷas. It is obvious that during the Chōḷa period music must have been a harmonious synthesis of song, dance and drama. It is also clear that there was a large body of literature on music, both theoretical and practical, with which the patrons were familiar in those times. The Śilappadikāram contains several references to this art.[1] A review of the music of of this period has necessarily to be on account of the great devotional hymns of the Nāyanmārs which came to be codified as the eleven Tirumurais by Nambi Āṇḍār Nambi under the guidance, inspiration and patronage of the Chōḷas. On this score alone the worth of the music of kthat periodcould be assessed. The Chōḷa kings really placed posterity under a dep debt of gratitude by their efforts in this direction which have left behind a priceless treasure of music.

The Tēvāram hymns which constituted the music of the Chōḷa period came out of the depths of emotional Bhakti. These hymns apeared at a time when they were most required by the Saivites for the revival of Hinduism. The collection and codification of these hymns was the work of Nambi Āṇḍār Nambi who flourished under the Court of Rājarāja I.[2]

That music was one of the fine arts which flourished under the generous and discerning patronage of the Chōḷas is also proved by the data provided by several inscriptions of this period. Some refer to the singing of Tiruppadiyam in temples set to tune. Some others mention musicians, instrumental accompanists and types of musical instruments. There is, however, no direct evidence about manner in which the science of music was practiced or the types of music in vogue then. But considerable research in this direction has been mooted.[3]

As will be obvious from the inscriptions, rulers of the Chōḷa reign, made several endowments for the regular recital of the Tiruppadiyam in temples and public places. Rājarāja I endowed land for fifty persons called '<u>Piḍārars</u>', fortyeight of whom were to sing, one to accompany in Uḍukkai and one on Maddaḷam daily in the Big temple at Tanjore.[4]

Another inscription of Rājarāja I from Tiṇḍivanam refers to an endowment of land for the musicians playing on the Vīṇa as well as singing of the Tiṇḍīśvara temple at Kiḍaṅgil.[5] According to another inscription on the north wall of the Tyāgarājaswāmi Temple at Tiruvāṟūr ascribed to Rājarāja I, music was to be provided during the time of Śrībali services by seven persons - three of them on Maddaḷam, one on Patākam and one on Śēkaṇḍigai. There is another inscription on the south wall of the Piplikēśvara temple at Tiruverumbūr which refers to an endowment of land for four persons who were to sing Tiruppadiyam daily in the temple to the accompaniment of Uḍukkai and Tāḷam. During Rājarāja's time various types of musical instruments were in use. They have all been mentioned in inscriptions with the epithets Tōṟukkaruvi, Tuṟaikkaruvi, Narambukkaruvi and Kañchakkaruvi. There were also sufficient inscriptions to confirm the presumption that music recitals were solo, vocal and instrumental. The fortyeight 'Piḍāras' of the big temple already referred to as beneficiaries of Rājarāja I could not have sung the tunes individually. It is possible that there were musicians attached to the Palaces and they gave recitals for the delectation of the king. From the inscriptions at Pālur, Tiruvāvāḍuturai, Andanallūr and Vriddhāchalam it is apparent that music culture was widely prevalent.

It is interesting to note that the gifts of Rājarāja I came largely from the booty captured in victories on the battlefield and included well over 41500 kaḷañjus of gold, 50650 kaḷañjus of silver etc. About 180 kaḷañjus of paddy a year were set apart to maintain 212 male musicians, drummers etc. They included three persons to sing Ariyam and four others to sing the Ahamārgas and Dēsi type of music. A choir of fifty on a daily wage of 3 kuruṇis of paddy was appointed to recite the Tiruppadiyam to the accompaniment of musical instruments.[6]

48 singers consisting of Brāhmins, Dēvadāsis etc., were brought to the Tanjore temple from various other temples in 1014 A.D. during the 29th regnal year of Rājarāja I. Some other inscriptions refer to the endowments given by this monarch.[7]

Regarding Rājarāja III, there is an inscription of Tiruvoṭṭiyūr during his 10th regnal year which refers to the king listening to music recital on the 8th day of the Āvaṇi Tirunāḷ Festival.[8] His consort Puvanamuḻututaiyāḷ was well accomplished and proficient in music. An inscription of this king during his 10th regnal year registers a Vīṇaikkaṇi - an endowment offered to one who played the Vīṇa in the temple.[9]

It is interesting to learn from a source that the Tēvāram songs of the first three Nāyanmārs were inscribed on copper plates through the efforts of Kaḷiṅgarāyan, the commaner-in-chief of Kulōttuṅga I. An inscription from Sīrgazhi Tirugañansambandhar temple refers to the preservation of such copper plates. During his time the recital of hymns was considered a privilege and Kulōttuṅga conferred this previlege on particular individuals.[10] There were also musicians attached to the court called 'Pāṇars' who set hymns and songs to tunes and trained singers to render them. An inscription from Tiruviḍaimarudūr[11] describes a Pāṇar called Tirumūrti Chōḻan Piran alias Pāṇapperu singing in the local temple after receiving appropriate training. Like other employees, musicians too were paid in kind and were also provided with living quarters.[12]

Given below is a list of inscriptions relating to music found in Tamilnadu and adjacent states.

Gift of land for reciting the Tiruppadiyam in the temple at Brahmadēśam, North Arcot District during the time of Rājarāja I alias Rājakēsarivarman in his 16th year of reign (ARIE. 199 of 1915).

Gift of land by the residents of Nerkuppai alias Mudukunṛam on the northern bank of Paravūrkunṛam to the local temple of Mahādeva for reciting the Tiruppadiyam hymns during the time of Rājarāja I in his 18th regnant year (ARIE. 40 of 1918).

The 11 verses of Tēvāram sung by the saint Tirugñānasambandhar in praise of the sacred Viḍaivai were engraged during the time of Rājakēsarivarman alias Tribhuvanachakravarti Vikrama Chōladeva at the Punyanāthasvāmin temple at Tiruvāvāḍuturai, Nannilam Taluk (ARIE. 8 of 1918).

An inscription mentions a certain Śembiyam Chedishaya Mūvendavēlan, a musician of the temple at Kīḷur, South Arcot District during the 5th year of the reign of Parākēsarivarman alias Uḍaiyār Rājēndradēva and records the provision made for the recitation of Tiruvēmbāvai on Tiruvādirai days by this musician (ARIE. 12 of 1905).

An inscription of the time of Parāntaka I in his 25th year of reign in front of the central shrine at Siddhaliṅgamaṇḍala mentions gift of land for providing music thrice a day during the time of worship in the temple of Vyāgrapādēśvara (ARIE. 387 of 1909).

An inscription in the Villināthaswāmi temple (on the third pillar of the inner verandhar) records that the assembly of Tiruviḷimilaḷi, a Dēvadāna village of the god in Veṇṇādu made due provision for the singing of the Tiruppadiyam hymns in the temple during the 22nd year of reign Rājarāja alias Rājakēsarivarman (ARIE. 423 of 1908).

An inscription on the south wall of the shrine records gift of land by the local assembly for singing the Tiruppadiyam in the Piplikēśvara temple at Tiruverumbūr with the accompaniment of Uḍukkai and Tāḷam during the reign of Rājarāja (ARIE. 129 of 1914).

An inscription of the 5th regnal year of Rājarāja II on the south wall of the Mandapa in the Viraṭṭēnśvara temple at Vaḷuvūr mentions gift of money for getting the Tiruvembāvai recital before the deity during the Tiruvādirai festival, with an endowment of 30 kāśus (ARIE. 421 of 1912).

An inscription records that the king granted to a certain individual the privilege of singing the Tiruppadiyam in the temple, besides a certain amount of land in his 2nd year of reign. King Rājakēsarivarman's inscription to this effect can be seen on the north wall of the Maṇḍapa of the Vēdāraṇya temple at Vēdāraṇyam (ARIE. 422 of 1904).

An inscription mentions the grant of land to a certain Rājarāja Pichchan and his troupe for singing the Tiruppadiyam by Rājakēsarivarman alias Tribhuvana chakravarti Kulōttuṅga during his 2nd year of reign. This inscription is on the east wall of the first prakāra of the Abhirāmēśvara temple at Tiruvāmattūr (ARIE. 433 of 1903).

An inscription of the 10th year of the reign of Rājarāja I on the south wall of the central shrine in the Tintriṇīśvara temple at Tiṇḍivanam refers to the grant of 2910 kuḷi of land for a musician who was to play on the Vīṇa and a Vocalist who was to accompany him (ARIE. 141 of 1900).

An inscription during the 27th year of Rājēndra I refers to the gift of land by the residents of Arpakkam for the maintanance of seven musicians for services in the shrine of Tirumagaral Udaiya Nāyanār on the belt round the local Ādikēśava Perumāḷ temple (ARIE. 145 of 1923).

Another inscription of the 11th year of the reign of Rājēndra I on the ṣixth pillar of the left door of the Vēdapurīśvara temple at Kiḷaiyūr records a grant of land for the maintenance of two persons singing the Tiruppadiyam hymns during the 3 services in the temple of Tirukkaḍaiyūr dēvar (ARIE. 96 of 1925).

An inscription of the 25th year of the reign of Parāntaka I on the south wall of the Gōmuktīśvara temple at Tiruvāvāḍuturai refers to the maintenance of pipers in the temple and records a purchase of11 mā of land for thispurpose (ARIE.126 of 1925).

An inscription on the southern wall of the Sundaravarda Perumāḷ temple at Uttiramērūr during the 26th regnal year of

Rājēndra I records a sale of land by the village assembly to the temple of Veḷḷaimūrti Āḻvāṛ for providing 7 kuruṇis of paddy daily to 3 persons reciting Tiruvāymozhi hymns in the temple (ARIE. 194 of 1923).

An inscription of the 13th year of the reign of Parākēsarivarman on the south wall of the Velvidainatha temple at Ṭirukkurugavur refers to a gift of land by Śembaṉ Aruḷan to 9 persons for beating drums in the temple of Tiruveḷḷāḍai Mahādēva (ARIE. 434 of 1918).

Another inscription of the 6th regnal of Vikrama Chōḷa on the south wall of the Maṇḍapa in front of the central shrine in the Karkaṭēśvara temple near Vēpaṭṭūr records a gift of land to a private individual for playing on the Vīṇa before the deity (ARIE. 47 of 1910).

An inscription of the 3rd regnal year of Rājarāja I on the north wall of the central shrine in the Maṇavālēśvara temple at Tiruvilakkuḍi records a gift of land by an assembly of Murugamaṅgaḷaṁ, towards the maintenance of 3 musicians for sounding the Kāḷam and beating the gong during the Śrībali offerings to the Maṅgaḷa Nakkar in the temple (ARIE. 116 of 1926).

An inscription of the 37th year of the reign of Parāntaka I on thesouth wall of the central shrine in the Saptaṛishīśvara temple at Lālguḍi refers to land given to two Brāhmins for chanting the Tiruppadiyam hymns thrice a day in the temple of Tiruttavaturai Mahādēva in Iḍaiyāṟṟunāḍu (ARIE. 19 of 1929).

An Uttiramērūr Inscription records a grant of land for provision of music during Śrībali at the temple of Uttiramērūr (SII., Vol. III, No. 194).

An inscription from Konērirājapuram of the 11th regnal year of Rājarāja I refers to a gift of land for singing the Tiruppadiyam at the local temple (ARIE. 631 of 1909).

Another inscription from the same place of the 26th year of the reign of Rājarāja I records grant of land to 2 persons for singing Tiruppadiyam in the temple at Tirunallam Uḍaiyār (ARIE. 624 of 1909).

An inscription at Tiruvāmattūr of the 2nd regnal year of Kulōttunga II refers to the grant of land toatroupe of Tiruppadiyam singers in the temple of Abhirāmeśvara (SII. Vol. VIII, No. 749).

An inscription in the inner gōpura of the Big temple at Tanjore mentions the deposit by a musician of 40 Kāśu yielding interest of 1/8th amount per year. This interest of 5 kāśus was to be distributed amongst five musicians who beat the Tiruppārai at the flag hoisting and five drummers who announced the procession of Āḍavallār (SII. Vol. II, No. 25).

Another inscription in the same temple refers to the daily allowance of paddy to fortyeight persons appointed for reciting Tiruppadiyam in the temple and for two persons who were to accompany them on drums - one on Uḍukkai and one on Koṭṭimaddaḷam (SII. Vol. I, No. 65).

An inscription at Galganāth, Hāveri Taluk, Dhārwār District of the reign of the Chālūkya emperor Vikramāditya VI contains a rather unusual reference to a musician named Mokari Bāramayya - that he bears the titles 'Samasta Gīta vīdya nrityanēka Śāstra sādhakaṁ, mūru rāya āsthāna biruda bāge kāra mukha darpaṇaṁ, ḍenka vilāsam, battīśa rāga kāla brahman' etc.

An undated inscription at Paṭṭadakkal (Bījāpur District) belonging to the time of Vikramāditya II (Western Chālūkya) records that thequeen consort Lōkamahādevi confirmed thecovenants, which had been given to the singers by Vijayāditya, thereby showing that this King, father of Vikramāditya II, also had been encouraging music and musicians (SII., Vol. IX, No. 89).

An inscription of Dharmasāgar records the gift of two portions of land for musicians, instrumentalists, etc.

Another inscription of Piḷḷālamaṛi records the grant of nineteen houses in the fort of Piḷḷālamaṛi to the musicians and dancers.

By virtue of the simplicity of language and the tremendous

enthusiasm by the kings who patronised musicians and music through various measures, the music of the Chōḷa period had its unhindered continuance in the later times as well. Till the end of the Chōḷa era, a single system of music was folowed in the whole country with local variations. It was only afterwards that the division into Carnatic and Hindustani music came into vogue. The Chōḷa period was an age of renaissance in many ways. The rulers of the dynasty founded by Vijayālaya were all ardent followers of Saivism. They made music part and parcel of the daily life of the people and emphasised not only the spiritual and emotional but even the educative aspects of this fine art.

NOTES

1. Vide Indian Music : A Perspective, 1980, Delhi.

   Vide Mrs. Leela Omcherry on Śilappadikāram in Music - Unpublished article.

2. One school of thought ascribes this inscription to Rajaraja I. Cf. Inscriptions of Erumibur, Āluvūr, Tiruvāvāduturai, Āllūr, Tiruttavatturai and Konērirājapuram.

3. It has been held by Prof. Veḷḷaivāraṇar that about 23 kinds of Paṇṇs were used during the Chōḷa period which have equivalent rāgas in Carnatic music.

4. South Indian Inscriptions, Vol. II, No. 65.

5. Ibid., Vol. VII, p. 154.

6. ARIE. 141 of1900.

7. Ibid., 40 of 1918, 423 of 1908 and 141 of 1900.

8. Ibid., 221 of 1912.

9. Ibid. 47 of 1910.

10. Ibid. 422 of 1904.

11. SII. Vol. V, p. 705.

TWO SYSTEMS OF MUSIC EDUCATION

Today, when the living current of the traditions of many of our arts has suffered a setback, the music tradition alone still clings to us and however much one may make himself a modern and bring himself under the impact of alien modes of life and thought, one cannot shake off the native music in which ones' being is so saturated.

As a fine art, music has been, from remote times, included in the scheme of studies which contributed to one's accomplishment and status as a man of culture. The tradition of the 64 arts in which man and women were expected to become proficient is headed by music and dance.

If there is one subject more than another which requires direct personal method of teaching, it is indeed practical music Books, charts, the blackboard, printed notation, even recorded music are no substitute for the living presence of the Guru. In carnatic music, the expression Rāgabhāva depends on the most careful employment of subtle modifications of svaras, delicate gamakas, anuswaras and characteristic sañcāras. The diverse rāga forms, each with its distinct physiognomy and aesthetic impression, have to be evoked correctly without intrusion of traces of allied forms. Certain pairs or groups of these are very close and there are also some new rāga forms, old and full of melodic delectation (Rakti). To imbibe all these from old teachers through systematic grinding and mastery of the definitive, descriptive and illustrative compositions and to make one's musical erudition as full as possible, the time hourned Indian way of intimate teacher-pupil relationship, Gurukula method, is the most suited. Subtle nuances which form the sound of beauty in Carnatic music cannot be imparted except by the mouth of the master and cannot be grasped except by the devout ear of the pupil. In other words, practical music proper, every svara or syllable has to be learnt directly from the voice of the Guru. The flexible living voice has to sing and the ear has to take in the music. The method by which the professional musician, till the beginning of this century, used to acquire his art was by personally living with his master intimately for many years, learning not by actual training but by constant listening and close observation followed by a period of apprenticeship when he assists and accompanies the master. Nothing can adequately replace the Gurukula system for learning music.

Music is essentially a gift of God. Musicians are born, not made. It is the internal urge of the aspirant that ultimately moulds one into an artist of lasting worth. But without the light lit by a great Vidwān the darkness in the heart of the aspirant remains ever thick and unrevealing. To attain eminence and Gñānam, Śraddha is essential on the part of the seeker of knowledge. The knowledge of music and musical attainment has to be obtained by an earnest student through dedication at the feet of the master and by unstinted devotion to him.

The system is something unique to our country not in the field of music but also in other branches of learning like philosophy, literature etc., but for reasons enumerated above, it has been particularly successful in the case of music.

Till the beginning of this century, the great Vidwāns were patronised by Mahārājas and also enjoyed sufficient leisure and freedom from want. In a feudal society, the rich stratum had the means and the inclination to support and encourage musicians. Since these princes and kings were men of cultured tastes and a good number of them were also musicians, composers of musicologists, the standard of music in such places was also high. The Vidwāns who enjoyed royal patronage settled down to a place and were always engaged in teaching to a few students. Since the art of printing was unknown and the system of notation was also not prevalent, oral instruction was the only worthwhile method of teaching available.

The teacher used to pronounce and sing while the student had to repeat exactly verbatim with particular emphasis on intonation and accent. It was essentially learning in parts based on imitation. The students received individual attention and were required to commit their lessons to memory. Individual attention led to intensive training in music. The student could ill afford to attend classes without thorough preparation. New lessons were not imparted until the old ones were thoroughly grasped and mastered.

This system of teaching did not compel the talented and brilliant students to wait for specific periods along with their duller class fellows. An intelligent, industrious or meritorious student could complete his education earlier. The advance students were enlisted for guiding and teaching juniors. A thirst for knowledge or the desire to preserve the traditions rather than examinations and diplomas or degrees were the incentives for learning. The Guru used to take the more promising Śishya along with him to accompany him during his concerts and the latter thus picked up Katchēri Dharma (concert technique) through constant and extensive listening. The Gurus' guidance was wholly and totally based on Lakshya Gñānam. Lakshaṇa was there only by implication. But later on, when the teachers had to go on tour to fulfil professional engagements, the teaching became more and more concert-oriented.

The Gurukula system might have had its defects but it did produce commendable results. The reasons for such success were atleast two : (1) The disciple who came to the masters was drawn to the art out of an inner compulsion. He was willing to learn the hard way. The risk that he took both economically and socially can be guaged by the fact that he had no degree or diploma awaiting him on the basis of which he could aspire for a job; (2) the preceptor was also willing to teach though in an exacting way; for he could realise the zeal of the disciple, having himself gone through this tortuous road earlier. The training imparted was vigorous, intense, meticulous and long drawn. There was no hurry to complete a syllabus within the stipulated time for the award of a degree.

The most desirable characteristic or attribute of the Gurukula is the fact that as opposed to an extensive exposure to different systems of music, it enabled the pupils to get an intensive training at the feet of their master. Till two or three generations ago, the professional musicians were not in the habit of frittering away their energies in too many directions. They believed in mastering a small area and did it to perfection. Within that sphere they could lay claim to superior authority. To mention only one example Mahāvaidyanātha Iyer is said to have had the smallest repertoire among any famous musicians of merit. But his mastery over it was so complete that the compositions in question gained a fullness and finality of aesthetic content and conotour never since altered. As a result the disciple who lived as a member of the Guru's family for a considerable length of time delved deep into this exclusive repertoire as well as the latter's intensive knowledge and musical attainments and thereby acquired a profound insight into his particular style of singing. This is even more true of the Gharāna system of North India. The Śishya stayed with his preceptor till the latter had exhausted all that he had to impart and then left only to take up his duties as a teacher himself. In the Gurukula system this helped to preserve for posterity a number of highly aesthetic forms of compositions by being passed on authoritatively from Guru to Śishya at a time when taking them down on notation was practically unknown. This is one of the brightest features of the Gurukula system.

On the other hand, the main defect of this system lies in the fact that owing to lack of means of mass communication as at present the disciple had to confine himself to listening constantly to his Guru and his co-students and had only limited opportunities to listen to after top-ranking musicians. This necessarily limited this outlook and capacity to appreciate and imbibe the best of the music of other great contemporary artists.

There was a time when no one had heard of a music school or college. That was two or three generations ago. But at the turn of this century socio-economic changes set in and the academic mind began to mould music teaching to institutionalised methods. An art that was taught as an intimate and creative transmission of tradition was taken over to schools and colleges.

Modern education brought with it a rediscovery of India's past and a critical appreciation of the cultural contributions of the country. On the one side appeared the expositions of Indian music savants and connoisserus like Captain C.R. Day, Fox Strangways and others and on the other, native musicologists arose like Rājā Surēndra Mōhan Ṭāgore and Paṇḍit Bhaṭkāṇḍe in the field of north Indian music and Vidwan Subbarāma Dīkshitar and Sri ChinnaswāmiMudaliār in the field of south Indian Music who collected and published all that was available on the theory and practice of Indian music in the two schools. The stage was now set to think of organising music institutions and courses of study in Music.

It is, however, only in so far as the Gurukula system in the modern condition of life is difficult of universal or extensive application that it becomes necessary to think of other methods to provide for music education of those who but for the other methods (courses in school and colleges) would have had to forego the benefit of the highest of all arts. The deterioration that is setting in the professional fields and the poor results of the short-cut methods evident today only bring to our attention with increased force the need for the upkeep for the desirable features of the ancient high class method of musical education (Gurukula system) to the extent possible in the present circumstances. So even in the modern methods of school and college education, it is necessary to preserve to maximum possible extent the essential element of personal instruction so pronounced in the Gurukula system. In the class-room the teacher meets his pupils who learn as a group and not as individuals though within the limit of time available, each pupil may receive individual attention. However, even after class hours the teacher-pupil contact unhindered by time and place should be possible and the value of the practical lesson would be in proportion to the direct personal attention.

In the Colleges, in respect of other common humanities or sciences, the work of the teachers in the higher aspect of learning is mostly confined to the guidance they give to the pupils. The higher the course of studies the less is the need for lectures. The scholars mostly study by themselves with the help of the masters. But in practical music proper every svara or syllable has to be learnt direct from the voice of the guru. So much so, even if the constant personal touch of the Gurukula system is not possible in the present set-up of society, still the personal element even in college education cannot be avoided. In the case of other humanities and sciences, libraries and laboratories are essential. In practical music, the only library worth mentioning is a good collection of recorded music.

This brings us to the question of the competence and accomplishments of the teacher. Without recruiting the services of the professional musicians, highly versed in practical music, music education in schools, colleges or Universities becomes a queer, lean, lopsided phenomenon. It is the professional teachers that helps to impart a higher standard to the student of music. Indeed the increasing worthwhileness of the school and college courses will depend on the extent to which they are able to harness more and more the services of expert professional teachers. The role of the professional musician is not merely confined to direct teaching. Every eminent master in the field is an indirect teacher; for it is by constant listening to high class recitals that the knowledge of the students in the art attains the needed dimensions. Our music exposition has two phases - the closed portion represented by compositions and secondly the free exposition of actual melodies. The ability to elaborate a pure melody (or rāga ālāpana) is indeed the invariable hallmark of proficiency and a young student learns to do this mainly by listening more and more and developing the imagination. There is no set teaching for this. It is listening that is particularly more important as the music education reaches higher and higher stages.

For this reason, more than printed materials, it is records of music (tape records, cassettes, etc.) that should constitute the major part of the music libraries of our schools and colleges. This is closely bound up with the preservation of our glorious musical traditions. However, none of the libraries are sufficiently equipped in this line and a lot of useful work can be done in this direction.

The organisation of music lessons in large classes in schools and colleges at the present day necessarily involves teaching in a mass. This is again a matter calling for some review. In group teaching and group singing, there is the general defect of less gifted and less qualified students not being noticed; apart from this, the nuances and graces of our music cannot be taught directly by taking a large class. Furthermore, each professional, belonging to a particular style and school has his own way of rendering and if different pieces or part of a curriculum are to be taught by 3 or 4 different teachers, there is a medley of styles and finer points of rendering, which is not at all desirable. One method of avoiding this would be to divide the class into small groups and allow each master to take charge of the whole education of this small batch, but it is doubtful whether this would be practicable.

The next subject of importance in teaching music is notation. No system so far devised can give even a rough picture of the melody. Subbarāma Dīkshitar's system of symbols is perhaps the most elaborate one for dealing adequately with the variety of graces characteristic of our music. But it is to be borne in mind that so far as our music and its subtelities are concerned, the written score is but a rough guide; without a live teacher the paper text may even prove harmful in the hands of the half-learned. Hence the traditional condemnation of learning pieces not from the mouth of the teacher but from a book. Still it cannot be said that notation has no use whatsoever. Every song properly learnt from a guru may be reduced to a notation to serve as a sort of memorandum to aid the memory. When a song has been thoroughly mastered as taught by a teacher, a notational rendering of it would ensure against its being forgotten altogether. But notation is but a cheap though poor substitute for tape recording.

It is to late Prof. P. Sambamoorthy more than anybody else, that music at the educational level owes its expansion in South India.

Lastly we come to the subject of musicology in the school and college curriculum. The extent to which musicology should be incorporated in a music course has been a subject of controversy. Essential, historical, biogrphical and theoretical information is necessary, but the tendency of musicology in some institutions is to encroach or even displace the practical side of the art which is after all the more important thing. Wherever practical musicians or professional are in charge of these institutions, they have invariably reduced the over-loaded musicological part of the syllabus to prevent the attention of the students being turned away from the practical training.

Considering the musical instruction at whatmay be called the College stage, there are several categories of institutions to be considered. In the first place there are the ordinary University institutions teaching music along with other subjects as optional. In these institutions emphasis is naturally laid on what may be called the theoretical and cultural side and only as much practical work as may be needed to illustrate the theory, history and practice, but the aim is to create a greater critical awareness of the several aspects of the art, the manysided development and history and hence there is necessarily a bias in this scheme towards musicology. Then there are the music colleges like the Central Carnatic Colleges of Music at Madras and Madurai, the Aṇṇāmalai University Music College, the Swāti Tirunāḷ Music College at Trivandrum etc., where only music is taught. Here the stress is essentially on the practical aspect of music; though theory is also generally provided for in the curriculum, it has only a secondary place. These institutions may be expected to train future professional musicians. Then there are Teacher's College to train music instructors as in the Madras Music Academy. The syllabi and modes of teaching in these institutions differ from what obtains in the other types of institutions. The topics of musicology which have to be taught for the different categories of institutions have to be carefully chosen, having clearly in our mind their objectives.

While every branch of applied knowledge has both the theoretical and practical sides, the relative emphasis varies with these branches. In music these two aspects, called generally Lakshya and Lakshaṇa have their own place; but lakshya is considered more important for obvious reasons. All Lakshaṇa should be subservient to the needs of Lakshya. Musicology diversed from the needs of practical music is only of limited value.

BHAJANA TRADITION IN SOUTH INDIA

Bhajana connotes worship of Gods through the medium of verses and recitation of His name with devotion. In a popular sense, it implies a congregational ritual of collective worship of Gods through songs, dance etc. Bhajan implies a genre of devotional music conveying traditional religious values. Bhakti represents the unappeased craving of the heart for God.

The supreme Indian ideal is spirituality. The dominant awareness in every traditional Hindu's consciousness is the omnipresence and omnipotence of God. Religion is so wedded to our daily life that the two are inseperable. The Hindu daily experiences the religion in entertainment, literature, folk-lore and music. Traditionally music in South India has been closely connected with the temple and is essentially devotional or reflects how religion has permeated into every aspect of life.

The most prominent tenets of the Bhakti doctrine are the efficacy of listening to the praise of God and of singing Hisholy names. The latter in particular refers directly to what is called the Nāma Siddhānta school - that persuasion in which the utterance of God's name is the potent means of gaining His grace. There are two ways in which this is achieved. The first method called Nāma Japa consists in repeating a name of God over and over again. The doctrine of the efficacy of the repetition of God's names is a vital aspect of the Bhakti approach to God. An important aspect of bhajana saṁpradāya is that which emphasises salvation through repeating the names of God as for example in the 'Sahasranāma' stanzas (on different deities) containing a catalogue of one thousand names and attributes of the deity. The second method is called 'Nāma kīrthana' or 'Nāma Sankīrthana' meaning singing the names and praises of God. It is this second mode of worship that is the important cornerstone of the musical aspects of bhajana ritual tradition.

Of the three-fold mārga of approaching the infinite viz., Gñāna mārga (knowledge of study and meditation), Karma mārga (right action and observance of rituals) and Bhakti mārga (devotional), the last is considered the easiest and most ideal. This is not, however, to deny the importance of the other two paths to God for the highest achievements of bhakti embrace them as well. Devotion itself has been conceived or as being nine-fold viz., Śravaṇa, Kīrthana, Smaraṇa, Pādasēvana, Archanạ, Vandana, Dāsya, Sakhya and Ātmanivēdana. It is significant that Śravaṇa or listening to the glories of God and Kīrtana or individual and collective singing of His glories, which have been accorded primacy in the order of development of bhakti, form in fact, the basis of bhajana.

According to Hindu traditions, sound or Nāda itself is considered a manifestation of God. 'Ōm' represents the primordial sound - the eternal fundamental source of all life, which encompasses the Universe. The participants of bhajana perform a form of Yoga - viz., Nāda yōga. Since one of the underlying principles of Yōga is that all things we concentrate upon we become by dwelling through song on the names of God epitomizing His glories and virtues, the sound gets related to the thought and to that extent provides the participants in the bhajana ritual with a mental condition conducive to union with the Nādabrahman.

In all devotional music, the words of the texts which are about God have special significance. When a devotional song is sung in bhajana, in contrast to a musical concert, the words are considered more important than the music. The latter is only a vehicle for the more important texts, but when repeated in a musical setting, the power of the words in the bhajana is certainly enhanced.

The concept or idea of bhajana can be traced to the Ṛgvēda whose hymns constitute the earliest outpourings of man praying to the divine power in the form of adulation of different members of the vast pantheon of Gods - Agni, Indra etc. - symbolizing the multifarious manifestations of the supreme God-head. The importance of bhajana as a means of salvation is also emphasised in the Bhagavad Gīta which represents the quintessance of all Hindu ethics and doctrines. One of the most striking features of Hinduism encountered everywhere in India is the overt personalisation of deities. The concept of God as revealed in the Bhagavad Gīta later changed from that of being at once remote and austere to a Krishṇa having qualities very closely associated with mortals as described in the Bhāgavatha relating to Krishṇā's antics with particular reference to his relationship with the Gōpis in a warmly human yet divine manner - qualities that are characteristic of contemporary Krishṇa worship. These stories from Krishṇa avatāra form the main legendary source from which has been generated much of the present day bhajana tradition. Many of the song texts, themes, symbolic acts and ritual dances connected with bhajana owe their origin to the Bhāgavatha.

The beginnings of the bhajana saṁpradya in South India may be traced to the appearance on the scene of a succession of great saint leaders - Nāyanmārs and Āḷwārs - who were respectively worshippers of Śiva and Vishṇu. These god-intoxicated poet singers preached complete surrender to God by way of Bhakti and used fervent devotional songs to convey their special messages. These hymns like the Tēvāram, Tiruvāchagam, Divyaprabandham, Tiruvāymozhi and Pāśuram represent the highest Saitivte and Vaishnavaite writings and to this day are regularly performed by Ōduvārs, Araiyans etc., in temples and they can be considered as the earliest progenitors of the bhajana tradition in South India. An important feature is the use of Tamiḷ for these song texts rather than the traditional Sanskrit. This was not only because not all these poet-singers were well-versed in Sanskrit but more importantly the bhakti movement involved the society in general and in order to ensure that the message of bhakti reached as many persons as possible, the vernacular was used. Although a great portion of the bhakti song texts are in Sanskrit, one of the hallmarks of the bhakti tradition in all parts of India is the use of regional languages. The Nāyanmārs and Āḷwārs made exhaustive pilgrimages to various shrines composing a greatpart of their works in these temples and dedicating their songs to the presiding deities of these sacred centres which consequently came to be known as 'Pādal peṭra sthalaṅgal'. The arrival of these poet singers coincided with the establishment ofthe Pallava empire in South India. The Nāyanmārs were instrumental in converting some of the Pallava kings from Vaishnavism back to Saivism and the latter in turn aided in the promulgation of the faith by founding new temples in and around which the religious activities were centered and all the arts and music flourished focussing on the idea of loving surrender to the Almighty. This work was continued with great zeal for many centuries by the Chōlas who followed the Pallavas.

Along with the Nāyanmārs and Āḻwārs, the three great Āchāryas - Śaṅkara, Rāmānuja and Mādhwa vedantic philosophical leaders who for the most part based their teachings on re-interpretations of the ancient scriptures - gave fresh impetus to the development of Bhakti movement and spread of the bhajan cult in South India. They travelled far and wide, preaching and debating, thereby bringing a philosophical vitality to the awakening. These Āchāryas helped provide, through their exemplary lives and teachings, inspiration not only for generations of poet-singers, but also activists of the bhajana movement like Rāmānanda in North India and Chaitanya in Bengal.

The Hindu revival of the 7th century which saw the beginnings of the bhajana cult in the Tamil country was taken up by other regions with populations speaking different vernacular languages. It first spread to the West and then to the North and eventually engulfted the whole of India. In Karnataka, the main protoganists of the movement were the Vīraśaivas (devotees of Śiva) and the Haridāsās who were comparable respectively to the Nāyanmārs and Āḻwārs and like them used the popular vernacular for emphasising the bhakti approach to God. The Haridāsās, who were ordent followers of Mādhwa, wandered from village to village carrying their message in song. The Dēvarnāmas of Purandaradāsa, the most well known among, the Haridāsās, form an important part of the present day South Indian bhajana repertoire as to the Abhaṅgs of prominent Maharashtraian poet-singers like Tukkārām centered round Pandharpur and the bulk of the Marathi devotional songs are in praise of the presiding deity, Paṇḍuraṅga. The most distinguished among the poet-singers of Northwest India are Narasimha Mēhta of Gujarat, Mīrabhai of Rajasthan and Gurunānak of the Punjab. Mīra, more than any other poet-singer, has captured and held the hearts of Indians all over the country down to the present day and her very thought is associated with the most ardent devotion to Lord Krishṇa. Coming to North India proper, a noteworthy feature is the emergence of Sufism out of Islamic elements which were compatible with Hindu bhakti; songs and dance were the essential parts of the worship of Sulfis who had much in common with Hindus. Kabīrdās represents a fusion of both the Hindu and Muslim ideologies. Rāmanānda, who hailed from Varanasi, was the chief architect of the bhajana cult in the region based on Rāmānuja's Vaishnavite doctrines and he provided inspiration to generations of distinguished Hindu bhajan composers such as Ravidās, Sūrdās and Tulasīdās. In Eastern India it was Chaitanya who gave impetus to the resurgence of Vaishnavism and he is hailed as the Mūlapurusha of the Nāma siddhāntha cult. Dominating the entire religious scene, he is unrivalled as the promoter of the bhajana tradition in the form of Bengali Kīrtans. Song and dance are reported to be integral parts of his Krishṇa worship. In fact Chaitanya is credited with having introduced dancing in the bhajana rituals. He is further said to have preached with great effectiveness the gospel of devotion to Vishṇu in the course of his pilgrimage to the temples in South India.

The great bhakti movement and its accompanying expression in the shape of bhajana, which initially originated in South India round about the 7th century A.D., seems to have moved clockwise round the country into Karnataka and Maharashtra and then through the Western and Northern regions east to Bengal and finally down the East coast back to South India once again nearly eight centuries later. The second half of the 15th and first half of the 16th centuries brought to fruition in great measure the essential formation of the present day bhajana ritual structures as at present performed by orthodox groups in South India. This task was begun by three generations of a family of poet composers from Tallapakkam in Andhra - Annamāchārya, Tirumalāchārya and Chinnayya, whose activities were centered round the Tirupathi temple. Among these, far less is known about Tirumalāchārya as compared to his more famous father and son. The importance of the Tallapākkaṁ composers lies in the fact that they began many of the conventions in bhajana paddhati that were continued and developed by those who came later. Indeed they are credited with having codified the present bhajana tradition and systematizing the orthodox bhajana ritual. They are also responsible for a largest output of diverse types of devotional songs. They composed the Tōḍayamaṅgalaṁ songs with which the first section of the bhajana invariably ends proclaiming victory to the Lord as well, as the Heccharika or the songs used in processions announcing the arrival of the deities. Chinnayya is responsible for the compositions used in different stages of Pooja during bhajana and he also set the order of songs performed during the last section of the bhajana ritual i.e., the Ḍōlōtsavam. More than anything else, the tradition of worshipping Rāma in song and ritual can be traced to Annamāchārya. Annamāchārya's imprint on the Rāmā cult was continued by Bhadrāchala Rāmadās but received its apex with Tyāgarāja. The devotional songs of Rāmadas who appeared on the Andhra scene two centuries later also form an important part of contemporary bhajana paddhati. He was instrumental in establishing Rāma Mandirams at different centres to facilitate the performance of bhajana rituals largely devoted to Rāma as regular religious and social functions in the lives of the people. After the Tallapākkam composers, Tyāgarāja is the contributor to the largest amount of musical literature performed in contemporary bhajana rituals. He owed much to the Tallapākkam composers as well as Rāmadās and closely followed their Rāma Nāma Siddhānta cult living his life of worship mostly by songs. In fact he had the opportunity of constantly listening to vast number of Rāmadās's compositions sung to him by his mother during his childhood and this is believed to have influenced his musical style considerably. He used to invariably sing Annamāchārya's Tōdayamangalams and other devotional pieces during his Uñchavṛitti and Chaturmāsya bhajanas. Tyāgarāja composed music for complete sections of bhajana paddhati as well as individual songs of varying standards, ranging from simple songs for the musically untrained to sing in unison to complex pieces sung ordinarily in solos by the musically initiated or by small groups within larger congregations. His important bhajana pieces include Divyanāma kīrtanas which form an important part of the second section of the bhajana ritual as well as Utsava Sampradāya Kīrtanas usually sung during the closing stages.

In addition to the above mentioned three architects of contemporary bhajana sampradāya who were all ardent votaries of Rāma Nāma Siddhānta, there are some exponents of the Krishṇa cult who have also contributed in large measure to the present day bhajana structure. Foremost among them is Jayadēva, the Oriyan poet of the 12th century whose Gītagōvinda has remained for eight centuries the highest symbolic example of bhakti and the single most influential musico-poetic work on subsequent individual poet singers and bhakti movements. The main theme of the Gītagōvinda is the estrangement of Rādhā and Krishṇa caused by the latter's solicitude for other Gōpis, Rādha's anguish at Krishṇa's indifference towards her and lastly the raptures which attend their final renunion. Another important savant of the Krishṇā cult in the context of bhajana is Nārāyaṇa Tīrtha whose magnum opus Krishṇa Līla Tharaṅgiṇi has noticeable connection with the Gītagōvinda both in point of poetic structure and thematic material. The Ashṭapadis of Jayadēva and the Tharaṅgas of Nārāyaṇa Tīrtha form indispensable constituents of the present day bhajana music repertoire. The complete set of Ashṭapadis from the entire Gītagōvinda are performed in some bhajana rituals like Rādhākalyāṇa. A noteworthy feature of the bhajana tradition based predominantly on the devotional songs springing from the Krishṇa Cult is the comparative preponderance of dance elements in the ritual.

A hallowed name in South Indian bhajana is Sadāśiva Brahmēndra whose Advaitic songs on the greatness of Nāma Siddhānta in fine and flowing Sanskrit with easy diction attract connoisseurs and laymen alike. Another such saint poet is Ūttukkādu Venkaṭasubbaier whose Rāsa Śabdha songs in both Tamil and Sanskrit are also quite popular in bhajana. Like some Taraṅgas, these compositions have Śolkaṭṭu appendages characterized by intricate rhythmic patterns. Venkaṭasubbier has also composed devotional songs on the different steps to union with God. The most prominent Tamil composer of bhajana songs is Gōpālakrishṇa Bhārati, some of whose Nandanār Charitra Kīrtanas find an important place in bhajana rituals as 'Naṭarāja Dhyāna'. The Tiruppugazh songs of Aruṇagirināthar are indispensable items in bhajanas dedicated largely to Lord Muruga.

In the bhajana tradition in South India, great emphasis is laid on the role of the devotees of God. Prominent preceptors of bhakti like Nārada and Prahḷāda are given the pride of place. Āñjenēya is lauded as the supreme bhakta exemplifying the highest ideals of love and fidelity towards God. Of great importance to the development of bhajana paddhati in South India was the appearance in the Cauvery delta of three bhajana Gurus - Bhōdhēndra, Śrīdhara Veṅkaṭēśa Ayyāvāḷ and Veṅkaṭarāma Sadguruswāmi - who are responsible for the bhakti revival during the late 17th and early 18th centuries. Realising the efficacy of Nāma-Saṅkīrtana as the ideal means of salvation in the Kali age and finding that the congregational singing of devotional songs in unison helped to inculcate bhakti into the minds of the people, they we instrumental not only in standardizing and codifying the contemporary bhajana structure but also founding Maṭṭhs in various centres which went a long way in popularising the bhajana cult. Compositions venerating these bhajana Gurus are an indispensable part of the bhajana format and are sung in the Gurudhyāna section following the Tōḍayamaṅgaḷaṁ.

The song types used in bhajana recitals fall into four categories - Puṇḍarīkam, Nāmāvaḷi, Ślōka and Kīrtana. The Puṇḍarīkam is a short responsorial song consisting of a few words used as a formula-like signal to the congregation indicating the beginning of a section of the ritual or the end of a longer song marking its conclusion. Nāmāvalis too are sung in a responsorial manner and are made up of comparatively short texts consisting of names and or praises of a deity or supplications directed to Him. Rhythmically and melodically simple, direct and free ofornamentation, they are the mainstay of congregational singing. Ślōkas or Viruttams are performed in invocative and meditative sections of the ritual usually by a leader or other solo singer in a rhythm-free manner. Kīrtanas constitute the vast bulk of the songs used in bhajanas; these refrain-like compositions include most devotional types like Ashṭapadis, Taraṅgams, Dēvarnāmas, Abhaṅgs etc. While simple Kīrtanas are sung by the entire congregation in unison, the advanced types are performed in solos by the musically trained. Forms of bhajana ritual itself vary from a solitary man singing unaccompanied songs about or to his God or the Uñchavṛitti moving from house to house singing, playing and dancing to his God to simple collective bha nas composed predominantly of Nāmāvalis or annual festivals wherein larger congregations take part involving the enacting of the comprehensive bhajanōtsavam. Such rituals are made up of four sections. The first section includes invocations to various Gods beginning with Gaṇēśa as well as salutations to the great preceptors and bhaktas and ends with Annamāchārya's Tōḍayamaṅgaḷaṁ compositions. The second section commences with Guru Kīrtanas on the three bhajana Gurus followed by Ashṭapadis, Taraṅgas, compositions of Sadāśiva Brahmēndra, Bhadrāchala Rāmadās, Gōpālakṛishṇa Bhārati etc., and lastly Upachāra Gītas. The third or Divyanāma Saṅkīrtana section is the most absorbing and elevating part of the whole ritual dealing largely with anecdotes from the Bhāgavata. The relevant songs are performed around Krishṇa represented by a Deepa followed by Gōpika Gītas and Abhaṅgs and this section concludes with an Ashṭapadi and Dhyāna ślōkas. In the last or Dhōlōtsavam section, Uthsava Sampradāya Kīrtanas are rendered relating to various aspects like Nalaṅgu, Shōbhānaṁ, Āraṭhi etc., and the whole ritual concludes with awakening the deity by singing suprabhātham the next morning.

The South Indian bhajana ritual, which was inaugurated by the Hindu revival of the Nāyanmārs and Ālwārs and consolidated later by Annamāchārya, received fresh impetus as a result of the establishment of Marathi rule at Tanjore which heralded the influx of large numbers of Marathi saints and singers. The current bhajana tradition is the result of developments from varying accretions which came from both North and South India. The influence of the Marathi Harikīrtanas and the highly devotional songs popularised by the Kīrtanakāras resulted in the evolution of a composite form of bhajana in which the fine elements of Maharashtrian devotional music got embedded. Their impact was even greater on the sister institution of Kathākālakshēpam which is verily the off-shoot of the Maharashtrian tradition. Whereas the essential feature in bhajana is the active participation of the devotees in the ritual involving the entire congregation, in Kathākālakshēpam it is the Kathā performer who gives a literary and musical exposition of the theme with members of the audience occasionally joining only in singing the Puṇḍarīkam and Nāmāvalis. The Kathākālakshēpam performance involves elements of drama, humour, satire etc., requiring diverse histrionic talents amounting to versatility on the part of the Harikathā exponent in addition to an intimate knowledge of bhakti lore and a large repertoire of devotional songs of diverse types. In the long line of distinguished Harikathā performers, Chidambaram Embār Srīraṅgāchāriar holds a prominent place. His original contribution lay in ceaseless working on the expansion of the songs and themes of the art through the preparation of Nirūpaṇas for whole series of epics and purāṇas like the Rāmāyaṇa and Bhāgavatha. That he was eclectic in the choice of his themes is borne out by the fact that in addition to becoming most celebrated in his time for his performance of the Śiva Charithram of Nandanār especially associated with Chidambaram where he lived, he was also the pioneer in performing the lives of many Nāyanmārs, who, as we have already seen, laid the foundations for the South Indian bhajana cult.

It is a matter of profound gratification to all the lovers of art that the present Annual conference of the Music Academy is being presided over by his distinguished son, Sri Embar Vijayaraghavachariar, who is so eminently carrying on the traditions of his illustrious father.

(This paper was presented at the Annual Conference of the Music Academy, Madras in 1982.)

AN IDEAL CONCERT HALL

Music is the finest of the Fine Arts. It has been cultivated and appreciated in India from times immemorial. The basis of all Fine Arts is to express beauty in form or colour orsound. A cultured mind can discover this beauty just as it is able to comprehend truth and goodness. More than any other art, music has always evoked an immediate sympathetic response from people in every land and in every stage of mental growth and education. Music holds an unique place as an indispensable accompaniment to the other popular performing art - dance and it is used to an extent in drama too. While the visual arts are static, music is dynamic. Sculpture and painting can be appreciated without hurry, but not music. The volatile character of sound makes it difficult formusic to be perceived at leisure.

An analysis of Indian music would reveal two distinct elements viz., rhythm and melody. Historically rhythm is the earliest aspect to be noticed in music. The appeal of most arts is primarily to our emotions rather than the intellect and this particularly applies to rhythm. That is the reason why primitive music is predominantly rhythmical in character. However, with the growth of music, the intellectual content of rhythm itself has become considerable. The large number of intricate time measures in Carnatic music bears testimony to the fact that rhythm now involves considerable thought and alertness in execution.

Melody emerges when a series of musical sounds rise and fall in pitch by definite intervals. This melody is the essential basis for Indian music. However, only certain series of sounds captivate us and keep us thrilled depending largely upon the tonal relationships of the various sounds that constitute the melody.

Though there are striking and characteristic differences between Indian music and European music as well as the music of other nations, each limits itself to definite scales or series of notes and the music invariably proceeds from note to note by determinate steps measured by the musical intervals.

Since music depends exclusively on sounds for its perception, the production and properties of sound assume importance. Sound is the effect on the ear of a wave-like motion of an elastic medium caused by vibrations. These vibrations impinge upon the ear drum of human beings and animals and set up the nervous disturbance which we call sound. Vibration is essentially a type of wave-like motion. The time taken for one vibration is known as the vibration period and the number of such vibrations taking place per second is known as the vibration frequency or cycles per second (c.p.s.). Sound has its origin in the vibration of material bodies. Material bodies are of 3 types - solids, liquids and gases. When the Vīṇa is played, its string, hemispherical bowl, stem and gourd all vibrate and emit sound. These are all solid bodies. When the Jalataraṅgaṁ is played, there is vibration in the water in addition to the vibration of the sides of the porcelein cups. In wind instruments like the flute - and this is also true of the human voice - air, which is gaseous, is made to vibrate.

There are 3 broad entities which characterize a musical sound - pitch, intensity orloudness and timbre or quality.

The pitch of sound is determined by the frequency of the vibration of the original sound-producing body. Slowly succeeding vibrations cause what we call low-pitch sounds while rapidly succeeding vibrations produce what we call high-pitch sounds. Quite early in the history of our music, musicians came to realise that a rapid vibration produced a tone of high pitch and a slow vibration produced a tone of low pitch and they also recognised differences of pitch known as intervals. Any particular body capable of being set in vibration has its own natural frequency of vibration, depending on such factors as size, density and tension. The human ear is sensitive to pitches ranging approximately from 20 c.p.s. to 16000 c.p.s.

Intensity, which depends on the extent or amplitude of the vibratory movements, regulates the loudness or softness of the sound. Where the vibrations of the generating agent of a note are extensive, we get an intense or loud sound; where the vibrations of the generating agent of that same note are small (with a small amplitude) we get a subdued sound. Whereas the frequency of vibration determines the pitch, amplitude of the vibrations is the principal factor which determines intensity. Pitch cannot be controlled without varying the conditions of the sounding agent itself. On the other hand intensity can be altered at will by changing the force of breath or bow or pluck.

It is the general experience that the same note produced by different instruments or for that matter even different human voices, having the same pitch and intensity, exhibit variations in character. Such differences are known as differences in quality or timbre. This timbre or tone quality or tone colour is not dependant on the vibration frequency or amplitude. It is determined by the form and complexity of the vibration, the wave shape and the manner in which the vibration is induced.

Sound vibrations are conveyed by material bodies from one place to another. This transmission takes place by means of the sound waves. The atmosphere air is the most common medium for the transmission of the sounds we hear including music. Sound travels at different speeds through different substances. While its speed is 1100 feet per second in air, it travels four times faster in water and fifteen times faster in iron. If the air is rarefied, the intensity of the sound is decreased. In a complete vacuum one cannot hear any sound at all.

Of all the music (sound) producing mechanisms, the human voice is the most perfect, the most vivid in expressing human emotions as also the oldest since music undoubtedly began with vocal singing. After all the ultimate goal of most music instruments is to produce melodic sounds closely approximating to those produced by kthe human voice.

The Brihaddharma Purāṇa - the last of the Upapurāṇas - asserts that musical talent is necessary for good singing but Sowrasyam or good tone is even more important. Wherever the merits of a singer are expounded in our Saṅgītalakshaṇa Granthas, right from Mataṅga's Bṛihaddēśi down to King Tulajā's Saṅgīta Sāmrāmṛita, while discussing <u>Gāyaka-guṇa-dōshas</u> the possession of a good voice is always pinpointed as one of the indispensable attributes of a good singer.

The human voice is a sound (music) producing mechanism just like any other musical instrument, but it has the additional capacity of articulating words and allying these with the tones. The voice should be capable of producing a wide range of controlled frequencies and must be able to sustain them for the required length of time at various intensities.

The organ by which vocal sounds are produced is the larynx. This is situated between the back of the mouth and the top of the wind pipe. Within the cavity are two horizontally stretched fibroid bands known as vocal chords. The chink between them is called the glottis. The human voice is able to produce musical notes through vibration of these vocal chords. The lungs act as a kind of bellows increasing the pressure of the air below the chords and the issuing air stream sets the vocal chords in vibration. Variations in frequency are made possible by the muscles which control the width of theglottis and the tension of the chords. Alterations in the intensity of the notes are brought about by controlling the strength of the air current through the glottis. The vocal mechanism resembles a stringed instrument in its vibration and a wind instrument in its generator.

Thus the vibration of the vocal chords plays an indispensable role in voice production. In men the natural length of these chords is greater than in women and that is the reason why the voices of women are in general shriller.

Every individual has a natural pitch of his or her own. It is the pitch level at which one can produce notes of the best quality with very little effort. The vocal mechanism works at its maximum efficiency at this pitch level.

An effective good voice should be capable of traversing 3 octaves. This entire range is classified into 3 sthayis - Mandra, Madhya and Tara (low, medium and high). In actual practice few people are able to sing in more than 2 octaves.

The intensity of the voice is dictated by the breath force which determines the amplitude of the vibrations of the vocal chords. In other words, the loudness or softness with which an individual sings a particular note depends on the greater or lesser force with which one directs the stream of air on the vocal chords.

The primary source of energy for voice production is the smooth flow of air provided by the breathing appartus - in particular the lungs. Disorders in voice production usually result from incorrect breathing. For artistic singing, voluntary control over the breathing mechanism is essential.

Singers and scientists all over the world agree that the style of breathing determines voice quality to a large extent. Hence correct breathing habits should be inculcated from the early years. The correct type of breathing enables the singer to inhale quickly so as to interrupt the song as little as possible and to have greater capacity of air and provides control to expel the breath in order to sustain on the notes steadily for a long period, to execute groups of notes in fast tempo at one stretch and to maintain the force and power of the voice in the lung passage up to the end of the musical phrase.

Voice, the most delicate and wonderful musical instrument, requires very careful nurturing and handling. The vowel mechanism can be brought into complete obedience to follow the will of the mind through diligent training. The process of bringing the voice under control is referred to as voice culture in the realm of music.

Voice training is an art. A good voice is the first requisite of a vocalist. It is true that not everybody is lucky enough to be endowed by nature with a rich voice. But it is also true that even ordinary voices can be improved substantially through proper training. Every singer should keep his voice sweet and melodious in order to exhibit his musical skill to the maximum possible extent.

The original nature of the vocal chords in an individual determines his innate voice quality, but through training he can improve both the action of these as well as some at least of the resonating passages. During voice culture proper control over the muscles regulating the air stream and those concerned in the mechanism of the larynx should be accomplished.

The quality of the voices depends largely on the resonant cavities. In the human voice the main resonating centres are the throat, mouth and nose. When the tone produced by the vocal chords is directed through the various sets of resonators, it assumes different colours depending upon the relative prominence given to the particular resonating cavity.

Voice quality mainly relies on vowel production. As the formation of vowels determines the quality of the voice great prominence is given to vocalisation excercises in voice training methods. The free passage of the breath stream through the mouth cavity without any audible friction results in vowel sounds. The consonants, which give intelligibility to the words, are produced by obstructing the breath in the mouth by the organs of articulation at one point or another.

Vowels are deemed more harmonious and deep-toned as compared to consonants. That is why a language is termed musical if it abounds in vowel sounds rather than consonants. In the West, the Italian language, which is replete with vowel sounds, is considered as the most musical language and the best studies for a singer are written in this language. A similar pride of place among the South Indian languages goes to Telugu because of the prominence imparted therein to the vowel sounds at the end of every word.

Let us pass on the subject of concert halls and auditoria for music. In recent years the study of the acoustic properties of large halls and auditoria has assumed prominence and it has helped architects to draw up designs with desirable acoustic features.

In the olden days in India, where the performances were held mostly in the open air theatres, there was no necessity nor possibility of taking precautions. The sound waves from the stage reached the listeners simply by direct radiation and there was no problem atall of the waves returning by reflection.

However, at present concert halls are necessarily in enclosed space and hence the sound waves, after reaching the listeners, strike the boundaries of the auditorium and undergo reflection. In the recent past auditoria of varying sizes have sprung up in different parts of the country. The biggest is the Shaṇmukhānanda Hall in Bombay with a seating capacity for 3000 persons. The Music Academy auditorium at Madras can accommodate 1500 persons at a time.

Complete design details of this auditorium have been published and are available. Other well-known auditoria are the Ravīndra Bhārati at Hyderabad, the Tata theatre at Bombay and the Chowḍiāh Memorial Hall at Bangalore.

It is not as though India was completely lacking in concert halls in earlier times. An instance in point is the well-known Saṅgīta Mahal built at Tanjore during the Nāyak rule. The acoustic excellence of this rectangular shaped hall has been highly acclaimed in the history of our music. But it has undergone far too many alterations and changes over the years to serve as the guide for our present day concert halls. Hence in the building of a modern auditorium devoted to Indian music, the only recourse left has been to use the principle evolved for Western music halls and to find out which of these conditions are subjectively acceptable to our own music performances.

Apart from the walls, different objects within the auditorium too reflect the sound waves. As sound travels quite fast, the waves are reflected not once, but many times before they disappear. Echoes may be heard as a result of these reflections. It has been found that echoes are not noticeable when the time interval between the arrival of the direct sound waves and of the reflected waves is less than 75 milli seconds. On the basis that the sped of sound in air is 1100 feet per second, this amounts to a path difference of 80 feet between the direct and reflected sound waves. Thus the question of echoes willnot arise except in large halls and auditoria with depth exceeding 80 feet. If curved surfaces are present in the auditorium, the echoes from such a surface will be enhanced at the place near the focus. A hall with an approximately rectangular section alone will be free from these focussing defects. The numerous sound reflections can also set up distortions and unequal intensities in the sound heard in the different parts of the auditorium. Sometimes dead spots may also be noticed in an auditorium. At such places the direct sound waves and reflected sound waves interfere and destroy one another with the result that no sound will be heard at all by the listeners sitting there. All these defects can be overcome through proper design.

On the other hand there is also a desirable effect of sound reflection, particularly in the context of music. This is reverberation or the persistance of sound due to its insufficient absorption by the boundaries as well as the objects in the auditorium. The time required for the sound to become inaudible after the source is discontinued is known as reverberation time. Each hall has its own reverberation time depending upon its volume and the sound absorption capacities of its walls and objects within. Two halls may be exactly similar in size and shape. In one the performer may sing with zest while in the other he may feel a lack of sympathy, the reason being the difference in the reverberation times. According to the criteria adopted for concert halls in the West, the optimal reverberation time is fixed at 1.7 seconds. However, in view of the fact that these concert halls are primarily meant for Orchestra performances consisting of numerous instruments of diverse types, it was felt that this reverberation time of 1.7 seconds might be on the high side from the clarity standpoint for concerts of Indian vocal music comprising only two or three accompaniments. Hence the Madras Music Academy auditorium has been designed for a reverberation time of 1.3 seconds at full audience load. Subjective appraisals of the performance characteristics of this hall have shown that this reverberation time is ideal for performances of classical vocal music.

The members of the audience themselves contribute the greater part of the sound absorbing power of the auditorium. This is borne out by the fact that while the reverberation time in the Music Academy Hall is 1.3 seconds with full audience, it is 1.5 second with 2/3rd audience attendance and 1.75 seconds with 1/3rd audience attendance.

Where the reverberation in a hall is higher than what is ideal, it can be brought down to the desired level through using sufficient quantities of sound absorbing materials like fibre board, asbestos and special acoustic plasters in the auditorium. If, on the other hand, the auditorium is found to be deficient in reverberation, its ceiling and walls ought to be made more massive and smooth to provide for greater sound reflectance.

From the point of view of evolving satisfactory listening conditions, the following criteria are important in the design of concert halls meant primarily for music performances.

1) LOUDNESS OF DIRECT SOUND :

The sound from the stage travels outwards from the site of the performance at the rostrum in the front with diminishing intensity and is required to reach the audience particularly in the back rows at a comfortable listening level. It is necessary therefore to restrict the depth of the hall or the distance between the stage and the last row of the audience as much as possible commensurate with the audience size.

2) LOUDNESS OF REVERBERATION SOUND

The reverberant sound, properly balanced with the direct sound, gives body to the music and helps in reinforcing the melodically soft passages. This is achieved not only through appropriate design of the hall in terms of reverberation time but also by suitable location of inflecting surfaces.

3) INFORMITY OF RESPONSE

A desirable feature of a good hall is that the sound intensity should be uniformly distributed over the listening areas without any dead spots or focal points.

4) TONAL DISTORTIONS

The original tonal quality of music can be adversely affected through lack of proper balance in the tones resulting from uneven absorption in the hall with respect to frequency.

5) ABSENCE OF ECHOES

Delayed echoes arising out of reflections from distant surfaces interfere with the overall music quality and need to be avoided. Care must be taken to ensure that strong reflections occuring after 50 milli seconds of the direct sound are not received in the listening areas.

6) FREEDOM FROM NOISE

Ambient noise, originating from sources within the hall such as fans, ventilating or air-conditioning systems etc., as well as intruding from sources outside like traffic, would cause interference with the performance and affect its quality.

In this context it may be pointed out that according to the Indian Standards Code of Practice for Acoustic Design of Auditoria and Conference Halls issued by the Indian Standard Institute, the noise level inside any auditorium should not exceed 40-45 Decibell Units.

In any auditorium design, the starting point is its size. From considerations, of comfort on the one hand and cost on the other, the optimum space that has to be provided for each member of the audience is 7-9 square feet and on this basis the total floor area can be calculated for a given audience number. As already pointed out, from acoustic considerations, the rectangular shape is the most ideal for concert halls. From the floor area, the length and breadth of the rectangle can be fixed keeping the difference between them as high as practicble. The stage should be at the centre of a long arm of the rectangle. In this way the distance between the stage and the last audience row can be minimized. Another feasible method of ensuring this is providing a balcony and this practice is followed in most instances. In the Music Academy auditorium, the wide fan shape of the hall tapering towards the stage is another device adapted with the same end in view.

But even with all these devices for minimizing the distance between the stage and the listeners as well as for improving the reverberation characteristics, one cannot do away altogether with sound reinforcement system particularly in large-sized and medium-sized concert halls. In these days, when each participant in a performance, including even percussionists like Mṛidaṅgaṁ and Ghaṭaṁ players, insist on separate microphones for each, there is a paramount need for proper balance in the sound output by the various participants. The sound reinforcement system should be used to amplify only to the extent necessary for the remote listeners to hear with comfort. Even so there should be sufficient feed back to the performer to hear distinctly his or her own voice. The microphone points should be suitably distributed over the entire listening area ensuring uniform intensity of sound throughout. Excessive amplification will adversely affect the melodic quality.

A word about chamber music would not be out of place here. The meaning of this term is different in our country from what it is in the West. Here it denotes just a performance without any microphone whatsoever. In Chamber music one can hear the delicate nuances of the human voice in all its original beauty and splendour. It is indeed regrettable that Chamber music is gradually going out of vogue mainly because of the reluctance of musicians to perform without microphone even in small concert halls.

The human voice consists essentially of four parts viz., the vibrator, the resonator, the motor and the articulator. Most musical instruments possess the first three parts in some form or other. But the articulator is the unique characteristic of the human voice alone. It is here that the human voice distincly scores over all music instruments. It is the most articulate mechanism since it can be made to utter words according to the musical laws by modifying the sound produced by the vocal chords into vowels and consonants throughout the shape of the lips and the placement of the tongue and the (soft) palate. When the pure vocal sound is backed up by good articulation shorn of the defects of phrasing, the beauty of vocal music becomes further enhanced. The appeal of vocal music is greater than the appeal of instrumental music because of the welding of the words lwith the music. Consequently the vocalist is in a position to sing with bhāva and to inculcate <u>rasānubhava</u> in the listener. The abundance of overtones too accounts for the richness of the human voice. It conveys poetic thoughts and hence produces impressive music. Other music instruments merely play the tone; the voice plays and says at the same time. Therein lies the splendour of vocal music.

REFERENCES

Pancholy, M., Chhapgar, A.F. and Davindar Singh : Journal of the Music Academy, Madras, 1966, Vol. 37, p. 145.

Ramakrishna, B.S. : Journal of the Institution of Electronics and Telecommunication Engineers, 1978, Vol. 24 (1) & 11), p. 506.

Ramakrishna, B.S. : Journal of the Acoustical Society of America, 1968, Vol. 43 (4), p. 734.

This paper was presented at the Seminar on 'Acoustics' at the Acoustical Society of India, December, 1987.

R

S